T0030625

# WHERE SHOULD WE CAMP NEXT?

## NATIONAL PARKS

# WHERE SHOULD WE CAMP NEXT?

## NATIONAL PARKS

The Best Campgrounds and
Unique Outdoor Accommodations in and
around National Parks, Seashores,
Monuments, and More

**STEPHANIE & JEREMY PUGLISI**

sourcebooks

Published by Sourcebooks
P.O. Box 4410, Naperville, Illinois 60567-4410
(630) 961-3900
sourcebooks.com

Library of Congress Cataloging-in-Publication Data

Names: Puglisi, Stephanie, author. | Puglisi, Jeremy, author.
Title: Where should we camp next? National parks : the best campgrounds and
    unique outdoor accommodations in and around national parks, seashores,
    monuments, and more / Stephanie & Jeremy Puglisi.
Other titles: National parks
Description: Naperville, Illinois : Sourcebooks, 2023. | Summary: "With
    America's national parks seeing rejuvenated interest from campers,
    whether it's in tents, RVs, cabins, or yurts, one question continues to
    float around camping communities more than any other: 'Where should I
    camp next?' Camping and RV experts Jeremy and Stephanie Puglisi are here
    with the answers. Where Should We Camp Next?: National Parks offers an
    expert but accessible guide to the best campgrounds and outdoor
    accommodations in and around over one hundred national parks,
    lakeshores, monuments, and more. The Puglisis will help you understand
    the different types of camping accommodations, find hidden gems across
    the country, and plan your family's next bucket list trip. It's time to
    make some memories in America's breathtaking national parks system!"—
    Provided by publisher.
Identifiers: LCCN 2022038851 (print) | LCCN 2022038852 (ebook) | (trade paperback) | (pdf) | (epub)
Subjects: LCSH: Camping—United States—Guidebooks. | Camp sites,
    facilities, etc.—United States—Guidebooks. | Family recreation—United
    States—Guidebooks. | National parks and reserves—United
    States—Guidebooks.
Classification: LCC GV191.4 .P84 2023 (print) | LCC GV191.4 (ebook) | DDC
    917.306/8—dc23/eng/20220923
LC record available at https://lccn.loc.gov/2022038851

LC ebook record available at https://lccn.loc.gov/2022038852

Printed and bound in the United States of America.
KP 10 9 8 7 6 5 4 3 2

Once again to Theo, Max, and Wes.
We have climbed to the top of so
many mountains together. And we
are not done yet. Not even close.

# CONTENTS

## Cape Hatteras National Seashore and The Wright Brothers National Memorial   106

## Gulf Islands National Seashore   112

## Everglades National Park and Big Cypress National Preserve   117

# *Midwest Region*

## Sleeping Bear Dunes National Lakeshore   123

## Pictured Rocks National Lakeshore   131

## Southwest Region

# Pacific Northwest and Alaska Region

## Denali National Park and Preserve   339

# HOW TO USE THIS BOOK

National park vacations are an iconic part of the American travel experience, and what better way to experience a national park than by camping in or near one?

Well, easier said than done.

Every national park has a completely different campground ecosystem—some have a dozen campgrounds, and some have none at all. Some require reservations, and some have only first-come, first-served sites. Some have a mixture of both. Certain national park campgrounds open for reservations six months in advance, and others open sixty days in advance. The campsite hookups, sizes, amenities, and number of RV sites all vary from campground to campground, even within the same national park.

It can be a very confusing system to navigate, especially for first-time campers or first-time visitors. The purpose of this book is to provide readers with the very best campground options around premier national park destinations throughout the country. We've picked favorite campgrounds both in and outside of the national parks' boundaries and provided details about everything from scenic beauty to reservation policies to on-site activities and amenities. For each national park, we've aimed to showcase a wide variety of campground types, from rustic boondocking sites to full-service RV resorts. No campground is perfect for everyone, but hopefully we can help guide you to the campground that is perfect for you in each bucket-list destination.

Each campground in this book was selected because we think it has great qualities that may satisfy and delight a certain type of camper. There are featured campgrounds inside the park for those looking for a more immersive national park experience. And there are featured campgrounds outside of the park boundaries for folks seeking more creature comforts, or perhaps an easier booking experience. Within each of these categories we've highlighted an "author's choice," which basically means if we were forced to pick a favorite—and we do love them all—that one would be the winner.

# PLANNING A NATIONAL PARK CAMPING OR RV TRIP

## Should You Stay Inside or Outside of the National Park?

We encourage you to pick a national park and do a little research before deciding what type of campground you want to stay at when visiting that particular destination. Some national parks have amazingly scenic campgrounds, and some simply do not. It is a well-acknowledged fact that the National Park Service has been woefully underfunded, and its infrastructure has suffered over the last few decades. In fact, in 2020, the U.S. Congress passed the Great American Outdoors Act, securing billions of dollars to fund the backlog of maintenance issues within America's public lands. As campers and national park enthusiasts, we hope to see the results of that funding over the next decade.

You may be the type of camper who always wants to camp within the national park proper. Or, after doing a little reading in this book, you may realize that a nearby state park or Bureau of Land Management (BLM) site is a better option. Consider all your options for each individual location before committing to a campground booking.

## What Type of Campground Is Right for You?

Even for national park trips, there are campground options in the middle of the action and campgrounds that are completely off the grid. Each one will come with a unique set of pros and cons, depending on your perspective. A remote national park campground may have the most beautiful views, but it also may lack any cell service or access to basic supplies. A campground in a nearby gateway town will make getting into the park every day take a bit longer, but you'll be able to enjoy dinner at a restaurant after a long day of adventuring and maybe even a swim in the campground pool. Decide how important basic amenities like RV hookups and Wi-Fi are to you, and make campground choices accordingly. Always make sure to check site length if you are traveling with an RV, and carefully review pet policies if you are traveling with a furry friend.

## How and Where Do You Make Campground Reservations?

Folks who are new to camping and RVing are often shocked at how difficult it is to navigate the reservation policies and systems for various public lands. Most national park campgrounds are available to reserve on recreation.gov, and that's also where you can purchase or reserve passes for national park activities and attractions. Once you've chosen a national park campground featured in this book, you can go straight to recreation.gov and search for that campground to learn more. Or you can go to the park-specific NPS website, find the camping page by using the top navigation menu, then click on the campground to find more information about reservations and booking windows.

We do recommend other public campgrounds or camping sites in this book, like state parks, national forests, and BLM lands. Each will have its own reservation or permit system. Some state parks have their own systems, and some use platforms like reserveamerica.com. If you are trying to nab a reservation at a very popular public campground, become familiar with the process before the booking window opens. We are not exaggerating to say that some of these campgrounds fill up within a minute of the reservation window opening.

Private campgrounds have their own unique reservation systems. Some franchises and chains—like KOA and Sun Outdoors—have a central reservations platform for all their locations. Independent private campgrounds may still require you to call to make a reservation. Note any cancellation policies when booking at a private campground. They are often much less flexible than hotels, and new campers and RVers are sometimes shocked at cancellation fees and penalties, which often include a nonrefundable deposit or campground credit only.

## What Are First-Come, First-Served Campgrounds?

You'll see in this book that some national park campgrounds are first-come, first-served or have some first-come, first-served sites. This means that the campground opens up any available sites at a certain time in the morning—usually at checkout time—and the first campers to arrive can claim that spot. This is a wonderful option if you are looking for a bit of flexibility and whimsy in your national park travel. If you are planning on staying at any first-come, first-served campground, research the policies at that particular campground. Know what time available spots open up, and be in line for those spots if it's a popular campground. You should also have a backup plan if the campground is known to fill up fast.

## Using Online Reviews

We never book a campground without doing our homework, and that includes researching campground reviews from a variety of our favorite resources. After choosing a recommendation from this book, you may want to do some extra digging—and that's a good idea. Don't just look at a star rating to make your decision. You'll also want to do a good amount of reading to make sure you are getting a holistic idea of the campground vibe. Here are some other tips for successfully navigating online campground reviews.

### Take Reviews Seriously

Sometimes we hear people complaining about a campground, and when we do a little research, it turns out that the place has years' worth of bad reviews with no response from management. If more than one review mentions late-night partying or dirty bathhouses, you should believe them. Also note when a review was left. Sometimes campgrounds change ownership or make a significant investment in amenities over the course of time. Don't believe everything that every reviewer writes but do look for patterns.

### Look for Reviews from People Who Have Similar Camping Styles to You

If you are tent camping, look for reviews from tent campers. The same is true for RVers or cabin renters. Different types of accommodations and campsites may have different issues, even at the same campground.

### Pay Attention to Specific Amenities That Are Critiqued

Some perfectly acceptable campgrounds in beautiful places have specific features and amenities that you might not care about at all. For example, we prefer to use our RV bathroom and rarely walk into the bathhouses at campgrounds. It really doesn't matter to us if a bathhouse isn't perfectly maintained. However, if you are tent camping, this may be the single most important campground amenity. The same could be true of playgrounds, pools, or fitness centers. Pay attention to feedback on things that are important to you personally.

### Follow Up with Additional Crowdsourcing

There are so many camping Facebook groups that make it easy to double-check your campground choices. In The RV Atlas Facebook group, people get feedback on campgrounds across the country in minutes, often confirming that they are picking a fantastic location. They also receive helpful tips from the crowd, perhaps being warned that the mosquitoes are bad in July, or the river sites tend to flood in spring. Crowdsourcing campground information is easier than ever, so take advantage whenever possible.

# Campground Pricing in and around National Parks

How much does it cost to camp? People ask this question over and over, and there's no easy answer. The truth is...it depends. It depends on the location, the type of campground, and the amenities the campground offers. However, it can also vary greatly within a campground itself. A single campground might offer tent sites for $30, electric and water RV sites for $60, and paved, pull-through, full hook-up sites for $80. Nevertheless, after more than a decade of camping all over the country, in private and public campgrounds, with rustic and resort-style amenities, we can offer some general price ranges that will help you weigh the affordability of camping and budget for your own national park adventures.

Remember: Campgrounds are real estate, and prices will often coincide with how expensive the real estate is in a particular region. Expect to pay significantly more for campgrounds near the most popular national parks in the country, like the Smokies and Glacier.

### Public Campgrounds

Public campgrounds are located in state parks, national parks, county parks, Army Corps of Engineers parks, national forests, or in any other government-managed land. These are hands down your most affordable campgrounds. Many of the campgrounds are also going to be rustic, with limited hookups or on-site amenities, although this is not the case across the board. Some public campgrounds, especially in the West, have camping fees as low as $10. Most, however, fall into the range of $20 to $40 for tent and RV sites. Cabins range from $50 to $100.

### Standard Private Campgrounds

Private campgrounds are owned by individuals or corporations, and there is a huge range of campsite quality and amenities in this category. For the purposes of giving a general price range here, we are talking about private campgrounds that offer full hookups and a standard level of amenities, which may include a camp store, laundry facilities, playground, and pool. They may also provide some organized activities on the weekends or during peak season. In other words, they have the basics, but nothing particularly fancy. This category would include the KOA Journey and Holiday campgrounds. These are perfect as a clean, safe base camp for your national park adventures. The price range for this type of campground is from $50 to $80, depending on the type of amenities offered and the location. Cabins cost anywhere from $75 to $200 per night. The biggest differentiator in the cabin pricing is the number of beds and bathroom or kitchen facilities.

### Private Campground Resorts

What's the difference between an average private campground and a resort? It's all about the on-site level of amenities and service. Campground resorts don't just have pools; they have multiple pools (probably heated pools) and additional water features like spray grounds or waterslides. Perhaps they have hot tubs and lazy rivers. True resorts also offer dining options and full activity schedules for kids and adults alike. The price tag for this type of campground ranges from $70 to $200 in general. Cabins cost anywhere from $150 to $300 per night.

### Dynamic Pricing

A decade ago, campgrounds offered pretty transparent pricing that was stable throughout an entire camping season. While most public campgrounds still have a standard price for each type of site (tent, electric, electric/water, electric/water/sewer), times have changed for many private campgrounds. It is becoming more and more common for private campgrounds, especially resorts, to use the dynamic pricing model that hotels have used for decades. Prices for the same site at the same campground will vary greatly depending on the day of the week and month of the year. A full hook-up campsite at a resort might be $70 per night on a Wednesday in early June and $125 per night on a Saturday in July. If you are looking for the amenities without the high price point, try to camp during the week or during the shoulder seasons. Also be aware that many private campgrounds are now offering a "site lock" fee option, where you can pay an additional fee to secure a particular site. While this is not a popular development in the camping community, it may be worth spending the money to guarantee the perfect site you want.

## Tips for Visiting National Parks

### Book Any Reservable Camping Accommodations as Early as Possible
If there's something worth repeating over and over again—this is it. National parks have always been popular vacation destinations, and camping is more popular than ever. The lack of available campsites is a common complaint among seasoned campers and RVers. Plan as far in advance as possible.

### Start at the Visitor Center for Personalized Tips
Upon arriving you might want to drive past the NPS visitor center and head straight into the park. That would be a mistake. Even if you have done your homework, speaking to a ranger and getting personalized recommendations is key to a great visit. Rangers are aware of current conditions throughout the park. They also have the uncanny ability to look at your family and figure out exactly what hikes or adventures will be perfect for your crew's (potentially) diverse ability levels.

### Read All Safety Recommendations on the Park's Website
Visiting a national park is not like visiting Disney World. A family trip to Yellowstone or Yosemite can be dangerous if you do not read and implement each park's safety rules and regulations. Most accidents that occur in national parks are easily avoidable. If you take the time to learn about the dangers that exist in each park, and apply common sense during your adventures there, you will avoid injuries that could easily ruin your trip.

### Avoid Crowded Spots at Busy Times
The overcrowding of our national parks has become a major story over the last few years. But are they really that overcrowded? Should we just stay home

or wait until next year? We don't think so. Yes, the most popular spots, in the most popular parks, at the most popular times, are jam-packed with visitors. But opportunities for off-the-beaten-path adventures exist in all our great national parks, especially if you can avoid weekends and visit during shoulder seasons. You might also decide to explore a less visited park—opting for North Cascades over Olympic, or Shenandoah over Great Smoky Mountains.

## Get Up Early and Go

The single most important tip we can give anyone who wants to enjoy a national park visit is to get up early. Popular sites and trailheads often have limited parking that can easily fill up by 8:00 a.m. The difference between crowds at entrance gates and visitors' centers in the early morning compared to after lunchtime is stunning. We've often heard folks say they are not morning people and will enjoy the late afternoon instead. In our experience, parks don't start to quiet down until dinner time, and by that time it may not be safe to head out on a hike. Consider becoming an early bird, at least for your national park adventures.

## Pack Tons of Snacks and Water

Nothing will ruin a day in the park more easily than someone getting hangry. Make sure you pack plenty of food and water for the day, and never assume you will be able to replenish supplies inside the park. Some national park newbies are shocked at the lack of concessions in many places. A cooler with sandwiches, fruit, and granola bars is always a good idea. You also need to calculate how much water to bring on every hike that you take. Filling up a few water bottles without making specific calculations could lead to dehydration on the trail.

## Attend Amphitheater Talks, Interpretive Walks, and Ranger Programs

Some of the most amazing national park experiences happen when rangers and guides bring the park to life during tours and talks. One of the best reasons to stay in a national park campground is that many host evening ranger talks right on site. We've learned about bear safety in St. Mary's Campground in Glacier, the moon phases in Cedar Pass Campground in the Badlands, and the lives of otters and weasels in Platte River Campground in Sleeping Bear Dunes. Make sure to get a program schedule when you first arrive and fit some into your itinerary.

### Always Get a Picture by the National Park Sign

It may feel corny, but most folks treasure those pictures when they look back through their camera roll. And framing those sign pictures is a great way to display your national park adventures. You can bring a mini tripod along with you on your trip, master the selfie, or find someone to take the picture for you. It's worth the stop.

## Tips for Visiting National Parks with Kids

### Get the Kids Educated and Excited before You Go

In the months leading up to a national park camping trip, we like to immerse ourselves and our kids in books, movies, videos, and music about the park we will be visiting. YouTube has also proved to be a terrific resource for destination videos. This process builds anticipation and excitement and often leads to the kids helping develop our travel itinerary. We always encourage this and try to empower them by implementing their suggestions for hikes, activities, and even restaurants.

### Participate in the Junior Ranger Programs

If you have kids between the ages of five and twelve, then plan on doing the Junior Ranger program at every park you visit. The activities are engaging and completely different at each park. Our kids loved the scavenger hunts and activity booklets and being sworn in as Junior Rangers after completing them. The badges from each location also became their favorite souvenirs from each and every trip.

Junior ranger booklets are available at national parks, national seashores, and national historic sites across the country. The booklets contain activities that are specific to that location, and children can earn badges or patches for completing the park booklets. Most of the Junior Ranger programs are free of charge, but a few parks like Yellowstone do charge a nominal fee for the booklets. These programs have captured our kids' imaginations across the country, from Olympic National Park to Sleeping Bear Dunes to FDR's Hyde Park. If you are camping with kids, this is an amazing way to get them excited about visiting our nation's natural and historic treasures. Here are some things to keep in mind if you'd like your children to participate:

1. Do some advance research. We like to look online or call to see what the general Junior Ranger requirements are for a particular park. Sometimes our visit will be too short to complete the program, and we like to know that in advance. For example, we only had about four hours at Crater Lake National Park, and we knew that we wanted to do the rim hike, so we let the kids know ahead of time that they wouldn't be earning Junior Ranger badges that day.

2. Pick up your Junior Ranger booklet before doing anything else in the national park. Every Junior Ranger booklet is different, so we like to know the requirements before we start hopping around a park. Often the booklets will require attendance at a ranger talk or two, so it's good to get the schedule and plan that at the beginning of your visit.

3. Celebrate the swearing in ceremony. Our boys earned their very first Junior Ranger badges at Cape Hatteras National Seashore. We took pictures, made a big fuss, and then celebrated with ice cream. We wanted them to look forward to collecting even more badges and patches in the future.

4. Check out the online Junior Ranger programs that can be completed from home. If your kids really connect with this type of learning, the National Park Service has programs you can complete at home when you aren't camping. Topics include fishing, exploring the wilderness, and learning about the night sky. Once they've completed the activities, you mail them in to receive the badge.

## Choose Hikes that Lead to Big Payoffs

There's a lot of hiking in many national parks, and if you're not careful, kids can burn out on the activity. Choose your hikes wisely. Look for adventurous climbs with big payoffs along the way. Our own kids love hikes that crisscross streams or lead us to waterfalls or summits with panoramic views. We have hiked to glaciers in Montana, and we have hiked above the clouds in Olympic National Park. There may be some grumbling along the way, but snacks usually help with that.

## Slow Down and Soak in the Beauty

It is possible to overplan a trip to a national park, just like it is possible to overplan a trip to Disney World. If you feel like you are rushing from place to place and stressing out about parking and squeezing in every last thing on your list, take a deep breath, slow down, and soak up the beauty around you. Always remember that you don't have to see and do everything in one trip. A return trip to a magnificent location is often as good or even better than the maiden voyage.

## Schedule Recovery Days and Downtime at the Campground

Make the most of your time in a national park with kids by scheduling some big, ambitious adventures, but also be thoughtful about planning downtime at the campground and what we like to think of as "recovery days." If we plan two to three straight days of rigorous biking, hikes, and scenic drives, we will often take a full day off for more relaxing activities like chilling at the campground, swimming, taking a guided tour, or doing some souvenir shopping in a gateway town.

## Sign Up for Every Kid Outdoors If You Have a Fourth Grader

Do not neglect to sign up for Every Kid Outdoors, and print out the pass before you head out to a national park with your fourth grader.

In 2015, the federal government launched Every Kid in a Park, an initiative to introduce more children to the natural wonders protected by the

National Park Service. A few years later the program was renamed Every Kid Outdoors and expanded to include hundreds of national parks and historic sites along with millions of acres of public lands.

Every Kid Outdoors offers all fourth graders a free entrance pass to hundreds of Bureau of Land Management, U.S. Fish and Wildlife Service, National Park Service, Bureau of Reclamation, National Oceanic and Atmospheric Administration, U.S. Forest Service, and U.S. Army Corps of Engineers sites. Go to everykidoutdoors.gov and follow the simple steps to apply and print the pass. Note that the pass must be printed (an unnecessary hurdle in our opinion) and presented for entrance. The pass covers the fourth grader and any other passengers in the vehicle. If the national park site charges per person, the pass will cover the fourth grader and up to three adults. No electronic receipts or proof of pass will be accepted—we, along with many other parents, have learned this the hard way.

There are certain NPS sites or attractions that are run by concessionaires and charge for amenities like parking, ferry rides, or tours. The pass will not cover those fees or any camping fees.

## Tips for Visiting National Parks with Pets

1. Do your research. Camping is an extremely pet-friendly way to travel; however, national parks camping trips can be an exception to this generalization. Many national parks are established to protect the natural environment, and if pets threaten the wildlife, plant life, or geological integrity of a site, the park service will restrict their access. Don't be surprised by pet policies when you show up at a national park. Make sure in advance they are allowed in the campground and know which activities you may have to forgo if you bring your furry friend.

2. Plan for your pet's safety at the campsite. You may have to make national park trips and campground decisions based on your pet's safety. You'll want to make sure you don't visit during extreme heat or cold temperatures. Make sure your pet is not left alone in a tent or RV during your stay.

Take precautions to keep them safe from wildlife—elk, bear, and bison roam through campgrounds in many national parks. Consider staying outside the park at private campgrounds with hookups, dog parks, and dog kenneling services. When we visited Badlands National Park in the summer, we reserved a less scenic campsite that offered electricity so we could be sure to keep our family cattle dog cool and comfortable.

3. Plan for your pet's safety while exploring the park. We love taking our dog along on our national park adventures, but we are also careful to prepare in advance to keep her safe and healthy. Check the forecast in advance to make sure temperatures will be mild enough for their comfort. Never leave your pet in a vehicle unattended while you go inside a visitor center or on a hike. Bring plenty of food and water. Be aware of park-specific hazards and follow park guidelines. We witnessed a dog being allowed to dip its nose in a geyser at Yellowstone, which could have caused serious injury. Snakebites and falls from cliffs are other common dog injuries in national parks. Be aware and be prepared.

4. Always leash your pet. No matter how well behaved your pet is, or how perfect their recall, pets are always required to be on a 6-foot leash while in national parks. This is as much for your pet's safety as for anyone else's. This is a nonnegotiable, so if you are bringing your pet to a NPS site, be prepared to follow this guideline.

5. Always clean up after your pet. The national parks were created to protect the land, and pet waste can put serious strain on an ecosystem. Just because you are in a remote location far from anyone else does not mean you stop cleaning up after your pet. Carry in the baggies and carry out the poop—every time.

## The B.A.R.K Ranger Program

Part of the Healthy People, Healthy Parks initiative, the B.A.R.K Ranger Program was launched within the last decade and has expanded quickly in the last few years.

The acronym stands for:

⇢ **Bag your pet's waste.**

⇢ **Always leash your pet.**

⇢ **Respect wildlife.**

⇢ **Know where you can go.**

The program is much more than a cute and memorable acronym. It encourages folks to understand the unique pet restrictions at individual parks and embrace the activities that are pet friendly. Many parks have developed their own B.A.R.K Ranger programs for pet owners to complete during their visit. Acadia—a very dog-friendly national park—has an activity sheet that dogs can complete to be sworn in as Bark Rangers, and Bark Ranger collar tags are available for purchase at the visitor center gift shop. Other national park sites offer Bark Ranger badges or stamps. General program information is available on the main nps.gov site, and park program specifics are detailed on individual park pages.

## National Park Designations

As of this writing, there are sixty-three official national parks, but there are a whopping 423 national park sites in the United States that are administered by the National Park Service, including national lakeshores, national monuments, and national battlefields. When choosing locations for this book, we aimed to feature the national park sites that offer the most phenomenal camping experiences, whether they are national parks, national seashores, or any other NPS sites. Here are some of the lesser-known federal units highlighted in this book.

### National Memorials

If you only visit NPS units that are designated as "national parks," you would miss out on classic road-trip destinations such as Mount Rushmore National Memorial, which is tiny compared to Yellowstone or Yosemite—but it is every bit as iconic.

### National Battlefields and National Military Parks

National battlefields like Antietam and national military parks like Gettysburg serve as historical feasts for Civil War buffs and casual tourists alike.

### National Recreation Areas

National recreation areas, such as the Delaware Water Gap, offer world-class hiking, kayaking, and fishing—less than two hours from both New York City and Philadelphia.

### National Seashores

Many families make annual pilgrimages to NPS units like Cape Hatteras National Seashore for miles upon miles of wild and windswept beaches and the best surfing on the East Coast.

### National Lakeshores

Our national lakeshores such as Sleeping Bear Dunes are every bit as stunning as our most famous national parks. This underrated Michigan gem was voted "Most Beautiful Place in America" by viewers of *Good Morning America* in 2011.

### National Parkways

National parkways—such as the Blue Ridge Parkway, which links Shenandoah National Park to Great Smoky Mountains National Park—are worthy destinations in their own right. Plan on making plenty of stops as stunning vistas and endless wildflowers abound.

## National Park Gear

Having the right gear can make or break a national park experience. Every national park requires a different packing list, but in our experience all-weather gear and wildlife safety gear are the two most important categories to ensure a great travel experience.

Many national parks are in places that see extreme temperature and weather changes over the course of a twenty-four-hour period. Many parks also have a wide range of elevation. Packing layered clothing is key to being comfortable. Always bring rain gear and more than one pair of comfortable, broken-in shoes. Wide-brimmed hats and light, long-sleeved shirts and pants are a must when visiting national parks with biting insects. Pack sunscreen and bug repellent as well.

Research the wildlife safety recommendations in advance. Purchase bear spray and bear bells before your trip to save money. Fragrance free toiletries are highly recommended. Make sure you can store all of your food properly at the campground, especially if camping in a tent or pop-up camper.

Other items to pack for national park trips include:

- **National Park passport book**
- **Emergency medical kit**
- **Hiking backpacks**
- **Emergency whistle**
- **Map and compass**
- **Knife or multitool**
- **Binoculars**
- **Refillable water bottles**
- **Headlamps**
- **Printed copies of all reservation information in case of no cell service**
- **Proof of vaccination for any pets**

## RV Driving and Parking Precautions

Never assume that you can drive an RV anywhere in a national park without specifically checking road restrictions. Just because we have recommended a scenic drive in this book does not mean that road is RV friendly. Many RVers tow trailers, and they can unhitch at the campground and drive to various places in the national park. Motor home owners may tow a smaller vehicle behind the RV and use that to explore a destination. If you plan on driving a motor home or towing an RV within any national park boundaries, do your research in advance to ensure that there are no extreme grading, hairpin turns, low tunnels, or other hazards. Also understand that while many visitor centers offer RV parking, it will be very difficult to park at any of the trailheads or park attractions.

## National Park Safety

National parks are, by design, wild places. These natural wonders experience floods, fires, and other extreme weather events throughout the year. One of the best resources for up-to-the-minute important safety information is the National Park Service website, NPS.gov. If you go to any specific park page (such as nps.gov/glac/ for Glacier National Park), you'll see a list of any current safety alerts for that park. These can include any reservation or timed entry requirements, road closings, fire warnings, and more. Download the free NPS app on your iOS or Android smartphone before your trip, and check for new alerts every day.

There's also a web page on specific safety concerns for each park. For example, you'll find information about the dangers of frigid glacier water and bear safety on the Glacier page. The Great Sand Dunes page talks about wind, sand, and lightning. Give this page a once-over before heading to the park, and you'll be much better prepared to experience our country's wildest places.

-------- **Favorite National Park Digital Resources** --------

**Apps**

▷ The National Park Service App

▷ National Park Pocket Maps

▷ GyPSy Guide

▷ National Park Trail Guide

▷ Just Ahead: Audio Travel Guides

▷ AllTrails: Hike, Bike, & Run

**Documentaries**

▷ *The National Parks: America's Best Idea*, PBS

▷ *Our Great National Parks*, Netflix

▷ *America's National Parks*, National Geographic

See book and show recommendations for individual national parks in the book chapters!

# Acadia National Park

Acadia National Park, located on Mount Desert Island in Maine, is one of the most visited national parks in the country. It's also a very popular RV destination with plenty of campgrounds both inside and near the park, but you'll have to book as far in advance as possible to score some of the more popular sites.

Most of the campgrounds open sometime in May and host visitors through mid-to-late October. It's a relatively short tourist season, so the crowds can be more intense—and campground booking more competitive— than at other popular national parks with longer shoulder seasons. Planning ahead and knowing reservation windows is an important part of planning a camping trip to Acadia National Park. Reservations, open sixty days in advance on a rolling basis, are required for all of the Acadia National Park campgrounds, and no first-come, first-served sites are available.

The black fly season traditionally spans from Mother's Day to Father's Day in Maine, so we have always preferred to schedule our visits at various times after mid-June. Late August is a heavenly time in Acadia, with warm days and cool nights and potentially fewer crowds. Fall foliage season is stunning but brief, with peak colors occurring from late September to mid-October.

Although three of the national park campgrounds have RV friendly sites, none of them have showers and cell reception is limited, if not nonexistent. If you are looking for hot showers and Wi-Fi, you'll probably want to check out one of the many private campgrounds on the island. Properties on the island along Route 3 offer easy access to both the park and the gateway town of Bar Harbor.

# CAMPGROUNDS INSIDE THE PARK

### Schoodic Woods Campground

▷ **Winter Harbor, Maine**

▷ **nps.gov**

▷ **RV and Tent Sites**

A rare modern national park campground, Schoodic Woods opened in 2015 and is the only Acadia National Park campground with electric hookups. It's also the only park campground that is located on the mainland, near Winter Harbor—an hour's drive from Bar Harbor and the park loop. If you are willing to drive a bit to see the park's most popular attractions, staying at Schoodic Woods is the perfect way to be surrounded by the famous Acadian scenery without battling the crowds. The campground is open from May 25 through October 9 (subject to change), and campsites can be booked two months in advance, on a rolling basis. Although seventy-eight of the eighty-nine sites offer electricity, there are no sewer or water hookups. The bathhouses have flushable toilets but no showers. The rangers will encourage guests to use pay showers and purchase items like ice, firewood, and propane in nearby Winter Harbor.

The campground amphitheater offers a robust schedule of ranger programs for all ages. Miles of hard-packed gravel bike paths are accessible

directly from the campground, leading riders through winding, wooded terrain and along stunning, rocky shorelines. The Schoodic Institute is just minutes away offering learning exhibits, educational programs, and even a touch tank for young visitors.

## Blackwoods Campground

▷   Mount Desert, Maine

▷   nps.gov

▷   RV and Tent Sites

Blackwoods Campground is a large, wooded campground on Mount Desert Island within walking distance of the ocean. The campground is only 5 miles south of Bar Harbor and close to many of the park's most famous attractions. Out of the 281 campsites, only 60 are available for RVs and the rest are tent sites. Like the other campgrounds in this park, there are no site hookups or showers for campers. Flush toilets, a dump station, and potable water are available.

-------------------- **Unique Attraction** --------------------

**Timber Tina's Great Maine Lumberjack Show**

Before Timber Tina became known as a contestant on *Survivor: Panama*, she was leading her crew of LumberJacks and Jills through nightly performances of log climbing, ax throwing, and crosscut sawing for Maine tourists. It's a roaring, interactive, and surprisingly educational seventy-five-minute show that you won't forget.

## Seawall Campground

▷   Southwest Harbor, Maine

▷   nps.gov

▷   RV and Tent Sites

Seawall Campground is located on the west side of Acadia National Park, often referred to as the quiet side of Mount Desert Island, near Southwest Harbor and the much-photographed Bass Harbor Head Lighthouse. Out of the 202 campsites, 59 can host RVs that are 20 feet or shorter in length. The coastline is within walking distance of the campground. Flush toilets, a dump station, and potable water are available. There are no showers in the campground, but vendors offer paid showers within driving distance.

## Other Campgrounds Inside the Park

→ **Duck Harbor**
→ **Wildwood Stable Campground**

# CAMPGROUNDS OUTSIDE THE PARK

### Bar Harbor/Oceanside KOA Holiday

▷ Bar Harbor, Maine

▷ koa.com

▷ RV and Tent Sites, Cabins

This is an amazing campground that you will want to return to over and over again...if you manage to nab one of the waterfront sites, labeled as "ocean-front" and "prime" sites on the KOA campground map. These preferred campsites only have water and electric hookups, but it's worth going without a sewer connection to enjoy uninterrupted views of the sunset in the evenings. To be frank, sites in the interior part of the campground are nothing spectacular, and for us it is waterfront-or-bust if staying at this KOA. An on-site cafe provides fresh-caught lobster dinners. Landlubbers can order a hotdog or cheeseburger if absolutely necessary. There's no guarantee of her arrival, but for years guests at this KOA have been enjoying homemade blueberry pies and other sweet treats delivered by the Pie Lady who drives through the campground a few times a week. Have your cash in hand.

## Bar Harbor Campground

▷   Bar Harbor, Maine

▷   thebarharborcampground.com

▷   RV and Tent Sites

Bar Harbor Campground offers some campsites with the same beautiful ocean views as the Bar Harbor/Oceanfront KOA Holiday, plus it has a heated pool and spotless bathhouses. However, it does not take reservations or credit cards, so this isn't going to be a perfect fit for every camper. When you arrive at the campground, the staff offer a site map and invite you to drive around and pick your favorite spot. Campground management recommends arriving no later than 9:00 a.m. in the summer to nab a site. If you are willing to risk it, the reward will be a clean, quiet, affordable campground just minutes from the main park entrance.

--------------- **Gateway Town: Bar Harbor** ---------------

You'll find both souvenir traps and local favorites in downtown Bar Harbor—a bustling and charming gateway town with views of Frenchman Bay. Depart on a whale watching adventure from the town pier, hike over to Bar Island via the land bridge that appears at low tide, or enjoy lobster ice cream from Ben & Bill's Chocolate Emporium. You can also rent bikes from downtown outfitters and explore Acadia's carriage roads or enjoy a guided sunset kayak tour.

## Under Canvas Acadia

▷   Surry, Maine

▷   undercanvas.com

▷   Glamping Tents

If you don't own an RV and you're not interested in pitching a tent, Under Canvas delivers on the glamping experience with classic coastal Maine views and its signature deluxe canvas tent suites. Be warned—despite the name, Under Canvas Acadia is not located on Mount Desert Island and it will take roughly 40 minutes to drive to the Park Loop Road area. Despite its distance from the park, Under Canvas Acadia is worth checking out for its spectacular water views, comfortable lounge areas, and curated local adventures with concierge-type service.

## Terramor Outdoor Resort

▷ Bar Harbor, Maine

▷ terramoroutdoorresort.com

▷ Glamping Tents

KOA recently jumped aboard the glamping train by changing one of its two Mount Desert Island properties into a Terramor Outdoor Resort, complete with luxury canvas tents for families and couples, a pool, spa, hot tub, lodge with ample common areas, and on-site dining with local food. There is also a bar so you can grab a cocktail around the campfire in the evening. The property has earned positive reviews thus far, and many insiders think KOA is going to expand the Terramor brand to compete with Under Canvas and Collective Retreats locations across the country. This location is just minutes from Bar Harbor and the Park Loop Road, but note that the property does not feature any water views—a must have for many Acadia visitors.

---

### Worth Braving the Crowds ----------------

**Jordan Pond House**

Yes, the crowds at Jordan Pond House will have you questioning whether any popovers could possibly be worth the hassle. The short answer is—they are. We recommend arriving when it first opens at 11:00 a.m. or during the mid-afternoon lull, around 3:30 p.m.

## Lamoine State Park

▷ Lamoine, Maine

▷ maine.gov

▷ RV and Tent Sites

If you want the rustic, public campground experience, but you can't get into the national park campgrounds, try securing one of the sixty-one RV friendly campsites at Lamoine State Park. This campground is about thirty minutes from Bar Harbor and the main entrance to Acadia, but you'll still enjoy sweeping views of Frenchman Bay. There are no hookups, but the bathhouses offer hot showers. The campground states that it can accommodate RVs up to 45 feet in length. Nevertheless, big rig owners do report having difficulty navigating the tight turns and unlevel sites. Reservations for Maine State Park campgrounds open for the upcoming season in February, so put a reminder in your smartphone.

## Other Campgrounds Outside the Park

→ **Smuggler's Den Campground**

→ **Hadley's Point Campground**

→ **Narrows Too Camping Resort**

------------------ **Know Before You Go** ------------------
Island Explorer is a free bus transportation system that operates on routes throughout Mount Desert Island and the Schoodic Peninsula. Most campgrounds will have a designated bus stop, and campground offices should provide route maps. Schedules and maps can also be found online. Free transportation is phenomenal. The added pet-friendly policies and bike racks make us swoon.

# Family-Friendly Hikes in Acadia National Park

## Ocean Trail

This easy, 4-mile roundtrip hike (also known as Ocean Path or Ocean Drive Trail) is the classic introductory hike to Acadia National Park. Starting at Sand Beach, the path brings you to Thunder Hole and Otter Cliffs, passing by one beautiful vista after another. There are many trail spurs that can lead to dramatic views and also dramatic drop-offs. There are also stretches where the path meanders alongside the Park Loop Road. Traffic can be fast and close, so beware. This hike is crowded during peak season.

## Gorham Mountain Trail

One of the more famous hikes along the Park Loop, this trail rewards its hikers with stunning views of Sand Beach, Otter Cliffs, and Cadillac Mountain. The summit offers incredible ocean panoramas and plenty of space for a snack or picnic lunch. The Cadillac Cliffs trail spur offers some fun rock scrambles.

## Wonderland/Ship Harbor Trails

Get away from the crowds clustered around the Park Loop, and drive past Southwest Harbor to the Wonderland and Ship Harbor Trails. Both of these trails can be done independently, or you can hike out to the water on the Wonderland Trail, then head west along the rocky beach to the Ship Harbor Trail and complete a loop back to the parking lot.

## Flying Mountain Trail

This 1.5-mile loop has a steep ascent at the beginning and ends with beautiful views of the Somes Sound. The trail then brings you down to a rocky beach and ends with an easy walk along a fire road back to the parking lot.

## Great Head Trail

This hike begins with a trek across Sand Beach and has some semi-challenging rock scrambles that lead to more of those famous Acadian Gulf of Maine views. Look up into the distance past the beach to watch adventure seekers navigate one of Acadia's most popular rung-and-ladder trails—the Beehive Loop.

# Cape Cod National Seashore

Cape Cod holds a surprising variety of experiences and landscapes for a skinny spit of land extending 65 miles into the Atlantic Ocean. Visitors can kayak in kettle ponds formed thousands of years ago by receding glaciers and climb 252 feet to the top of the Pilgrim Monument in Provincetown. They can hike along the marshy paths at the Wellfleet Bay Wildlife Sanctuary and bike along the 25-mile Cape Cod Rail Trail, stopping for a cup of chowder and an ice cream cone at any one of a dozen charming towns.

Time on Cape Cod offers visitors the opportunity to experience a completely unique beach vacation—one that combines lazy days spent in beach chairs with outdoor adventures and historical learning. The Cape Cod National Seashore seems to blend seamlessly into its environment, protecting dunes and beaches nestled alongside bustling, charming towns like Brewster, Orleans, Eastham, Wellfleet, and Provincetown.

The Upper Cape is the region closest to the mainland, and the majority of the RV, resort-style campgrounds are located in this area...along with the majority of the crowds. The Lower and Outer Cape regions are closer to the bulk of the National Seashore, and this is where we prefer to camp when we visit. At the Cape, we tend to trade amenities like pools and tennis courts for easy access to bike trails and beaches, but if you need a hot tub, we've got campground recommendations for you too.

Before making reservations, think about where you will spend the majority of your time during your stay. During peak season, it can take hours to navigate from Falmouth to Provincetown on the roads choked with summer tourists. Also think about whether you can visit during the shoulder seasons. The Cape is surprisingly quiet in the weeks leading up the Fourth of July. Early September can be magical weather wise, but note that many businesses close their doors right after Labor Day weekend. There are no designated camping areas inside the Cape Cod National Seashore. But don't fret—there are amazing camping options, both public and private, spread throughout the rest of the Cape.

# CAMPGROUNDS OUTSIDE THE PARK

### Nickerson State Park

▷     Brewster, Massachusetts

▷     mass.gov

▷     RV and Tent Sites, Yurts

There are more than 400 campsites spread throughout the pine and oak forests of Nickerson State Park. The fresh water kettle ponds in the park, formed when glaciers retreated from the Cape thousands of years ago, are stocked with trout, and a couple—Flax and Cliff ponds—allow swimming, canoeing, and kayaking. An 8-mile bike path within the park connects to the longer Cape Cod Rail Trail. Campers can easily ride to the Cape Cod Bay beaches. Note that alcohol is prohibited in all Massachusetts State Park campgrounds. Reservations can be made up to four months in advance on a rolling basis. There are no hookups at any campsites in Nickerson State Park, but there are potable water spigots, bathhouses with flush toilets and showers, and a dump station.

## Wellfleet Hollow State Campground

▷ Wellfleet, Massachusetts

▷ mass.gov

▷ Tent Sites Only

This state park does not permit RVs, but this is an inexpensive and rustic place to pitch a tent close to the National Seashore. Duck Pond, a half-mile hike from the campground, permits swimming and non-motorized boating. Some of the sites have 20-amp electric service. There are flush toilets and outdoor showers. Pets are not allowed, and reservations are required.

## Atlantic Oaks

▷ Eastham, Massachusetts

▷ atlanticoaks.com

▷ RV and Tent Sites, Park Model Rentals

Located in Eastham, this campground is just a half mile from the National Seashore Salt Pond Visitor Center and 20 miles from Provincetown. There is also access to the Cape Cod Rail Trail directly from the back of the campground. The sites are wooded, with a rustic feel, but offer water, electric, sewer, and cable hookups. The bathhouses are modern and clean. There are RVs available on-site to rent on a weekly basis. Atlantic Oaks is open in the winter by reservation only for campers who would like to explore the Cape off season.

# Unique Attractions

### Off the Beaten Path

Art's Dune Tours has been taking folks off-roading through the Provincetown Dunes for more than seventy-five years. Driving through the National Historic District of the Cape Cod National Seashore, the one-hour tours run daily from March into November. Art's also offers two-hour sunset tours, with optional dinner and bonfire add-ons.

### Cape Cod Baseball League

This amateur summer baseball league has been around since 1885 but grew increasingly popular when it began using wooden bats in 1985. Players for the ten-team league are recruited from top NCAA schools across the country, and the nonprofit claims that one out of every six MLB pros played in its league. The ten teams are spread out around the Cape with each field offering a unique experience for visitors, and fans enjoy ranking their favorites. Our opinion? You can't go wrong finding a game nearest wherever you are camping.

### Church of the Transfiguration

This religious community, founded on the principles of the Benedictine monastic tradition, has been located on Cape Cod for more than forty years. The church itself is a work of art, with limestone and tile murals designed to tell the story of Christianity. Tours are offered daily throughout the week, leaving from the gift shop, and there is an organ demonstration after 3:00 p.m.

## Sun Outdoors Cape Cod

▷ **Falmouth, Massachusetts**

▷ **sunoutdoors.com**

▷ **RV and Tent Sites, Cabin Rentals**

This RV resort is located in the Upper Cape—the area nearer the mainland— close to Falmouth. If you are interested in visiting Martha's Vineyard or Nantucket, and you don't mind being a drive from the national seashore and P-Town, this may be the perfect location. There are three pools and a lake within the campground. There's also mini-golf, a playground, and an arcade for the kids. Full hookup sites are available for RVers, and there are also tent sites and cabin rentals.

--------------------- **Coffee and a Donut** ---------------------

### Hole in One Bakery & Coffee Shop

This pastry shop opens at 6:00 a.m., and the line can get long for the famous hand-cut donuts and other sweet treats. They make 250 dozen donuts every day during the summer season, so hopefully you can nab a dozen before they run out.

### Beanstock Coffee Roasters

Beanstock's organic, fair-trade coffee is available in dozens of stores and restaurants around the Cape. Our favorite place to grab a cup of this heavenly brew, though, is at the actual roasting facility in Eastham. There's a small retail shop attached where you can stock up on pounds of your favorite blend while you watch the magic being made.

## Shady Knoll Campground

▷ **Brewster, Massachusetts**

▷ **shadyknoll.com**

▷ **RV and Tent Sites**

Shady Knoll, the sister campground to Atlantic Oaks, is located in Brewster and offers a simple, quiet, clean place to park your rig or pitch your tent. There are no bells and whistles at this campground, but guests are about a mile away from the beautiful bay beaches and Nickerson State Park. Full hookups are available, and RVers with big rigs will appreciate the pull-through sites.

## Autocamp Cape Cod

▷ Falmouth, Massachusetts

▷ autocamp.com

▷ Airstream Rentals, Lodging

Located near Falmouth, Autocamp Cape Cod is a good hour's drive from the National Seashore's Salt Pond Visitor Center, but staying in a beautiful Airstream park may be worth battling the summer traffic. In addition to Airstreams, there are luxury cabins and canvas tents available for guests. Complimentary cruiser bikes are available on a first-come, first-served basis, or visitors can splurge for an e-bike rental. There's an on-site cafe plus a general store for basic provisions.

## Race Point ORV Beach Camping

▷ Cape Cod National Seashore

▷ nps.gov

▷ Self-Contained RVs

The National Seashore calls this "Self-Contained-Vehicle Camping in the Off-Road Vehicle Corridor." There are very strict guidelines for the types of campers that can obtain a permit to overnight at Race Point Beach, but if you have one, this is an amazing place to experience the magic of the Cape. Only one hundred vehicles are allowed per night, and the spaces are on a first-come, first-served basis.

----------------- **Where to Whale Watch** -----------------

There are a lot of whale watching options along the Cape, but we highly recommend the Hyannis Whale Watcher Cruises. We recommend taking the earlier tour. The afternoon trips are significantly more crowded. This outfit definitely delivers a breathtaking wildlife viewing experience, but it also places an emphasis on education and conservation efforts. An intern tours the ship, teaching guests about whales, allowing them to touch baleen and bones, and explaining why no sonar or bait is used to attract animals to the boat. The ship doesn't spend too much time in any one location so as not to disrupt the whales, and yet the chances are good that you will be treated to fabulous demonstrations of breaching and blows.

There are two trips per day offered by the Hyannis Whale Watcher Cruises and as we disembark, we see a long line of people ready to board and are relieved we took the early tour since the afternoon trips are significantly more crowded.

## Other Campgrounds Outside the Park

- **Coastal Acres Campground (P-Town)**
- **North of Highland Camping Area (tent campers only)**
- **Adventure Bound Cape Cod**

# Biking in and around Cape Code National Seashore

There are three bike trails within the Cape Cod National Seashore, and biking is one of the most popular ways to explore the park.

▷ Province Lands Bike Trail is a 5.5-mile loop (with additional spurs along the way) that includes steep hills and sharp turns. You can depart from the Province Lands Visitor Center.

▷ Nauset Bike Trail is a paved, hilly 3.2-mile, out-and-back ride that departs from the Salt Lake Visitor Center and brings you to the Coast Guard beach, a popular place for swimming.

▷ Head of the Meadow Bike Trail is an easy 4-mile, out-and-back trail that you can hop on from either High Head Road in Truro or Head of the Meadow Beach.

▷ The Cape Cod Rail Trail is maintained by the state of Massachusetts—not the National Park Service—and runs 22 miles from South Wellfleet to South Dennis. It is a perfect way to travel from town to town along the Cape, especially in the highly trafficked summer months. Many famous Cape Cod dining options, like Arthur's Lobster & Clam Bar, are located along the trail.

# National Parks of New York Harbor

New York City is not the first place that comes to mind when talking about national park camping trips, but there are a whopping nine national park sites around the Port of New York City, and there are indeed places to camp nearby.

Why would someone want to camp near New York City instead of staying at a hotel? It's mostly economics that drives some folks to make this choice. City hotels—even the budget options—are quite pricey. Parking and food can also drive up the costs of staying in the Big Apple. Bottom line? This is one of the most expensive cities in the country, and camping is a great way to control costs. It's also a good way to balance out the hustle and bustle of a city vacation. Some people enjoy visiting a busy and vibrant urban location, and then retreating to the comfort of their own home away from home at the end of the day.

Urban camping isn't for everyone. But if you are looking for a national park adventure you'll never forget, try camping near New York City. There are more great options than you might expect.

# CAMPGROUNDS OUTSIDE THE PARKS

## Liberty Harbor RV Park

▷  **Jersey City, New Jersey**

▷  **libertyharborrv.com**

▷  **RV and Tent Sites**

Let's make this clear right away: Liberty Harbor RV Park is not for the faint of heart. It is basically a waterfront parking lot in Jersey City with tight sites that offer water and electricity hookups. The drive into the RV park can be highly trafficked and a bit nerve-racking depending on your tolerance for towing a trailer or driving a motor home through the city. But you can't get any closer to New York City in an RV, so this quirky spot is sought after by adventurous RVers who want easy access to the Big Apple. It even has a grassy corner section of the property designated for tent campers. But light sleepers beware. You are in the middle of a busy and bustling city, and it can be noisy, even late at night. But the facility is secured 24/7 and you can hop on the New York Waterway Ferry right on the property and head directly over to Wall Street. Other public transportation options are also nearby. You can also see the Statue of Liberty and Ellis Island right from your site...if your neighbor's RV is not blocking the view. A restaurant and a bar are also located on-site. Both get excellent reviews. The park's prices are dirt cheap when compared to any other kind of New York City accommodation, and it is open all year.

## Cheesequake State Park

▷  **Matawan, New Jersey**

▷  **nj.gov**

▷  **RV and Tent Sites**

Cheesequake State Park is an intriguing option for those who want to camp close to the city but can't stomach the thought of driving into Jersey City for Liberty Harbor. Cheesequake is only 35 miles or so from New York City, and if you time the traffic correctly, you can make it into Manhattan in forty-five minutes or less. Cheesequake has some hiking trails and offers up nice, wooded sites, but there is an 11-foot height restriction on the way into the campground, and some of the sites are hard to back into even if your rig is moderately sized. This is mostly marshland, and New Jersey mosquitoes are known to feast on out-of-staters during the summer months, so bring your bug spray. Lots and lots of bug spray.

## Croton Point Park

▷ **Croton-on-Hudson, New York**

▷ **parks.westchestergov.com**

▷ **RV and Tent Sites, Cabin Rentals**

The campground at Croton Point Park is a bit of an undiscovered gem for those who want a peaceful campsite within striking distance of New York City. The Metro North picks up right outside of the campground. The city is about 40 miles away, and depending on traffic, it will take at least an hour to an hour and a half to drive there. Croton Point Park campground wins points for proximity and also for having large, shaded sites with full hook-ups. Cabin rentals offer direct views of the Hudson River.

## New York City North/Newburgh KOA Holiday

▷ **Plattekill, New York**

▷ **koa.com**

▷ **RV and Tent Sites, Cabin Rentals**

This charming KOA is a family favorite and serves as a destination in its own right, but driving into New York City can take almost two hours. However, if you want to spend some quality time camping in the Hudson Valley and then venture into the city for a day or two, this could be a terrific base camp. There are plenty of fun amenities for the kids here, like a playground and bounce pillow, and the pool area is a lovely place to cool off on a hot summer day.

## Black Bear Campground

▷  Florida, New York

▷  blackbearcampground.com

▷  RV Sites

Black Bear Campground is located about 60 miles from New York City and offers yet another full-service camping option within reasonable driving distance of New York City. The campground has a rustic country feel and offers full hook-up sites for RVers at reasonable prices. It is also one of the rare campgrounds in the Northeast that is open year-round. Most campgrounds in the region close in October and reopen in April. So if you're up for a winter camping trip to the big city, this could be your place.

# Getting to the Statue of Liberty and Ellis Island

Although there are eleven NPS sites in the Port of New York City, Ellis Island and the Statue of Liberty are the two bucket-list, must-see attractions for most visitors. These monuments are only accessible by ferry, so planning ahead is a critical part of an enjoyable experience. Here are the most important things you need to know:

1. Ellis Island and Liberty Island are open year-round, except for on Thanksgiving and Christmas Day. Inclement weather or security risks can shut down the islands at times, so check the park websites for alerts before visiting.

2. The only ferries that land at the islands are run by Statue City Cruises, an approved NPS concessionaire. Other vendors sell tickets that tour around the islands but do not land and disembark. Some first-time visitors mistakenly purchase the wrong tickets, so beware.

3. Statue City Cruises ferries depart daily from Battery Park in New York City and also from Liberty State Park in Jersey City. So you don't have to venture into Manhattan to get to the islands. Pick a ferry departure location that works best for you.

4. Ferry tickets can be purchased in person from Statue City Cruises, but they often sell out weeks in advance during busy times of the year. Buying tickets in advance is highly recommended.

5. There is a security screening before boarding the ferry, so arrive at least thirty minutes before your boarding time to be safe.

6. There are no additional fees for park entrance aside from the ferry tickets. Audio tours are included free of charge and can be picked up at each island.

7. If you wish to visit the top of the pedestal at the Statue of Liberty (a ten-story climb), you must make timed reservations—free of charge—in advance through Statue City Cruises. There is additional security screening to enter the pedestal.

## Ranger Tours

Audio tours are included free of charge for all monument visitors, but attending the daily ranger programs will truly bring these historic locations to life.

▷ Liberty Island: Meet a park ranger at the Liberty Island Flagpole for a thirty-minute talk that covers the construction and restoration of the Statue of Liberty. Tours run throughout the day.

▷ Ellis Island: A park ranger gives a fifteen-minute talk before each showing of the thirty-minute *Island of Hope, Island of Tears* film.

## Escape the City: Hyde Park

Just a couple hours' drive north of New York City, you'll find the Home of Franklin D. Roosevelt, a National Historic Site worth a visit. The historic home of the longest serving U.S. president is nestled along the Hudson River, and the grounds offer a fascinating look at the lives of both Franklin and Eleanor Roosevelt through permanent and rotating exhibits. Take a guided tour of Roosevelt's childhood home and then visit the Franklin D. Roosevelt Presidential Library and Museum. Other nearby attractions include Eleanor Roosevelt National Historic Site, Vanderbilt Mansion National Historic Site, and the Historic Hyde Park Train Station.

# CIVIL WAR NATIONAL PARK TOUR

Civil War buffs—or anyone with an interest in American history—will enjoy a camping road trip to Gettysburg, Antietam, and Harpers Ferry. They are geographically close to each other, and there are excellent camping locations near each. Some folks also choose to use Gettysburg as a base camp and take day trips to Antietam and Harpers Ferry—both of which are less than an hour's drive away.

Touring these battlefields is serious and somber work, but it's worth the emotional investment. William Faulkner famously said that "the past is never dead. It's not even past." Nowhere is this more true than on the battlefields of Gettysburg, Antietam, and Harpers Ferry, where the past seems to be a living, breathing force that can help explain our present moment with clarity and force...if we take the time to listen.

There are no campgrounds open to the public inside these three NPS sites. However, Rohrbach Campground inside Antietam National Battlefield is open to civic organizations such as scouts and school groups.

# Gettysburg National Military Park

Gettysburg, Pennsylvania, may be the most famous Civil War NPS site as both the location of the war's bloodiest battle and the focal point of President Lincoln's famous Gettysburg Address. Visiting can be either a moving experience or a tedious drive through grassy fields. The key to getting the most out of a visit to Gettysburg National Military Park is engaging with the exhibits, ranger programs, and living history demonstrations. Plan ahead to make the trip a memorable one.

## CAMPGROUNDS OUTSIDE THE PARK

### Gettysburg/Battlefield KOA

▷ Gettysburg, Pennsylvania

▷ koa.com

▷ RV and Tent Sites, Camping Cabins and Deluxe Cabins

This bucolic and cheerful campground is located only minutes away from one of the Civil War's most famous sites. History buffs will love the proximity to all that Gettysburg has to offer, and campers of all ages and inclinations will love this campground's cozy and secluded location. We visited in April and the wooded areas that surround this KOA were filled with colorful wildflowers. Our boys loved the jumping pillow and games in the common area near the camp store. We spent hours playing mini-golf, carpet ball, and life-size checkers and Connect 4—all of which were a welcome reprieve after spending our mornings touring battlefields and other NPS sites. The nature trail that cuts up into the woods above the campground makes for a lovely ramble. Bring a cup of coffee and contemplate the quiet before heading to the battlefields.

## Gettysburg Campground

▷ **Gettysburg, Pennsylvania**

▷ **gettysburgcampground.com**

▷ **RV and Tent Sites, Cabins**

The best sites at the Gettysburg Campground are located directly on Marsh Creek—and thankfully, there are a lot of them. Fishing is allowed in Marsh Creek, and the sound of the water is calm and relaxing. The rest of the campground is also good, so don't fret if you can't get a waterfront site. This campground isn't fancy, but it's reliable and centrally located to all of the historical sites. After a long day of exploring Gettysburg, make sure you get a hand-dipped Hershey's ice cream cone in the camp store.

## Artillery Ridge Campground

▷ **Gettysburg, Pennsylvania**

▷ **artilleryridge.com**

▷ **RV and Tent Sites, Cabins, Horse Camping**

Located just 1 mile from the NPS visitor center, and 1.5 miles from downtown, Artillery Ridge is a solid if not spectacular option. Ongoing construction can disturb the tranquility of the setting—but the staff is friendly and the potential is obvious.

## Granite Hill Campground

- ▷ Gettysburg, Pennsylvania
- ▷ granitehillcampingresort.com
- ▷ RV and Tent Sites, Cabins, Bed and Breakfast

Traveling with friends who don't own an RV and don't really love cabin camping? Consider getting an RV site while they stay at Granite Hill's own on-site bed and breakfast. The campground hosts an excellent twice-annual bluegrass festival in May and August. Book early if you want to enjoy terrific music just a short walk away from your site.

# Antietam National Battlefield

This Civil War battlefield in Maryland is the location of the single bloodiest day in American history, where almost 23,000 soldiers were killed, injured, or went missing over the course of a day of fighting on September 17, 1862. The battle led to President Lincoln issuing the Emancipation Proclamation, freeing the 3.5 million slaves in the Confederate states. Join a park ranger's battlefield talk to get the most out of your visit.

## CAMPGROUNDS OUTSIDE THE PARK

### Yogi Bear's Jellystone Park Camp-Resort: Williamsport, Maryland

▷ Williamsport, Maryland

▷ jellystonemaryland.com

▷ RV and Tent Sites, Lodges, Cottages, Bungalows, Luxury and Rustic Cabins

Visiting the somber sites at Antietam during the morning hours and then returning to this boisterous Jellystone for family fun in the afternoon may seem like a discordant way to spend a vacation. But it also might be exactly what you need to keep the whole family happy. This is family-style resort camping at its best. This Jellystone manages to have off-the-hook amenities like huge water slides, laser tag, and jumping pillows while still offering campers large, semiprivate sites that are not stacked right on top of each other like they are at so many other RV resorts. Mini-golf is free and so are many other activities like outdoor movie nights and family kickball. But the park also offers a bunch of fun add-on items for an extra fee. You can rent golf carts, hammocks, pool cabanas, private hot tubs, and much more. If you want to blow your kids' minds, schedule a personal visit from Yogi or Cindy Bear. Our kids love it here and always place it near the top of their list of all-time favorites. Hey, Boo Boo! We hope to see you again soon.

## Antietam Creek Campsite

▷   **Near Sharpsburg, Maryland**
▷   **Chesapeake and Ohio Canal National Historical Park**
▷   **nps.gov**
▷   **Tent Sites**

Adventurous tent campers who don't mind parking nearby and walking to their sites might check out Antietam Creek Campsite. It's budget priced and just a few miles away from the battlefield. The pit toilets are not for the faint of heart, and it can get noisy on the weekends during the warmer months. But the twenty sites are large and all of them are located directly on the canal. No RVs of any kind are allowed.

## Hagerstown/Antietam Battlefield KOA Holiday

▷   **Williamsport, Maryland**
▷   **koa.com**
▷   **RV and Tent Sites, Cabin Rentals**

This is a solid choice near Antietam if you want full hookups and fun amenities for the kids. The sites can be tight, but the service is friendly.

# Harpers Ferry National Historical Park

The location of Harpers Ferry, West Virginia, at the confluence of the Potomac and Shenandoah Rivers prompted the establishment of a national armory there in 1796. That same arsenal led abolitionist John Brown to raid the armory in 1859—the first in a series of important events that took place there leading up to and during the Civil War. Harpers Ferry changed hands fourteen times during the war, and the well-preserved historic town offers a much different experience than the typical Civil War battlefield tour.

## CAMPGROUND OUTSIDE THE PARK

### Harpers Ferry/Civil War Battlefields KOA

- Harpers Ferry, West Virginia
- koa.com
- RV and Tent Sites, Camping Cabins and Deluxe Cabins

Civil War buffs will delight in a camping trip to Harpers Ferry, and this KOA is our top pick for the region. This campground has a delightful setting and is just minutes away from Harpers Ferry National Historical Park, where visitors can participate in historic trades workshops or learn about the area's rich history on a guided hike with a park ranger. Back at the campground, families can play a game of mini-golf, jump on the covered bounce pillow, or take a dip in the pool. Older kids love the indoor and outdoor basketball courts and game room—especially on a rainy day. Adults love Grapes & Grinds, the campground's specialty wine and coffee store. Start the day there with a piping hot cup of coffee and make sure you don't miss one of the afternoon wine tastings. There are a wide variety of tent and RV sites and plenty of cabins to choose from. If you are in a big rig, take turns slowly—the campground has a few tight corners and it gets quite crowded during peak season.

--- **Read These Pulitzer Prize Winners before You Go!** ---

*Team of Rivals: The Political Genius of Abraham Lincoln* by Doris Kearns Goodwin is about much more than the battles at Gettysburg, Antietam, and Harpers Ferry. It offers a panoramic view of our sixteenth president and his cabinet. Reading this book will enrich your understanding of the battlefields you visit on this trip, and of the American experiment in all of its complexity and grandeur.

*The Killer Angels: A Novel of the Civil War* by Jeff Shaara is a magnificent historical novel that brings the battlefields of Gettysburg to life like no other book. Ken Burns credits the book for inspiring his epic nine-part documentary about the Civil War.

# The Dos and Don'ts of Dragging Your Kids to Gettysburg Military National Park

We love national parks, and our kids do as well. But you know those stories of children getting dragged around to battlefields by their boring parents? They probably originated in places like Gettysburg. On our first visit, we decided to save money and avoid guided tours, opting to purchase an audio tour from the gift shop. Don't make the same mistake. Gettysburg, and most other historic sites, are brought to life by ranger programs, living history demonstrations, and guided battlefield tours. Plan ahead, and history will come to life.

## Start with the Film, Cyclorama, and Museum Experience

These tickets are timed, and if you get an early start, it will help the rest of the day flow a bit more smoothly. The whole experience should take about an hour.

## Pick a Battlefield Tour Option

Gettysburg is very unique in that it has a couple of different ways you can explore with a Licensed Battlefield Guide. You can reserve a car tour, bus tour, or bicycle tour. The weirdest part is that the guide drives *your car* if you choose the car tour option.

## Choose the Ranger Programs You Wish to Attend

Look at the online schedule ahead of time to get the most value out of your visit. The ranger programs run all day and vary from guided hikes to interactive programs using your personal devices. Definitely plan on visiting the Soldiers' National Cemetery where Lincoln gave his famous address. From Memorial Day to Labor Day, "Taps" is played at 7:00 p.m.—a very moving experience.

## ------ Good Grub in Shepherdstown, West Virginia ------

Downtown Shepherdstown is quirky and quaint, with lots of good food and cool local shops to explore. Here are two of our favorites for a hearty meal after a long day of touring the area.

The jacked mac and cheese with bacon at the Blue Moon Cafe is not the healthiest option on the menu at this eclectic local favorite, but it sure did taste good after a long day of exploring Harpers Ferry.

Maria's Taqueria may have the freshest, tastiest tacos in all of West Virginia. The huevos rancheros are also delicious. Vegetarian and vegan options are also available.

# MID-ATLANTIC REGION

# Delaware Water Gap National Recreation Area

Overshadowed in reputation by Acadia National Park to the north and Shenandoah National Park to the south, the Delaware Water Gap National Recreation Area has actually welcomed more visitors than Yellowstone or the Grand Canyon in recent years. Its close proximity to major population centers like New York City and Philadelphia has made this a favorite outdoor retreat for millions of hikers, paddlers, and anglers each year. There is a serious campaign underway to turn this into a designated NPS site, so stay tuned.

There are no established campgrounds within the boundaries of the Delaware Water Gap National Recreation Area. Instead there are "river campsites" at fifteen locations along the edge of the Delaware River. There are anywhere from one to twelve sites at each of these campsites, and camping is strictly limited to a one-night stay at each location. Currently, there are a limited number of river campsites available to reserve in advance at recreation.gov. Efforts are being made to expand the pool of reservable sites in the future. If you are visiting this recreation area for the first time and thinking about river camping, connecting with a local outfitter is highly recommended.

Twenty-eight miles of the Appalachian Trail pass through this national recreation area, so some fun bucket-list hiking should be on the agenda. When planning your visit, be sure not to overlook nearby Worthington State Forest and High Point State Park. Both offer great hiking, fishing, and boating opportunities. They are also very popular destinations for hunting.

# CAMPGROUNDS OUTSIDE THE PARK

### Worthington State Forest Campground

▹   Columbia, New Jersey

▹   camping.nj.gov

▹   RV and Tent Sites

Worthington State Forest Campground is nestled right alongside the banks of the Delaware River and offers seventy-eight spacious sites that can be challenging to book on busy summer weekends. Twenty-eight of those sites are tent only, but the rest can accommodate RVs. The sites located directly on the banks of the river are the most desirable. They are large and private, and you can see (and hear) the Delaware River through the trees. Take caution if you are camping with small children, because the sites are elevated above the river and drop-offs can be dangerous. Three group campsites are also available, which can make the campground loud on the weekends. Your best bet for a quiet stay is to book during the week in a shoulder season. This rustic campground has restrooms with running water but no showers, so a self-contained RV would be ideal here. Excellent hiking abounds in the immediate area, and there are several waterfalls nearby.

## Driftstone Campground

▹   Mt. Bethel, Pennsylvania

▹   driftstone.com

▹   RV and Tent Sites

Driftstone Campground (a.k.a. Driftstone on the Delaware) offers up a classic family camping experience that harkens back to summer camps of old. This delightful campground is situated directly on the Delaware River in a quiet, country setting. There is a long, thin island right in front of the campground that creates a separate channel in the Delaware that is perfect for tubing. You can launch a tubing run on one side of the campground, de-tube on the other, then walk back and repeat the process until you are exhausted. Which is what kids and families do all summer long. The non-natural amenities, like the pool, are also delightful. The activity barn (with pool table and Ping-Pong) is terrific for rainy days.

## Camp Taylor

▷ Columbia, New Jersey

▷ camptaylor.com

▷ RV and Tent Sites, Cabin Rentals, Trailer Rentals

Camp Taylor has been family owned and operated for almost sixty years. It is a rustic and deeply wooded private campground that looks more like a state park. The sites here are large and many are private, and some have peaceful little streams with crystal clear water running in between them. Amenities and activities are limited here, but the campground hosts the locally famous Lakota Wolf Preserve. Reservations are required for the preserve and must be booked separately from your campground reservations. You can hear the wolves howling at night while you relax around your campfire in one of New Jersey's prettiest natural settings. Hiking options near the campground are abundant. You can depart for the trail right from your site.

## Delaware Water Gap/Pocono Mountain KOA Holiday

▷ East Stroudsburg, Pennsylvania

▷ koa.com

▷ RV and Tent Sites, Cabin Rentals, Trailer Rentals, Conestoga Wagon Rental

If you are looking for full hook-up sites with lots of amenities near the Delaware Water Gap National Recreation Area, then this might be the place. This KOA Holiday has all of the private RV park fixings: a pool, playground, puppy park, basketball and volleyball courts, plus mini-golf and hayrides. It also loves to throw fun themed weekends, and makes a mean pancake breakfast. In many ways, this campground offers the quintessential KOA experience. The sites are not as big and naturally beautiful as the other campgrounds in this chapter, but they have all of the fun stuff here for kids and families that like to spend part of each day at the campground.

---------------- **Park Highlights on Land** -----------------

### Hike to the Top of Mount Tammany

This 3.6-mile loop trail offers sweeping views of the Delaware Water Gap. It can be a crowded trail, so try to hike it during the week or earlier in the day.

### Visit Historic Millbrook Village

This preserved mid-1800s agricultural town offers a glimpse into the past with living history demonstrations of woodworking, weaving, blacksmithing, and more. There's also a picnic area for visitors.

### Take a Waterfall Tour

Visit the picturesque Ramondskill Falls, the tallest waterfall in Pennsylvania. Silver Thread Falls and Dingmans Falls can be found along the accessible Dingmans Creek Trail.

## Get Out on the River

### Edge of the Woods Outfitters

Located in Delaware Water Gap, Pennsylvania, this outfitter offers 4-mile, 6-mile, and 10-mile self-guided tours in kayaks, canoes, or rafts. It will provide you with equipment and instructions, send you on your way, and then pick you up downriver. It also offers custom guided tours for groups. If you want to try river camping in the park's primitive campsites, this is a great place to rent canoes for your overnight adventure.

## Great Views

### High Point State Park

The highest elevation in the state of New Jersey can be found here at 1,803 feet above sea level. The High Point Monument at the summit is dedicated to New Jersey veterans, and the top of the monument can be accessed by climbing 291 steps.

## On the Horizon

### Camp Margaritaville RV Resort

Set to open in 2024, this luxury RV resort will follow in the footsteps of its cousins in Tennessee, Georgia, and Florida, offering premium RV sites along with restaurants, pickleball courts, kids clubs, and swim-up bars. It's five o'clock somewhere.

------------------ **Poconos Water Parks** ------------------

If your kids are on nature overload, head to one of the many waterpark resorts in the region. Locals will argue with each other about which is the best, but they all offer fun waterslides and wave pools.

### Kalahari

Day passes are available here, and the waterpark has both indoor and out-door resort areas. Older kids love the 5-foot wave simulator for surfing and bodyboarding.

### Aquatopia and Camelbeach

Part of the Camelback Resort, these sister indoor and outdoor waterparks claim to be the biggest in Pennsylvania. There's also on-site opportunities to zip-line, bungee jump, or head out on a UTV tour.

### Split Rock Resort

This indoor waterpark is a bit smaller and more affordable than the other options. It's also better suited for younger children.

# Assateague Island National Seashore

Assateague Island National Seashore is home to one of the few unspoiled beachfront camping experiences you can find along the northeastern coastline of the United States. The seashore is famous for the herd of wild horses that roam freely on the island, but visitors also enjoy fishing, crabbing, kayaking, and birding. It's a magical place that we return to as a family year after year—although we personally prefer to camp inside the neighboring state park, which offers the same beautiful landscape paired with a few more campground amenities.

Camping on Assateague Island is not for the faint of heart. If you read camper reviews, you will hear folks talking about swarms of mosquitoes and abundant sandburs with sharp needles that attach to clothing and pop bicycle tires. You will need to be prepared for the possibility of strong winds and fierce riptides. Nevertheless, people fall in love with the ocean sunrises and bay sunsets, along with the sheer wonder of watching a herd of wild horses gallop down the beach.

This is a very popular camping destination, and both public and private campgrounds are often booked solid far in advance of the peak season, which traditionally runs from Memorial Day to Labor Day along the East Coast. Pay close attention to the reservation windows noted here, and mark your calendar if you want to snap up an oceanfront site.·

# CAMPGROUNDS INSIDE THE PARK

### Assateague Island National Seashore Campgrounds

▷   Berlin, Maryland

▷   nps.gov

▷   RV and Tent Sites

### Oceanside

All of the camping areas in the national seashore are open year-round. From November 16 to March 14, campsites are first-come, first-served. From March 15 through November 15, reservations are required and can be made up to six months in advance. Sites are $30 per night, but keep in mind you will also have to pay the park entrance fee. All sites have a picnic table and fire ring, but there are no hookups in the park. Vault toilets and cold water showers make for a very rustic camping experience, so come prepared. In addition to drive-in sites, there are walk-in sites for tent campers who are looking for a more remote beach camping experience.

### Bayside

Although we prefer the oceanside sites, many campers appreciate the bayside campsites for ease of fishing, kayaking, and paddleboarding access. The sunsets are an additional perk. Insects will be an issue no matter where you camp on Assateague Island, but the bayside does come with an extra helping of mosquitoes and horse flies, especially during the hottest summer months. Just like the oceanside campground, bayside has no hookups, vault toilets, and cold showers. There is a generator-free zone in the Bayside B-loop if you are seeking a truly peaceful rustic camping experience

---------------- **Backcountry Camping** -----------------

There are six backcountry—two oceanside and four bayside—campgrounds in Assateague Island National Seashore that are only accessible by backpacking or paddling. Permits are required and are only issued day of departure on a first-come, first-served basis. Some of the camping areas require up to 13 miles of hiking to reach, and rangers are strict about departure times.

# CAMPGROUNDS OUTSIDE THE PARK

### Assateague State Park

▷     Berlin, Maryland

▷     parkreservations.maryland.gov

▷     RV and Tent Sites

Just minutes away from the national seashore is Assateague State Park's campground, which offers the same beautiful scenery along with some additional amenities that will make for a much more comfortable beach camping experience. The majority of the 342 sites do not have hookups, except a single loop with electric hookups along with a handful of sites on a second loop. However, there are modern, clean bathhouses with flushing toilets, hot showers, and dishwashing stations—a luxurious upgrade from the rustic national seashore experience. These amenities come along with even more competition for coveted reservations, which can be made 365 days in advance of your arrival. When booking at this campground, we try to nab a site nestled up against the beach dunes, and a few sites away from a beach access footpath.

## Yogi Bear's Jellystone Park Chincoteague Island

▷ Chincoteague, Virginia

▷ campjellystone.com

▷ RV and Tent Sites, Cabins and Yurts

Located in Virginia, this Jellystone is a bit of a drive from the main national seashore visitor center in Maryland and the Assateague State Park beaches, but it's only a few minutes from the Toms Cove Visitor Center, the South Pony Corral, and the Assateague Lighthouse. The resort is next door to Maui Jack's Waterpark, and campers can purchase discounted passes with their reservations. The campground is also conveniently located near historic downtown Chincoteague, which has plenty of delicious restaurant and ice cream parlor options.

## Sun Outdoors Frontier Town

▷ Berlin, Maryland

▷ sunoutdoors.com

▷ RV and Tent Sites, Cabins and Cottages, Conestoga Wagons, RV Rentals

If you want to combine a visit to the national seashore with a Wild West–themed camping experience, then look no further. Sun Outdoors Frontier Town is less than ten minutes away from the Assateague Island Visitor Center and offers full hook-up RV sites, tent sites, cabins, and cottages. There is an on-site waterpark with a lazy river as well as bay access for fishing, kayaking, and jet skiing. The western-themed 1880s downtown has stagecoach rides, panning for gold, and live-action performances of bank holdups and gunfights.

## Sun Outdoors Ocean City

▷ Berlin, Maryland

▷ sunoutdoors.com

▷ RV and Tent Sites, Cottages

Formerly called Castaways, this campground is the best resort option near Ocean City that does not include any Wild West shenanigans. There are hundreds of RV sites, tent sites, and cottage rentals along 50 acres of bay-front property. The on-site dining, tiki bar, pool, and splashpad are some of our favorite amenities. There are also boat rentals and a courtesy shuttle to the area beaches.

### Camp Tip

Campers are not allowed to bring firewood from out of state into the national seashore. Rangers are strict in enforcing this, and plenty of firewood is available locally.

### Safety First

Sunscreen and insect repellent are your best friends when it comes to packing for a camping trip to Assateague Island National Seashore.

### NPS Memories

My family used to camp at Assateague State Park every year with a group of friends. On the last night of our stay, the kids would bring our sleeping bags down to the beach and spend the night under the stars. Many times we woke up in the morning to a herd of wild horses galloping up the beach.

—Stephanie

# Unique Camping Experiences & Attractions

## Assateague Cottage

If you wish to enjoy the beauty of Assateague State Park without the hassle of pitching a tent or parking an RV, book one of Assateague Cottage's delightful tiny homes, which can be delivered right to the campground. You'll have to book the campsite on your own, then head to AssateagueCottage.com to reserve one of the small, brightly colored abodes. There are no bathrooms or kitchens in the cottages, but they come with a comfortable bed, table and chairs, plus 12-volt lighting powered by a solar panel.

## NASA Wallops Flight Facility

Most folks don't think of rocket launches when they plan a trip to the eastern shore of Virginia, but check the launch schedule before your visit. You may get lucky and see a rocket take flight. Or just stop by the visitor center, which offers free educational programs and exhibits throughout the year.

## Chincoteague Island Pony Swim

The pony swim takes place every year at the end of July, and you may want to either plan a trip to see this historic event or avoid the crowds altogether. Tens of thousands of spectators come to watch the saltwater cowboys round up the wild ponies on Assateague Island and swim them across the bay to Chincoteague where they are auctioned off to control the size of the herd.

# Shenandoah National Park

Shenandoah National Park is often overshadowed by Great Smoky Mountains National Park and may be one of the most underrated national parks in the country—especially when it comes to camping. Shenandoah has five excellent campgrounds inside the park that are easier to book than campgrounds at many other national parks. There are also several excellent private campgrounds outside the park that offer a wide range of amenities and experiences. If you want off-the-hook family fun, then book a site at Jellystone Luray. If you want something quieter and more peaceful that still has hookups and amenities, then book a site at Spacious Skies Shenandoah Valley. There is also a small but fantastic state park—Shenandoah River State Park—located less than 10 miles away from the park's northern entrance at Front Royal.

Overall, this is a great national park for RVers and campers to visit. When we think of Shenandoah, we think of easy family hikes that lead to cool waterfalls or spectacular views of the valley below. We also think of driving along Skyline Drive with the windows down and the music on as we pass by fragrant wildflowers and look for black bears gallivanting in the woods right along the side of the road.

# CAMPGROUNDS INSIDE THE PARK

## Big Meadows Campground

▷ Stanley, Virginia

▷ nps.gov

▷ RV and Tent Sites, Lodge Rooms Nearby

There are five campgrounds in Shenandoah National Park, but Big Meadows is our favorite for several reasons. Some of the park's most popular hikes are nearby, including Dark Hollow Falls and Stony Man. The Byrd Visitor Center is within walking distance as is a well-stocked camp store. Big Meadows has over 200 sites that are excellent for tents and smaller RVs, and most are level and easy to get into. Evenings here are lovely, and dozens of deer can often be seen around the campground as families settle in for dinner and campfires. The amphitheater also offers excellent ranger-led programs and talks that educate campers about bear safety, the night sky, and local wildlife, among other topics. We also love Big Meadows Lodge right next store to the campground. Guest rooms are fairly affordable if you want to visit the park with friends who do not camp. The Great Room is a cozy and comfortable place to play a game of checkers, read a book, or relax and watch a spectacular sunset light up the park. Those staying at the campground can walk right in and enjoy this public space. There is live music on summer nights in the downstairs pub, and the snacks and beer will hit the spot after a long day of hiking.

## Matthew's Arm Campground

▷ Rileyville, Virginia

▷ nps.gov

▷ RV and Tent Sites

Matthew's Arm is located at mile marker 22.1 on Skyline Drive. The campground is pretty and close to a waterfall hike to Overall Run Falls. This is a perfect spot for tent camping, and there is a dump station for RV owners who want to camp inside the park. Matthew's Arm is the closest campground to the northern terminus of Skyline Drive and the gateway community of Front Royal.

## Lewis Mountain Campground

- ▷ **Standardsville, Virginia**
- ▷ **nps.gov**
- ▷ **RV and Tent Sites**

Lewis Mountain Campground (located at mile marker 57.5) is the smallest campground in the park and almost looks like a smaller version of Big Meadows. It is pretty like Big Meadows, but it is also simpler. However, reservations are first-come, first-served, and there is no dump station for RVs. If you are a tent camper and don't care about being near the lodge for dinner or drinks, then this might be the spot for you.

## Loft Mountain Campground

- ▷ **Crozet, Virginia**
- ▷ **nps.gov**
- ▷ **RV and Tent Sites**

Loft Mountain may win the prize for having the National Park Service's prettiest amphitheater with mountain views, so make sure you catch a ranger talk while you are camping here. The entire campground is also gorgeous and has mountain views to the east and to the west. More adventurous souls will want to check out the nearby hike to Doyles River Falls—it is one of the best hikes in the park. Loft Mountain is located at mile marker 79.5 on Skyline Drive and has a dump station and camp store on-site.

# CAMPGROUNDS OUTSIDE THE PARK

## Jellystone Luray

▷ Luray, Virginia

▷ campluray.com

▷ Deluxe and Camping Cabins, Tent and RV Sites

We think that Jellystone Luray is one of the best family campgrounds in the country. The pools and water slides are epic, and most of the campground has stunning views of the Blue Ridge Mountains. It is rare to find a full-fledged resort campground located just minutes from the gates of a national park. Jellystone Luray *is* that rare campground. You can spend mornings hiking in Shenandoah National Park and afternoons relaxing back at the pool or bounce pillow with your kids. Hey Hey Rides and photo ops with Yogi and Friends will charm younger campers, while laser tag and full-sized sports facilities will keep teenagers busy for hours at a time. Spend your evenings relaxing under the stars and enjoying a crackling campfire or watching a movie together in the campground's delightful outdoor theater. Food options at the campground are better than average, and mini-golf is free.

## Shenandoah River State Park Campground

▷ Bentonville, Virginia

▷ dcr.virginia.gov

▷ RV and Tent Sites, Cabin and Lodge Rentals

Shenandoah River State Park Campground is located less than 10 miles north of the Rockfish Gap Entrance Station to the park. It may be the perfect base camp for those who want a bucolic setting without having to tow their RVs into the park. You can see Shenandoah National Park to the east and rent a canoe or launch your own right inside the park. Sites are large, but they can be difficult to come by, so book well in advance to get a spot.

Well-equipped cabins and lodge rentals are also available for those traveling with friends who don't camp. The campground and lodging options are
open year-around.

## Spacious Skies Shenandoah Valley

▷ Luray, Virginia

▷ spaciousskiescampgrounds.com

▷ RV and Tent Sites, Cabins and Yurts

Spacious Skies Shenandoah Valley is a charming and quieter alternative to
Jellystone Luray for campers who want full hookups and amenities near the
national park. The RV sites are large and lovely, and so are the views of rolling hills and farmland that surround the campground. This campground
has enough fun amenities to keep kids busy, but it could also serve perfectly
for couples looking for a romantic weekend retreat.

---

### ---------- Hiking in Shenandoah National Park ----------

Hiking is among the best things to do in Shenandoah National Park. It doesn't
get much better for the casual day hiker or for families with young kids. You
can reach spectacular summits in Shenandoah on relatively short roundtrip
hikes like Stony Man (1.4 miles round trip) and Hawksbill (2.8 miles round trip).
You can also descend into the cool and shaded world of Dark Hallow Falls for
a waterfall hike that is not to be missed (1.4 miles out and back). Our favorite hike in Shenandoah National Park is Bearfence Mountain (1.2-mile lariat).
Climbing and scrambling through this trail's jumbled rocks has just the slight-
est whiff of danger, but is oodles of fun. You'll feel accomplished and winded
when you reach the top. Thankfully, there is an easy section of the Appalachian
Trail that leads right back down to the parking lot.

# Other Favorite Shenandoah National Park Experiences

## Cruise on Skyline Drive

Skyline drive is more than 100 miles long with stretches that are breathtakingly beautiful. If you are looking for things to do in Shenandoah National Park, don't forget to just roll the windows down, put on some good music, and cruise. This classic American drive starts at Front Royal in the north, then it deposits you onto the Blue Ridge Parkway at its southern terminus. We recommend pulling over at whatever overlooks catch your fancy. Take your time and breathe in the cool mountain air, particularly at sunset.

## Grab Lunch or Dinner on the Back Deck of Big Meadows Lodge

The Spottswood Dining Room at Big Meadows Lodge is open to the public, and it is surprisingly easy (especially at lunch) to get a table on its gorgeous back deck. Your blackberry lemonade will taste better with mountain views.

## Learn about the Park's History

The history of Shenandoah National Park is not without controversy. In the West, conservation often came well before development, but in the East, development came before conservation. The end result? In order to create Shenandoah National Park, over 500 families were displaced against their will. The permanent display in the Byrd Visitor tells this story without simplifying the human complexity of these events.

## Become a Junior Ranger

This beloved program is available at NPS sites across the country, and it has a different flavor in each location. Ask at the front desk for a Junior Ranger booklet and let your kids get to work. They will never forget the experience.

## Black Bears in the Park

The American Black Bear is the only species of bear that calls Shenandoah National Park home. In the early 1900s they were almost extinct in the area that now constitutes the park. The park was founded in 1935, and in 1937 only two bears were thought to live within its boundaries. Now that number ranges into the high hundreds depending on a multitude of variables. We have seen black bears every single time we have visited Shenandoah. They can often be spotted in the woods right alongside Skyline Drive. If you spot one while driving please take great caution and consider pulling off onto the side of the road until it crosses or disappears back into its native woods.

## Blue Ridge Parkway

Between Shenandoah National Park to the north and Great Smoky Mountains National Park to the south runs the 469-mile Blue Ridge Parkway—a U.S. National Parkway often referred to as "America's Favorite Drive." This long, winding road is dotted with scenic views, wildlife viewing opportunities, historical landmarks, and unique towns to explore. Since driving the entire length of the park would take between ten to twelve hours without stops, visitors will want to identify the areas they wish to explore and choose campgrounds accordingly. Milepost markers are included in the campground listings to aid in planning.

An important note for RVers: While some portions of the Blue Ridge Parkway are accommodating for travel trailers and motor homes, there are many curves, elevation changes, and tunnels that may not be suitable for larger rigs. In addition, the eight NPS campgrounds along the parkway do not have any hookups, and many have a very limited number of sites that can accommodate anything other than tents or small (under 20 feet) RVs. Because of these factors, most RVers tend to stay at one of the many private campgrounds located just off the parkway, and then day trip along the Blue Ridge Parkway proper.

The Blue Ridge Parkway welcomes visitors year-round with stunning wildflower displays in spring, hiking and swimming in the summer, and leaf peeping in the fall. Many visitors enjoy hiking, snowshoeing, and cross-country skiing in the winter. However, be warned that the road is frequently closed to vehicles on account of icy conditions in the winter months.

# CAMPGROUNDS INSIDE THE PARK

### Mount Pisgah Campground

▷    Canton, North Carolina (Milepost 408.8)

▷    nps.gov

▷    RV and Tent Sites

Choosing a "top pick" among the eight campgrounds along the Blue Ridge Parkway is difficult work and makes for a great conversation around the campfire for those who have sampled several of them. Mount Pisgah Campground earns our top pick because of its location. This thickly wooded campground is carved into the side of a mountain that you could spend the rest of your life exploring—and as with the other campgrounds along the Blue Ridge Parkway, most sites are not accommodating for larger rigs. A few of the sites are pull-offs that can handle larger rigs, but most of the sites are small and favor van lifers and tent campers. Some of the tent sites are downright wonderful. They are cool and shaded and private. You are camping in bear country here—so please take caution and secure all of your food according to the park's specifications. And please make sure to bring comfortable hiking boots. There are trails on this mountain that look like they belong in fairy tales, folk songs, and Japanese haiku.

## Otter Creek Campground

▷ Bedford, Virginia (Milepost 60.8)

▷ nps.gov

▷ RV and Tent Sites

Scoring a creekside site at Otter Creek is one of the most desirable camp-ing experiences that the Blue Ridge Parkway has to offer. The roads can be crumbling in places, and many of the campsites themselves are in a state of disrepair, but the natural beauty of this campground still shines through. Loop A is tent only here, but the sites are still small and cannot accommodate very big rigs. Once again, this Blue Ridge Parkway gem favors tent campers, those who own pop-up campers, and van lifers. Loop B is for tent campers only. Both loops have sites by the creek. Get one if you can!

## Julian Price Campground

▷ Blowing Rock, North Carolina (Milepost 297.0)

▷ nps.gov

▷ RV and Tent Sites

Those traveling with kayaks and fishing gear will love a stop at Julian Price Campground. Boat rentals are also available if you are not traveling with your own. The 2.3-mile loop trail around the lake is also lazy and relaxing for those in search of an easy hike. The forest around the campground is filled with wildflowers in the spring and brilliant, bright red and orange foliage in the fall.

## Crabtree Falls Campground

▷ Micaville, North Carolina (Milepost 339.5)

▷ nps.gov

▷ RV and Tent Sites

Crabtree Falls Campground may be the prettiest little campground along the Blue Ridge Parkway. Wildlife like coyote and deer roam freely through the park (especially in the evening hours), and mist often hangs in the air in the morning. You can reach nearby Crabtree Falls via a 2.5-mile moderate loop trail. The waterfall is elegant and lovely as it cascades down a 60-foot rock cliff. It is a photographer's delight.

### Other NPS Campgrounds on the Blue Ridge Parkway

- ⇻ **Peaks of Otter Campground, Bedford, Virginia (Milepost 85.9)**
- ⇻ **Rocky Knob Campground, Floyd, Virginia (Milepost 167.1)**
- ⇻ **Doughton Park Campground, Laurel Springs, North Carolina (Milepost 239.2)**
- ⇻ **Linville Falls Campground, Newland, North Carolina (Milepost 316.4)**

# CAMPGROUNDS OUTSIDE THE PARK

## Mama Gertie's Hideaway

- ▷ Swannanoa, North Carolina
- ▷ mamagerties.com
- ▷ RV and Tent Sites, Camping Cabins

We enjoyed a magical stay at Mama Gertie's a few years back. The rear bed of our pop-up camper was hanging directly over a gurgling stream behind our site. We fell asleep each night to the gentle sound of that stream and have been recommending Mama Gertie's for Asheville-area stays ever since. Since we camped there, it has added breathtaking new mountain view sites that accommodate large RVs. The setting here is gorgeous, but the amenities are limited—there is no playground and no pool, and while kids are welcome, this will probably not be their favorite campground. But that's okay, Mom and Dad count too, right? The location is also excellent. Mama Gertie's is less than twenty minutes from Asheville (depending on traffic—yes there is traffic in Asheville) and less than ten minutes from Black Mountain. Folks come here to visit Asheville for its food, culture, and craft beer, but we always implore them to take a drive into Black Mountain too. It's like a mini Asheville with tons of charm and great food of its own.

## Fancy Gap KOA

▷  Fancy Gap, Virginia

▷  koa.com

▷  RV and Tent Sites, Deluxe Cabins and Camping Cabins

This delightful campground is carved into the side of a shady hill, and the elevation keeps it cool and comfortable during the hot summer months. The pet-friendly "backyard sites" are absolutely incredible for dog owners who want to give their pups extra room to roam. This KOA is also close to Mount Airy, North Carolina—a.k.a. Andy Griffith's Mayberry. The entrance to the Blue Ridge Parkway is right outside of the campground. Hungry travelers can have pizza and barbeque delivered to their sites after a long day of exploring the area.

## Davidson River Campground

▷  Pisgah National Forest

▷  Near Brevard, North Carolina

▷  fs.usda.gov

▷  RV and Tent Sites, Cabin Rentals

The Davidson River Campground is located along the banks of the Davidson River in a sparkling and almost magical spot in Pisgah National Forest. The campground has eight loops, and five of them have waterfront sites that are among the most desirable in western North Carolina. Bring your tubes to Davidson River and you can easily spend an entire summer day (or weekend) floating and splashing in the crystal clear water. Family-friendly hotspot Sliding Rock (a natural waterslide) is also nearby for those willing to take the plunge.

## Fun Gateway Towns to Explore along the Blue Ridge Parkway

- ✧ Afton (Milepost 0)
- ✧ Roanoke (Milepost 120)
- ✧ Fancy Gap (Milepost 199)
- ✧ Blowing Rock (Milepost 293)
- ✧ Asheville (Milepost 382)
- ✧ Cherokee (Milepost 469)

# A Day in Mount Airy: America's Main Street

Visitmayberry.com

Main Street may be disappearing from small towns across America, but it's alive and well in Mount Airy, North Carolina—the birthplace of actor Andy Griffith and the inspiration for Mayberry on *The Andy Griffith Show*, a popular TV series from the 1960s. Mount Airy fully embraces its claim to fame and has enshrined iconic locations from the show throughout the town. If you are traveling the Blue Ridge Parkway, plan to spend a day in Mount Airy, located just miles from the Fancy Gap parkway access point along the Virginia–North Carolina border.

Start your day with a Squad Car Tour in a vintage 1962 replica of what Andy Griffith and Barney Fife used to patrol the town of Mayberry. Your "sheriff" tour guide will take you to all of the famous locations from the show, including Wally's and the iconic jail. You'll also stop for a photo shoot in front of Andy's real-life childhood home.

After the tour head to Snappy Lunch—the only true-to-life Mount Airy business ever name checked on *The Andy Griffith Show*—and order a pork chop sandwich with all the fixings. Don't be phased by the line out the door; it moves quickly and is worth the wait. Save room for dessert at Walker's Soda Fountain and enjoy a classic chocolate malt or root beer float. If you need a haircut or shave, the most practical tourist stop ever is just 200 feet away at Floyd's City Barber Shop. Inside, the scene is straight out of the 1960s with old timers sitting in chairs anxious to school you on life.

Finish up your day by visiting the Andy Griffith Museum, which, not surprisingly, houses the world's largest collection of Andy Griffith memorabilia. Before you head out of town, snap a selfie with the Andy and Opie statue located next door in front of the Andy Griffith Playhouse.

# Six Top Attractions on the Parkway

## Humpback Rocks (Milepost 5)

Located at the northern end of the parkway, this stop hosts a visitor center and museum, along with a historic 1890s farm, picnic area, and hiking trails with access to Appalachian Trail.

## Peaks of Otter (Milepost 85)

If picking just one stop on the northern section of the parkway, this is a great choice. There's a lodge, campground, living history farm, historic tavern, a lake with fishing access, and plenty of hikes.

## Mabry Mill (Milepost 176)

Known as one of the most photographed spots along the Blue Ridge Parkway, this is where Ed and Lizzy Mabry built their family gristmill in 1910 and worked it for years, grinding corn, blacksmithing, and sawing lumber. A lovely trail allows for views of the historic building, and an on-site restaurant serves up hearty comfort food. Visit on Sunday afternoons for live music and dancing.

## Blue Ridge Music Center (Milepost 213)

The biggest draw to the Blue Ridge Music Center is the outdoor amphitheater, which hosts live mountain music concerts on Saturday evenings. But even if you can't attend a formal concert, the venue provides an immersion in the tradition of American folk music and dance through daily live music performances in the center's breezeway and rotating exhibits. There are also a couple of hiking trails at the center.

## Mount Mitchell (Milepost 355)

The highest point east of the Mississippi River, Mount Mitchell State Park is accessible directly from the Blue Ridge Parkway. A 0.3-mile hike will take you from the parking lot to the mountain summit where you can enjoy spectacular views of the Blue Ridge Mountains. There are many hikes of varying levels of difficulty here, but the easy and peaceful 1-mile Balsam Nature Trail Loop is our favorite, offering interpretive signs throughout the fir forest. At 6,684 feet above sea level, it can be chilly up there no matter the season, so bring extra layers when you visit.

## Mount Pisgah (Milepost 408)

This stop hosts the only lodge along the parkway in North Carolina, and along with that lodge comes a bustling restaurant, gift shop, and country store. Visitors can access the moderately difficult 2-mile, roundtrip hike to the summit of Mount Pisgah from the parking lot. The trailhead for the popular 16-mile, one-way Shut-In Trail is also located here if you're looking for more of a challenge. There's a picnic area where you can enjoy a bite to eat after the effort.

# Five Top Attractions off the Parkway

## Natural Bridge (Off Milepost 61)

This beautiful 215-foot limestone natural bridge is a gorge carved by Cedar Creek. The Cedar Creek trail—2 miles out and back—takes visitors from the entrance down under the bridge and then onto the historical Monacan Indian Village. Continue down the trail to see the picturesque Lace Falls. After your visit, enjoy lunch at the iconic Pink Cadillac Diner.

## Explore Park (Off Milepost 115)

This recreational center features hundreds of acres designed to immerse visitors in Blue Ridge Mountain outdoor experiences. There are obstacle courses, ziplining, mountain biking trails, disc golf, and even a 1-mile wooded path with animatronic dinosaurs from four time periods. When you've had your fill of adventure, enjoy a local craft beer or wine at the Twin Creeks Brewpub.

## Chimney Rock State Park (Off Milepost 384)

This location has plenty of cinematic history—Chimney Rock was one of the filming locations for *The Last of the Mohicans*, and famous scenes from *Dirty Dancing* were filmed in nearby Lake Lure where there is a cute downtown and swimming beach. Hike to the top of Chimney Rock via the Outcroppings Trail, which includes a challenging 494 steps. An elevator is available for those looking to avoid working up a sweat. The state park has on-site rock-climbing concessionaire that offers hourly, half-day, or full-day adventures.

## Biltmore (Off Milepost 388)

The historic Biltmore Estate is one of the most famous draws to Asheville, offering tours of the lavish Gilded Age marvel built over the course of six years by George Vanderbilt beginning in 1889. Self-guided and guided tours of the house and grounds are available, as well as rotating and seasonal exhibits. Advance reservations are required, and house entry tickets are timed.

## Sliding Rock (Off Milepost 413)

Nestled in the Pisgah National Forest, Sliding Rock is a 60-foot natural water slide that empties into an 8-foot-deep, frigid pool of water. Although on public land, the area is operated by a concessionaire, and there are observation platforms, lifeguards, and bathhouses open during the summer season. Expect crowds—this immensely fun experience is no hidden gem for local folks.

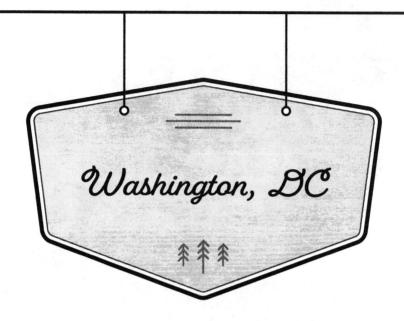

# Washington, DC

This NPS-designated site in our nation's capital includes more than a dozen memorials and monuments, hundreds of statues and fountains, and more than 1,000 acres of green space. Although it's not technically a national park, according to the park service more than twenty-five million people visit every year—more than Yosemite, Yellowstone, and the Grand Canyon combined. And yes, there are actually some great campgrounds and RV parks nearby that offer easy access to this popular destination.

Traffic is notoriously horrific in the DC metro area, so consider your transportation game plan when picking a base camp. On-site or nearby public transportation options or shuttle service should be considered a major bonus. If you plan on driving downtown, avoid rush hour in the morning and evening hours at all costs.

The National Mall and Memorial Parks can offer visitors a unique experience no matter the time of year. If you're willing to bundle up, the winter is a great time to avoid the crowds. Our favorite time to visit is in spring after the throngs of cherry blossom tourists have dispersed in April and May, or in early fall when the summer temperatures have dropped and school field trips haven't started en masse. Entrance to the National Mall and all of the Smithsonian museums is free, but some of the most popular sites—think Washington Monument and Ford's Theatre—require advance timed reservations, so planning ahead is critical. First-time visitors should also make a must-see list and prioritize attractions since doing everything in one whirlwind tour is just not possible.

# CAMPGROUNDS OUTSIDE THE PARKS

### Cherry Hill Park

▷   College Park, Maryland

▷   cherryhillpark.com

▷   RV and Tent Sites, Log Cabins, Glamping Pods, Yurts, and Rental Houses

You will adore this clean and well-managed resort campground and its incredibly convenient location just outside of the capital. First-time visitors to Cherry Hill are often amazed at just how close it is to downtown Washington, DC, which is only a twenty-to-thirty-minute drive away. The metro line is also so close that you don't even have to take your own vehicle into the city if you don't want to. Many urban campgrounds near big cities are just parking lots with RV hookups—but not Cherry Hill. This is a real campground with trees, shade, and wide-open spaces for walking the dog and going for a morning walk with a cup of coffee in your hand. A loud, multilane highway is right next to the campground—so tent campers who are light sleepers may want to look elsewhere. RV owners might also consider asking for a site away from the highway to mitigate the noise. Despite the road noise, coming back to Cherry Hill after a long day of sightseeing in the National Mall and Memorial Parks is blissful. The solar-warmed pools, splashground, and playground areas are large, and the indoor hot tub is a big hit with kids and weary travelers of all ages. The park also has decent food offerings on-site at the Capitol Cafe. Cherry Hill offers Washington, DC, tours that leave right from the campground; call ahead for tickets because they sell out all summer long.

## Washington DC/Capitol KOA Holiday

▷   Millersville, Maryland

▷   koa.com

▷   RV and Tent Sites, Cabin Rentals

The Capitol KOA is a solid if not spectacular option within striking distance of downtown Washington, DC. It is farther away from the city than Cherry Hill, but there is still road noise to contend with here. The pull-through sites in front of the camp store are good for those in big rigs and they are fairly spacious, but some of the smaller sites in other sections of the campground are difficult to navigate. Overall, this is a solid backup plan if you can't get a site at Cherry Hill.

## Lake Fairfax Park Campground

▷   Reston, Virginia

▷   fairfaxcounty.gov

▷   RV and Tent Sites

Lake Fairfax Park Campground provides a clean, safe, and affordable option for RV and tent camping about forty minutes away from Washington, DC, depending on traffic. The campground offers spacious sites and clean bath houses—but it is located inside of a very busy county park that is often bustling with local activity and locals who wander into the campground. It can be noisy here until about 10:00 p.m., but it usually quiets down soon after. Overall, this is a terrific value for those who don't want (or need) to stay at a more expensive private campground with full hookups.

## Greenbelt Park Campground

▷ **Greenbelt, Maryland**

▷ **nps.gov**

▷ **RV and Tent Sites**

Greenbelt Park Campground is a solid option for those who are camping on a budget and want to be close to Washington, DC. The park is only 10 miles away from the city's major attractions. There are 172 sites here for RV and tent campers, so getting a site is surprisingly easy considering its proximity to the nation's capital. Ticks can be bad in the summertime, and the bathroom facilities are not always the cleanest, so those in self-contained RVs who are just using the park as a base camp after a day in the city may be happiest here.

# Reservations Required (or Strongly Recommended!)

You can enjoy most of the monuments and memorials on the National Mall for free, but some of the bucket-list attractions require timed tickets that book out in advance and charge a nominal fee when reserving online. These requirements can change often depending on crowds and security concerns, so carefully research current procedures to avoid disappointment if you have your heart set on an experience. Here are some popular attractions with special reservation requirements.

## The White House

You will have to go through your congressional representative to book a White House tour. Reach out by calling or emailing the representative's office no more than 180 days in advance, and be prepared for a background check.

## The Capitol

While everyone can visit the Capitol Visitor Center and guided tours of the public areas are available without advance reservations, if you want to visit the Senate or House galleries you will need to contact your senator or representative to arrange a tour.

## The Washington Monument

While a limited number of same-day passes are available, your best bet is reserving timed tickets far in advance at recreation.gov for a nominal processing fee.

## Ford's Theatre National Historic Site

Timed same-day passes sell out fast, so reserve guided tour tickets in advance at fords.org for a small fee up to ninety days in advance of your visit.

## National Museum of African American History and Culture

Timed-entry tickets are required and released thirty days in advance on a rolling basis.

## Smithsonian National Zoo

Timed-entry passes are required for all ages and can be reserved online up to thirty days in advance. Passes are released on a rolling basis, so if your preferred date is booked, check back one week or one day in advance. If you purchase a parking pass in advance for $30, you do not need to reserve additional timed-entry passes.

# Sample the Smithsonians

There are more than twenty Smithsonian museums, galleries, and zoos in Washington, DC, and you'll want to narrow down your list of must-see exhibits before you visit. The Smithsonian website (si.edu/museums) has a very user-friendly list of all the locations, plus operating hours and tips for visiting each one. Start your visit by heading to the Smithsonian Institution Building, otherwise known as "The Castle"—which basically serves as a visitor center. Note that although all the Smithsonians offer free admission, many have special exhibitions, events, or IMAX shows that do have a fee. Here are five Smithsonians perfect for your first visit to DC.

1. **National Air and Space Museum.** This museum houses the *Wright Flyer*, *Spirit of St. Louis*, and an Apollo lunar module, bringing the history of flight and space exploration to life. This location just received a full remodel, so you'll want to check it out even if you have visited in the past.
2. **National Museum of Natural History.** This museum is huge— larger than eighteen football fields according to the Smithsonian Institution—so you may want to pick and choose what displays you explore. David H. Kock Fossil Hall and Sant Ocean Hall are always big

hits. It's worth it to pay a bit extra for timed tickets to the Butter-fly Pavilion.

3. **National Museum of African American History and Culture.** This newer Smithsonian requires timed tickets and promises a moving and emotional experience for visitors. All guests follow a one-directional flow with exhibits that bring you chronologically through the experiences of African Americans in the United States.

4. **National Zoo.** Also requiring timed tickets or a parking pass, the National Zoo is located in Rock Creek Park and houses giant pandas, Sumatran tigers, and Asian elephants.

5. **National Postal Museum.** This is a hidden gem in the Smithsonian system, but don't miss out on the truly engaging exhibits and hands-on demonstrations. Explore the history of mail from colonial times to present, sort through thousands of stamps, and design your own stamp collection.

## U.S. Botanic Garden

This isn't a part of the Smithsonian Institution, but this is another free "living museum" that you don't want to miss. The garden is open daily and timed tickets are not required. The conservatory has everything from a tropical rain forest to an orchid display to a desert. The children's garden offers hands-on activities from spring through fall. The themed annual holiday train display is worth braving the crowds.

## Independence National Historical Park

Philadelphia is the birthplace of our nation, and it's also a vibrant, accessible, and incredibly family-friendly city that is especially welcoming for first-time visitors. The Independence National Historical Park includes the Independence Visitor Center and Liberty Center, both free and open year-round, and the surrounding area includes many more historic locations. You'll also want to make time for other important activities like running up the *Rocky* steps and maybe visiting the Philadelphia Museum of Art after the photo op with Rocky's statue. This is a great year-round location, with late spring and early fall being ideal for enjoying the outdoor points of interest. The winter months can be cold, but the crowds are much lighter, so pair a visit with a stay at the Philadelphia South/Clarkboro KOA—open year-round—for a unique winter camping trip.

Some of the main attractions on and around Independence Square require timed tickets or are by guided tour only. Check out more details in this chapter and visit the national park website for up-to-date information when mapping out your day-to-day plans. Visiting Independence National

Historical Park can be a very budget-friendly excursion as many of the high-lights are free. If there is room in the budget to splurge, buy tickets to one of the many available walking tours, as the guides bring the history of the cobblestones and brownstones to life.

# CAMPGROUNDS OUTSIDE THE PARK

### Philadelphia South/Clarksboro KOA Holiday

▹ **Clarksboro, New Jersey**

▹ **koa.com**

▹ **RV and Tent Sites, Cabins, Glamping Tents**

Location wins the day at this KOA. If it was in the middle of nowhere it would be just fine. But because it is located about twenty minutes away from downtown Philadelphia, we think it is the cat's meow. At least if you adjust your expectations accordingly. Urban camping rarely feels rustic, quiet, and peaceful, but this KOA comes pretty close. It has a lovely parklike common area that is perfect for whiling away a summer night with your family. This charming area near the pond has community grills, cornhole, a playground, a bounce pillow, and other games that will keep the kids busy for hours. The RV sites here are a little tight, and nothing to write home about, but the deluxe cabin rentals are cozy, and the glamping tents are semiprivate and nicely shaded. The pool is small and gets crowded on summer weekends, but it makes for a nice place to take a quick dip after a long day in the city of Brotherly Love. The camp store is cute and well stocked, and the customer service is very friendly.

## Atsion Family Campground

▹ **Shamong, New Jersey**

▹ **state.nj.us**

▹ **RV and Tent Sites**

The Atsion Family Campground inside of Wharton State Forest is plain-and-simple and rustic. The sites are spacious, and those closest to Atsion Lake are the most desirable. The campground is not a destination in and of itself, but it puts you closer to downtown Philadelphia than any of the campgrounds in Pennsylvania's state park system—and the price is budget friendly. The bathhouses are not great, so those with self-contained RVs will be happiest here. There are other camping options inside Wharton State Forest (like Godfrey Bridge), but Atsion is your best bet for an outside-of-the-box base camp for a visit to Philadelphia.

## Lums Pond State Park

▷  **Bear, Delaware**

▷  **destateparks.com**

▷  **RV and Tent Sites, Yurt Rental**

The campground at Lums Pond State Park is just over an hour away from Philadelphia, but it is an excellent campground that could easily serve as a base camp for Philadelphia. Just make sure you time the traffic getting in and out of Delaware and in and out of downtown Philly. The campsites at Lums Pond are spacious and pretty and offer full hookups at a bargain basement price. Lums Pond is the largest freshwater pond in the state of Delaware, and the trails around it are lovely. Those traveling with kayaks will be in heaven. Don't forget to check out the zip-lining and ropes courses at Go Ape's Adventure Park, which is located within the state park and is an absolute hoot.

## Philadelphia/West Chester KOA Holiday

▷ Coatesville, Pennsylvania

▷ koa.com

▷ RV and Tent Sites, Cabins, Glamping Tent

This delightful KOA is nestled alongside the banks of the Brandywine River—making it a perfect place for those who like to fish, kayak, or SUP. Downtown Philadelphia is a bit of a hike depending on traffic, but the campground is very close to Longwood Gardens and Winterthur—both breathtaking DuPont properties that shouldn't be missed. Combining tours of those gorgeous estates with a couple of day trips into Philadelphia would make for a terrific family vacation, despite the drive into the city.

---------------------- **Tips for Visiting** ----------------------
### Independence National Historical Park

▷ Reserve timed tickets for the Independence Hall tour online in advance.

▷ Get in line early to see the Liberty Bell. There is a security checkpoint entering the building, and the line can get long in the late morning and early afternoon.

▷ Avoid school hours during the day, Monday through Friday. This is a very popular school field trip destination, so arriving at 9:00 a.m. sharp or visiting after 2:00 p.m. is a good bet.

▷ Go straight from the Liberty Bell to Congress Hall, where entrance is by tour only March through December, and tours are first-come, first-served.

▷ Don't miss the America's National Parks Museum Store located in Old City Hall and featuring some great national park merch.

## -- Other Must-See Attractions in the Historic District --

There are many historic attractions near Independence Square that are not officially part of the National Historical Park, but you should see them anyway.

▷ The National Constitution Center is located adjacent to Independence Square and operated in partnership with the NPS. The museum is full of engaging, interactive exhibits, and each day's schedule offers live educational programs and performances.

▷ At the Museum of the American Revolution, visitors can see George Washington's actual Revolutionary War tent and a full-scale replica of his field headquarters.

▷ The Betsy Ross House offers a self-guided tour and rotating exhibits that focus on life in colonial Philadelphia.

▷ It's hard to imagine coming to Philly and not visiting the Benjamin Franklin Museum, which explores the life and inventions of the man who put his stamp on so much of this city.

▷ Carpenter's Hall is where the First Continental Congress gathered in 1774. Admission is free and there is a scavenger hunt for children.

# Where's the Best Philly Cheesesteak?

That's really a trick question. Every native Philadelphian will try to convince you that their personal favorite cheesesteak joint is the only one worth visiting. But we lived in Philly for a couple of years, tried them all, and learned that there are a ton of really delicious ones to be had. It is definitely worth it to track down some of the legendary locations, just to experience the long lines and cranky grill masters. To place your order like a local, name your cheese preference (provolone, American, or Whiz) and then your onion preference (with or without). We usually order "Whiz with" at these iconic cheesesteak destinations:

▷ Jim's South Street is our personal go-to. The cheesesteak is, of course, delicious, but we also love the location and the view of South Street from the upstairs dining room.

▷ Geno's Steaks is one of the two most famous Philly cheesesteak empires, and it's open 24/7 so you can satisfy your craving at any hour.

▷ Pat's King of Steaks has been open since 1930 and claims to be the originator of the cheesesteak. Located across the street from Geno's, these two places are locked in a permanent Philly cheesesteak stare down.

▷ Sonny's Famous Steaks is located in Old City, so those exploring the Historic District can get an authentic cheesesteak without going too far out of the way.

▷ Reading Terminal Market, established in the late 1800s, has a dizzying number of vendors offering baked goods, meats, cheeses, and flowers. But there are also a few solid cheesesteak places here, so you can satisfy your craving and bring some groceries back to the campground.

# New River Gorge National Park and Preserve

Until recently, New River Gorge was a National River beloved by serious rock climbers and river rafters but was not as well known by the typical national park tourist. That changed when the location was redesignated in 2020 as America's sixty-third national park. The accompanying fanfare and media coverage has led to a rapid increase in the area's popularity—600,000 more people visited in 2021 than the previous year—and many national park enthusiasts are discovering wild and wonderful West Virginia for the very first time.

As you'll see in this chapter, the campgrounds in the New River Gorge National Park are about as rustic and remote as they get for an NPS site. Upgraded, modern camping facilities are at the top of the agenda for the new national park, and the many new RVing visitors will look forward to those improvements when they are complete. For now, if you don't want to really rough it, you'll have to find a private or state park campground nearby.

New River Gorge was redesignated as both a national park *and* a preserve, allowing some 65,000 acres to remain open for hunting—something not typically permitted in national parks but an important part of the outdoor recreation culture in the region. The park is open year-round, but to truly enjoy the highlights, you'll want to visit when you can get on the river.

# CAMPGROUNDS INSIDE THE PARK

## Primitive Camping Areas within the Park

▷ Stone Cliff Beach, Army Camp, Grandview Sandbar, Glade Creek, War Ridge/ Backus Mountain, Brooklyn, Thayer, Meadow Creek, Gauley Tailwaters

▷ nps.gov

▷ RV and Tent Sites

Camping inside of New River Gorge National Park and Preserve is challenging in several ways, and those with local knowledge will benefit when it comes to scoring sites. All nine of the campgrounds inside the park are first-come, first-served, and many of them are far off the beaten path and would require an adventurous drive just to find out if a site is available. But all of the sites are free, so driving around to score a great one could certainly be considered part of the fun. Calling these primitive camping areas "campgrounds" is also a bit of a stretch, as the smallest of them (Thayer) has only four sites, and the largest (Meadow Creek Campground) has only twenty-six sites and is for tent camping only. There are no hookups at any of these campsites, so come prepared. Tent campers love these remote and often scenic campsites, and so do adventurous van lifers and those with small RVs. Those with big rigs will need to camp at Meadow Creek or look outside of the park. Thankfully there are several great private campground options and more coming.

# CAMPGROUNDS OUTSIDE THE PARK

### Adventures on the Gorge

▷ Lansing, West Virginia

▷ adventuresonthegorge.com

▷ RV and Tent Sites, Cabins, Glamping Tents, Vacation Home Rentals

Adventures on the Gorge is not so much a campground as it is an all-in-one adventure resort with accommodations for all kinds of travelers. Its location near the gorge is just about perfect and boasts excellent views of the water in several locations. It is also the largest outfitter for all things New River Gorge. Whether you want to go whitewater rafting, zip-lining, mountain biking, rope climbing, or more, it has everything you need for an exciting day in and around America's newest national park. RV sites are limited at the time of this writing, but a significant expansion is underway. Tent camping options in a variety of different locations within the resort are also excellent in every way, though some are a distance from the main resort area and pool. The sites are almost all private and shady, and tent platforms are spacious and level. The cabin options here are also absolutely delightful and range from rustic to what the resort calls "hotel style." Many campers come here with their RVs and tents, and then come back for a second trip and treat themselves to a gorgeous cabin or glamping tent. Each type of accommodation here offers up a different experience that is well worth having.

## The Outpost at New River Gorge

▷ Fayetteville, West Virginia

▷ outpostnrg.com

▷ RV and Tent Sites, Cabin Rentals, Vintage RV Rental

At the time of this writing The Outpost at New River Gorge was completing construction and preparing for a soft opening. Located less than a mile from the New River Gorge Bridge and boasting comfortable new facilities and a great location, this campground looks to provide a more relaxed and down-to-earth version of Adventures on the Gorge. It also offers a wide range of rustic accommodations that are moderately priced. If its Grateful Dead–themed vintage camper rental is an indication of the vibe at this new outpost, then those who are not adrenaline junkies might feel right at home here. There are a handful of new campgrounds breaking ground or opening around New River Gorge because of the massive national interest in our newest national park—we think this one will have staying power.

## Babcock State Park

▷ **Clifftop, West Virginia**

▷ **wvstateparks.com**

▷ **RV and Tent Sites, Cabin Rentals**

Babcock State Park Campground is a lovely option for quiet state park camping that is just a short twenty-minute drive away from New River Gorge. Locals love to fish in the delightful trout stream that runs through the park, and photographers love to capture images of Glade Creek Grist Mill—a completely functional replica of the original mill. Some of the sites here are a bit unlevel, so bring leveling blocks. For those who want to cabin camp, Babcock offers up twenty-eight awesome options, including almost twenty classic CCC cabins that were built by the Civilian Conservation Corps in the 1930s. Many of these are located near the Grist Mill and offer up a cozy wood fireplace, a fully equipped kitchen, and a comfortable outdoor porch and picnic area.

# A Quick Guide to New River Gorge National Park and Preserve

## Gateway Town: Fayetteville, West Virginia

Located on the rim of the gorge, this town is just minutes from some of the park's main attractions like the New River Gorge Bridge and the Canyon Rim Visitor Center. It already hosts a variety of restaurants, shops, and outfitters. More will certainly crop up as the park gains popularity.

## Visitor Centers

There are four visitor centers spread throughout the park. At the north end of the park, Canyon Rim Visitor Center is open year-round and located near many of the park's most popular attractions. At the southern end of the park, Sandstone Visitor Center is a green design and has educational displays that focus on the natural and cultural history of the New River. Grandview Visitor Center is at the highest elevation in the park and offers visitors dizzying views from the rim down almost 1,400 feet to the river. Thurmond Depot Visitor Center is located in a restored railroad depot and focuses on the history of coal in the region.

## What to Do

### New River Gorge Bridge Walk

Bridge Walk offers two-to-three-hour guided tours along the 24-inch-wide catwalk that crosses the river 25 feet under the bridge. Brave souls are fastened to a safety cable for the entire 3,030-foot, one-way trip and then shuttled back to the Bridge Walk headquarters.

### New River Gorge Scenic Drive

This 83-mile loop will give you a variety of river and gorge views, passing through many of the more popular overlooks including Grandview and the Endless Wall areas. The scenic loop encompasses both the Canyon Rim and Sandstone Visitor Centers.

## Fayette Station Road

The 7.5-mile loop drive begins at the Canyon Rim Visitor Center and takes you under the New River Gorge Bridge. Interpretive roadside exhibits teach about the history of mining and culture in the gorge.

## Endless Wall Trail

One of the more popular hikes in the park, this 2.3-mile point-to-point trail can easily be turned into a loop trail by walking 0.5 mile at the end along the road back to your starting point. The fairly easy trail is a favorite for its great New River Gorge overlooks.

## Castle Rock Trail

This short, challenging 1-mile loop trail will offer up spectacular vistas and steep drop-offs. This trail can be combined with the Turkey Spur or Grandview Rim Trail for a longer adventure.

## Whitewater Rafting

If you want to get out on the river, try one of Adventure on the Gorge's guided rafting tours. Families and beginners will be happy exploring the Upper New River with calm pools and smaller rapids. Adrenaline junkies can experience class III and IV rapids on the Lower New River.

## Rock Climbing

If you know what you are doing, pick one of New River Gorge's 1,400 established rock climbs and start scrambling up the sandstone. Need a little guidance? Tap into the expertise of one of the many local climbing outfitters like ACE Adventure Resort, which offers climbs for everyone from beginners to experts.

## Biking

Ride a traditional bike (no e-bikes permitted) along the 12.8 miles of easy-to-intermediate Arrowheads Trails. Class I and II e-bikes are allowed only on the Stone Cliff Trail, a 2.7-mile one-way ride along the bank of the New River.

## Bridge Day

Held on the third Saturday of every October, Bridge Day commemorates the 1977 completion of the New River Gorge Bridge. The popular festival includes BASE jumpers, rappelers, and high-line riders, as well as spectators who enjoy walking the bridge and watching the daredevils fly over the gorge. Plan ahead if you want to attend the largest single-day festival in West Virginia.

# Mammoth Cave National Park

Mammoth Cave National Park is home to the world's largest known cave system with over 400 miles that have been charted and explored. Besides being a gem in the crown of America's best idea, it is also a UNESCO World Heritage Site and an International Biosphere Reserve. In other words: it's kind of a big deal.

However, the NPS goes out of its way to let you know that it is not just a cave by promoting the park's hiking, biking, kayaking, fishing, horseback riding, and stargazing options. So if you are wondering if Mammoth Cave can sustain a weeklong family camping vacation, the answer is an absolute *yes*. Thankfully there are a handful of excellent campground options both inside and outside of the park. You can keep it simple and tent camp inside the park, or park a big rig at one of the private campgrounds located just outside of the park. No matter how you camp, you have to make reservations in advance to enter the caves. We recommend booking a tour right after you book your campsite.

# CAMPGROUNDS INSIDE THE PARK

## Mammoth Cave Campground

▷ Mammoth Cave, Kentucky

▷ nps.gov

▷ RV and Tent Sites

Looking for a quiet, rustic base camp for exploring Mammoth Cave National Park and don't need the hook-ups and kid-friendly amenities that the Jellystone provides? The wooded, shady sites offered by the NPS at the Mammoth Cave Campground are spacious and affordable. The visitor center is also a short walk away.

## Maple Springs Group Campground and Houchin Ferry Campground

▷ Mammoth Cave, Kentucky

▷ nps.gov

▷ RV and Tent Sites

Maple Springs Group Campground and Houchin Ferry both offer a limited number of sites in quiet, more remote parts of the park. Maple Springs can accommodate larger RVs, tent campers of all kinds, and those camping in groups or with horses. But Houchin Ferry is for tent campers only. Neither of these campgrounds has cell reception or staff on-site, nor do they sell firewood. So come prepared with what you need and prepare to be unplugged during your stay. If you are looking for simplicity, simplicity, simplicity, then both of these campgrounds will fit the bill.

# CAMPGROUNDS OUTSIDE THE PARK

## Yogi Bear's Jellystone Park Mammoth Cave

*Author's*
☆☆☆
**CHOICE**

▷ Cave City, Kentucky

▷ jellystonemammothcave.com

▷ Cabins, Cottages, Bungalows, RV and Tent Sites

An off-the-hook Jellystone Park with tons of fun family activities located just minutes away from an epic National Park that is also a UNESCO World Heritage Site? Sign us up now. After a morning of exploring Mammoth Cave's underground trails you will love heading back to this Jellystone Park for swimming, waterslides, pedal carts, mini-golf, jumping pillows, and the campground's own sandy beach and 2.3-acre lake. Yogi and his friends can also be seen throughout the park and are available for bear hugs and fun photo ops. We do always like to emphasize that Jellystone Parks are not just for little kids. Teenagers will love the huge inflatable sports park on the lake (known as the Wibit!), and they will also spend hours playing softball, basketball, and volleyball. A wide variety of RV and tent sites is available, and they can accommodate the biggest of rigs and the smallest of tents. This Jellystone also has more than ninety-three air-conditioned cabins, making it a perfect place for glampers who don't own an RV and don't want to sleep in a tent. The Cindy Bear Cottage and Ranger's Retreat are just two of their cozy options.

## Horse Cave KOA

▷ Horse Cave, Kentucky

▷ koa.com

▷ RV and Tent Sites, Cabins, Conestoga Wagon, Tree House, Home Rental

The Horse Cave KOA is just a short drive away from Mammoth Cave National Park. It gets high marks for natural beauty, the cleanliness of its bathrooms, and basic (but fun) amenities for the kids. This KOA is also an excellent choice for cabin campers or those who like alternative types of campground accommodations, like its Conestoga Wagon and tree house rentals. It even has two rental options in a cozy and well-equipped duplex. The roads can be a little tight for larger rigs, and some of the sites are not perfectly level—so bring extra leveling blocks if you are staying in an RV.

## Wax Campground at Nolin River Lake/ U.S. Army Corps of Engineers

▷  Clarkson, Kentucky

▷  nps.gov

▷  RV and Tent Sites

If you want to visit Mammoth Cave and camp in a peaceful and natural setting, then this Corps of Engineers park might be perfect for you. Wax Campground is located on the tranquil shores of Nolin River Lake and is surrounded by rolling hills. Canoe and kayak lovers will enjoy hitting the water and utilizing the campground's easily accessible launch points. But make sure you bring plenty of groceries and supplies, as the campground is in a fairly remote location with few shops around. Most sites here offer water and electric hookups so you can run your RV's air conditioning during the hot summer months. Tent campers might choose to stay here during the shoulder seasons when the heat and humidity are milder.

## Diamond Caverns RV Resort and Golf Club

▷  Park City, Kentucky

▷  thousandtrails.com

▷  RV and Tent Sites

Diamond Caverns is part of the Thousand Trails network of campgrounds, but non-members can also camp here. This campground is pretty, with rolling open lawns and lush green trees. It has fewer than eighty RV sites, and booking one during peak months can be quite competitive, but not impossible. There is an eighteen-hole golf course on-site if you want to unleash your inner Tiger Woods and visit the world's longest known cave system on the same trip. Those who are less ambitious may also choose to play a game of mini-golf or go for a dip in the pool. There are also hiking trails on-site and a comfortable indoor game room for rainy days or chilly nights.

# A Quick Guide to Mammoth Cave National Park

## Where to Stock Up

Cave City is 6 miles from the main entrance of Mammoth Cave National Park and is the place to grab groceries and other provisions.

## Regularly Scheduled Ranger Programs

▷ Coffee with a Ranger

▷ Porch Talk

▷ Heritage Walk

▷ Junior Ranger Nature Track

▷ Echo River Springs Walk

▷ Sloans Crossing Pond Walk

▷ Evening Program at the Amphitheater

## Cave Tours

It's imperative to research cave tours ahead of time to find the right ones for your family. You'll also want to make reservations in advance, as the most popular tours fill up not only during the summer months but also during the spring when local schools visit for field trips. There are age restrictions for many of the tours. Strollers and child backpack carriers are prohibited on all cave tours, so plan accordingly.

### Easy Cave Tours for the First-Time Visitor

▷ Frozen Niagara Tour, 0.25 mile

▷ Mammoth Passage Tour, 0.75 mile

▷ Discovery Tour, 0.75 mile (unguided)

### Moderate Cave Tours for the Adventurous Visitor

▷ Historic Tour, 2 miles

▷ Domes and Dripstones Tour, 0.75 mile

▷ Gothic Avenue Tour, 1 mile

## Strenuous Cave Tour for the Bold and Brave Visitor

▷ Violet City Lantern Tour, 3 miles by lantern

## Caves Outside of the National Park

▷ Cub Run Cave

▷ Diamond Caverns

▷ Hidden River Cave

▷ Onyx Cave

▷ Outlaw Cave

## Additional Activities Outside the National Park

▷ Dinosaur World

▷ Kentucky Action Park

▷ Kentucky Down Under Adventure Zoo & Mammoth Onyx Cave

▷ Hidden River Cave and American Museum

▷ Diamond Caverns

# Great Smoky Mountains National Park

Great Smoky Mountains National Park regularly wins the award of America's Most Visited National Park, with more than fourteen million people entering the park boundaries in 2021. Why does this park attract so many visitors year after year? For starters, it is only a day's drive from the many densely populated areas in the East. It also offers a compelling mix of wildlife viewing, historical sightseeing, scenic drives, and hikes. Add in bustling tourist destinations like Gatlinburg, Pigeon Forge, and the iconic Dollywood theme park, and you end up with one of the country's favorite vacation destinations.

The good news for campers is that there is an almost overwhelming number of campground options to consider when planning a Smokies camping trip. The bad news is that the sheer volume of annual visitors makes it difficult to reserve the most popular campsites, especially in the national park campgrounds.

If you are determined to camp in one of the national park campgrounds, pay close attention to the six-month rolling reservation window, and try to reserve a spot immediately when the window opens for your desired dates.

You'll have better luck securing a site during the off-season than in the summer, but note that fall is also a very popular time to visit the park and take in the colorful foliage. Private campground sites will be easier to find, but note that some of the most popular campgrounds fill up over a year in advance. In other words: don't try to wing it when visiting the Smokies.

Consider where you want to spend time and what you want to explore before choosing a campground as a base camp. This national park is sprawling, and if you stay at a campground far from the attractions you are interested in, you may spend hours in the car driving from site to site. We've separated our campground recommendations according to state—there is a North Carolina side of the park with Cherokee and Bryson City as hubs, and a Tennessee side with Gatlinburg, Pigeon Forge, and Townsend as gateway towns. If you have an extended period of time, think about campground hopping. On a previous two-week trip, we stayed at three different campgrounds and enjoyed the experience tremendously.

# CAMPGROUNDS INSIDE THE PARK

There are no sewer hookups, electrical hookups, or showers at any of the campgrounds in Great Smoky Mountains National Park. There is also no Wi-Fi—and very spotty cellular service—so plan accordingly.

### Elkmont Campground

▷   Gatlinburg, Tennessee

▷   nps.gov

▷   RV and Tent Sites

Located about twenty minutes from the gateway town of Gatlinburg, this beautiful campground is a family favorite on account of the size and riverfront location. The Little River and Jakes Creek run right through the campground, and visitors love fishing and swimming in the crisp mountain water. Most of the 200 sites will accommodate RVs, but read descriptions

carefully to note any size limitations. Some campsites have a steep grade, which makes it challenging to level a larger RV. The sites are spacious with a picnic table and fire ring. Firewood is available for purchase on-site. The bathhouses have flush toilets, but no showers.

## Cades Cove Campground

  ▷  Townsend, Tennessee

  ▷  nps.gov

  ▷  RV and Tent Sites

Elkmont may be the perfect place to enjoy a classic Smokies river experience, but Cades Cove Campground puts you in the middle of the most iconic wildlife and scenic loop and about 15 miles from the charming gateway town of Townsend. Bears, deer, turkeys, and coyotes are regularly spotted in the valley, especially during the early morning and evening hours. The campground has a well-stocked store with supplies, souvenirs, and ice cream. You can also rent bikes right on-site, which will help visitors more easily navigate the traffic along the popular 11-mile Cades Cove Loop Road. This campground is open year-round and has flush toilets, potable water, and a dump station for guests.

## Cosby Campground

  ▷  Cosby, Tennessee

  ▷  nps.gov

  ▷  RV and Tent Sites

A smaller, more secluded and peaceful campground, visitors may have a better chance at nabbing a site at Cosby Campground than the more popular national park campgrounds listed above. There are a handful of RV sites with an additional tent pad and a handful of sites for van campers with a tent pad. You'll have to drive a bit to get to the main park attractions, so if you are looking for a quiet Smokies retreat, this may be the perfect campground.

## Deep Creek Campground

- Bryson City, North Carolina
- nps.gov
- RV and Tent Sites

Located in the southeastern corner of the park on the North Carolina side, Deep Creek is one of the most popular creeks in the park and the campground fills up quickly in the summer with visitors looking to fish, tube, and swim surrounded by beautiful mountain scenery. The ninety-two campsites include spots for both tents and RVs, all equipped with fire rings, picnic tables, and grills. Flush toilets and potable water are available, but there is no on-site firewood for sale. The gateway town of Bryson City is just minutes away and hosts plenty of stores for stocking up on provisions, plus an array of outfitters for tubing, rafting, ziplining, horseback riding, and more.

## Smokemont Campground

- Cherokee, North Carolina
- nps.gov
- RV and Tent Sites

One of the two national park campgrounds that is open year-round, Smokemont is located on the North Carolina side of the Smokies, about fifteen minutes from the gateway town of Cherokee. It offers both tent and RV sites, each with a picnic table, fire pit, and grill. River views and a large, open field for a game of catch are favorite campground features. Sites are more exposed and closer together than in some of the other Smoky National Park campgrounds. Flush toilets, potable water, and a dump station are available for campers. There is a camp store, and firewood is sold at the campground.

## Other Campgrounds Inside the Park

- **Abrams Creek**
- **Balsam Mountain**
- **Big Creek**
- **Cataloochee**

# CAMPGROUNDS OUTSIDE THE PARK

## Little Arrow Outdoor Resort

▷ Townsend, Tennessee

▷ camplittlearrow.com

▷ RV and Tent Sites, Glamping Tents, Cabin Rentals, Lodge Rentals

The Little Arrow Outdoor Resort may be the buzziest, most on-trend campground in the Smokies. The property changed owners a few years ago, and the new management dove right into developing the hip glamping vibe that is all the rage right now. Framed as a wilderness retreat, it offers RV sites, tiny homes, cabins, glamping tents, and even an Airstream all with direct access to the Little River. The luxury RV sites are 90 feet long, featuring a covered cabana, outdoor sink, and paver patio. There is a swimming pool, hot tub, river access, and organized activities like bingo, trivia, and riverfront drumming class. Book a massage at the Little Arrow Spa as a treat after a long national park hike.

## Greenbrier Campground

▷ Gatlinburg, Tennessee

▷ smokymountaincamping.com

▷ RV and Tent Sites, Cabin and Tent Rentals

The Little Pigeon River runs right through the Greenbrier Campground, offering guests a swimming hole, private beach, and on-site trout fishing. There are full hook-up sites, some with water access and some wooded options, plus tent sites and cabins. Campers rave about the pet-friendly policies and cleanliness. This campground offers plenty of recreation for families, including volleyball, ga-ga ball, badminton, bocce ball, and corn hole. Greenbrier is less than a half mile from the Greenbrier entrance to GSMNP. It's close enough to Gatlinburg to easily access the bustling town, but far enough away enjoy the peace and quiet of the Smokies.

## Imagination Mountain Camp-Resort

▷ Cosby, Tennessee

▷ imaginationmountaincamping.com

▷ RV and Tent Sites, Cabin rentals

Imagination Mountain Camp-Resort is located in Cosby, which is only about twenty minutes from Gatlinburg but feels like a million miles away. Almost all of the campsites and cabin rentals are creekside, and the friendly workers will help you back into your campsite. There is a heated saltwater pool, arcade, ice cream parlor, and well-stocked camp store. An oversized chess board, basketball court, and club house will keep the kids entertained when you aren't exploring the park. Organized activities are available on a daily basis for the kids during the summer season. The combination of natural beauty and family-friendly amenities makes this campground a favorite for many campers.

## Pigeon Forge/Gatlinburg KOA Holiday

▷ Forge, Tennessee

▷ koa.com

▷ RV and Tent Sites, Cabin Rentals

This family-owned KOA opened in 1966 and is legendary among area campgrounds. Located right off the main drag in Pigeon Forge, a trolley is available to take you into town and a few minutes up the road to Dollywood. It has all the amenities you would expect in a KOA: pool, hot tub, snack bar, and dog park. Plus it has some extras like a waterslide, outdoor cinema, and fun train. Some visitors are not big fans of the tight sites and general hustle and bustle, but this is not a campground for anyone looking for peace and quiet. Reserve a spot here if you want to be in the heart of all the glorious touristy action the Smokies has to offer.

## Townsend/Great Smokies KOA Holiday

▷ Townsend, Tennessee

▷ koa.com

▷ RV and Tent Sites, Cabin Rentals

Located on what is known as "the peaceful side of the Smokies," this is one of the most beloved and recommended campgrounds in the Smokies, likely because it combines the best features of many different types of campgrounds. The Townsend KOA is right on the river and offers on-site tubing and fishing. Plus, it has all the amenities KOAs are known for, such as a pool, playground, wagon rides, and scheduled activities. The managers create a warm and cozy family-friendly atmosphere, and people return year after year. This is a great campground choice if you are looking for proximity to Cades Cove but can't get into the Cades Cove national park campground.

## Anchor Down RV Resort

▷ Dandridge, Tennessee

▷ anchordownrvresort.com

▷ RV Sites

Located about forty-five minutes north of Gatlinburg in Dandridge, this RV resort opened up less than a decade ago and quickly grew in popularity. The campground is on the shores of Douglas Lake, and the most popular campsites are legendarily Instagrammable, with large stone fireplaces and stunning water and mountain views. Anchor Down also has all the resort amenities you could want, including a pool and lake beach with swimming, inflatables, and watercraft rentals. There are pickleball courts and a basketball court. The sparkling clean bathrooms get rave reviews.

## Cherokee/Great Smokies KOA Holiday

▷ Cherokee, North Carolina

▷ koa.com

▷ RV and Tent Sites, Cabin Rentals

On the North Carolina side, the Cherokee/Great Smokies KOA Holiday is open year-round and offers a true camping resort experience. There's an indoor and outdoor pool, hot tub, and sauna. There's also a jump pillow, go-cart rentals, snack bar, community fire pit, and movies under the stars. You'll find a packed recreation schedule during the peak travel season. Some of the best RV sites back up right to the river, and guests can enjoy tubing and fishing on-site.

## Under Canvas Great Smoky Mountains

▷ Pigeon Forge, Tennessee

▷ undercanvas.com

▷ Glamping Tents

This Under Canvas property is located in Pigeon Forge about 10 miles from downtown Gatlinburg. All of the gorgeous safari tents offer luxurious bedding, and some offer private bathrooms with hot water, but there's no electricity and your only source of heat is the in-tent, wood-burning stove. On-site dining is top-notch, and evenings come along with live music and complimentary s'mores around the community fire pit.

## Camp Margaritaville RV Resort and Lodge

▷ Pigeon Forge, Tennessee

▷ margaritavilleresorts.com

▷ RV Sites, Lodging

Camp Margaritaville is a new player on the RV resort scene and is already winning positive reviews from RV owners who like to fancy camp. Its pool and water recreation area are extensive and will please parents who want to chill out in the sun, and kids who want to race down the looping water slides. Options for on-site dining are also extensive, so if you don't feel like busting out the old two-burner camp stove, you don't have to. We also love the Lodge building here. The rooms are downright luxurious for those who don't have an RV, or who just want to leave their rigs at home and try something different. When compared to RV Resorts in the Northeast, the prices are also reasonable. The location here is also very good. The National Park is just a short drive away.

## Worth the Splurge

### Dollywood

There are so many free things to do in the Smokies—hiking, tubing, fishing, and long, scenic drives—that the cost of a ticket for Dollywood can give many visitors pause. If there's room in the budget for a splurge, skip the Ripley's Aquarium, SkyLift Park, and Gatlinburg T-shirt shops, and head straight to Dolly Parton's theme park. Top-notch rides for all ages, live music, great food, and entertaining shows make for a truly unforgettable experience.

## The Main Event

### The Firefly Event Lottery

Synchronous fireflies put on their stunning reproductive display for a few weeks every year in late May through early June in the Elkmont area of the national park. Event and lottery dates are announced in early spring, and hopeful visitors can enter the lottery via recreation.gov. Eight hundred lucky winners will receive a date-specific parking pass to enter the managed area and view the natural wonder.

# The Many Gateway Towns of GSMNP

## Gatlinburg

Gatlinburg is arguably the most popular tourist hub in the Smokies. It's known as the main gateway to Great Smoky Mountains National Park, and Sugarlands Visitor Center is just minutes from the downtown area. Some of the most famous hikes and drives are close to the main drag as well, like the Roaring Fork Motor Nature Trail and Chimney's Picnic Area.

## Pigeon Forge

People seem to either love or hate staying in the Pigeon Forge area of the Great Smoky Mountains. If you want to be surrounded by nonstop action, this is the place for you. Parents of preteens and teenagers often give this area two thumbs up. They particularly enjoy the trolley that allows everyone to get around independently. Plus, Dollywood is right there.

## Townsend

Townsend is located in "the quiet side of the Smokies." People who loathe the touristy commercialism of Gatlinburg and Pigeon Forge often choose this area when visiting Great Smoky Mountain National Park. But don't let the nickname fool you. Even though Townsend is quiet, there are so many outdoor activities—and endless seasonal festivals—in the area. Townsend is close to the Cades Cove park entrance, a favorite area for many visitors.

## Cherokee

Staying near Cherokee, North Carolina, allows visitors to be immersed in the history of the Great Smokies region. The Museum of the Cherokee Indian is an engaging, educational, and interactive experience, and the outdoor show "Unto These Hills" tells the story of the Cherokee people from 1780 to the present day. There's also a casino if you're feeling lucky. Bryson City, just fifteen minutes away, is a hub for outdoor recreation experiences.

## Dreamy Drives

Great Smoky Mountains National Park was designed with motoring in mind. In fact, back in the 1920s and '30s, auto clubs played a pivotal role in its formation. When President Franklin D. Roosevelt dedicated the park in 1940 for "the permanent enjoyment of the people," many of those people were doing so from the comforts of their automobiles.

That legacy lives on today. **The Roaring Fork Motor Trail** is easily accessible from downtown Gatlinburg, but it feels like you are making a great escape into the heart and soul of the Smokies. The road follows the path of a crystal clear mountain stream and crosses it over picturesque wooden bridges.

Other drives not to be missed? **The Cades Cove Loop Trail** and **Newfound Gap Road**. By the way, leave your rig at the campground and plan on using your tow vehicle or your dingy. These roads were designed for roadsters, not RVs.

## Heavenly Hikes

Strap on your hiking boots, pack the snacks, and head out for an easy ramble or a strenuous climb. Great Smoky Mountains National Park has amazing options for both. Start at the Sugarlands Visitor Center on the Tennessee side or the Oconaluftee Visitor Center on the North Carolina side, where a park ranger will recommend a hike that is just right for your skill level and physical ability. That's how we discovered the **Kephart Prong Trail,** one of our all-time favorite hikes. Crossing back and forth over a rushing mountain stream on narrow wooden bridges with just a single handrail was a highlight for the whole family.

Other hikes not to be missed? **The Cosby Nature Trail** is a peaceful, easy, wooded walk along streams, and the hike out to **Abrams Falls** is perfect for the more adventurous.

## ----------------- Wild Water Adventures -----------------

If you love tubing in cool water on a hot day, there is no place better than Great Smoky Mountains National Park. Several reputable outfitters along the Little River can get you set up for your adventure, and many private campgrounds in the area are nestled along rivers. You can rent tubes directly from the camp stores and float back to your own campsite.

For the best tubing, head to the **Deep Creek Tube Center and Campground** located in Bryson City, where you can rent tubes for $7 a day. The mountain stream at Deep Creek has an upper and a lower section. The upper section has fast-moving white water, and the lower section is quiet and gentle. You pass by a waterfall and a natural swimming hole on your way back down to the campground. Then head back up and do it again.

# Cape Hatteras National Seashore & The Wright Brothers National Memorial

A camping trip to Cape Hatteras National Seashore is always a bit risky. Excessive wind can break RV awnings and send tents flying with very little warning. Driving rain can flood campsites and turn them into massive 12-inch-deep puddles in just a few hours. But when the weather cooperates, the beaches here are unmatched for their accessibility and wild, natural beauty. The surfing is the best on the entire East Coast, and the fishing and paddle sports are equally epic. We've camped here almost every single year since we were teenagers, even though we occasionally get skunked by wind and rain.

The national seashore and its surrounding beaches offer up a wide variety of camping options, from rustic campgrounds inside the national seashore to the RV-centric resorts in Waves and Rodanthe. Choosing the right campground is important for this type of NPS trip. Why? Because while there is much to explore in and around the national seashore, you will probably spend most of your vacation hanging out on the beach near your campsite. Ask us how we know...

On your way into or out of Cape Hatteras National Seashore, make sure you check out the Wright Brothers National Memorial. It will make you feel like flying.

# CAMPGROUNDS INSIDE THE PARK

### Cape Point Campground

▷   **Buxton, North Carolina**

▷   **nps.gov**

▷   **RV and Tent Sites**

▷   **No Hookups**

The Cape Point Campground is the largest of the four NPS campgrounds on the Outer Banks—and because of its prime location just a short walk away from some of the best surfing and fishing on the East Coast, it is also the most popular. We tent camped here when we were teenagers during some fairly epic wind and rain storms hoping that the waves would get good. Thankfully, most of the time they did and we surfed until our hearts were content. Cape Point is also near the famous lighthouse, so it is also a popular choice for those sightseeing in the area. But for the most part, this campground is filled with surfers and fisherman and those in search of sun and sand. This is the only NPS campground on the Outer Banks that does not accept reservations in advance. At Cape Point, you can only use its reservation system on a same-day basis. Why have such a quirky policy? Because the campground is so prone to flooding that it wants campers to actually inspect their site before paying for it. We can personally attest to the wisdom of this policy because we have seen our own sites flood while tent camping here. So yes, conditions can be challenging at Cape Point. But when the sun is shining, and the wind is behaving, this is one of the best spots for beach camping in the entire country.

## Oregon Inlet Campground

▷ **Nags Head, North Carolina**

▷ **nps.gov**

▷ **RV and Tent Sites**

Oregon Inlet Campground is located closer to the hustle and bustle of the more touristy section of the Outer Banks, and those who want more options for food, shopping, and entertainment might choose to stay here over spots over the bridge and closer to the lighthouse. This campground is open year-round and offers some hookups for RV owners. It can also handle big rigs. The surfing is not as good here as in other spots farther south, but the fishing is great and the beaches are lovely.

# CAMPGROUNDS OUTSIDE THE PARK

## Cape Hatteras/Outer Banks KOA Resort

▷ **Rodanthe, North Carolina**

▷ **koa.com**

▷ **RV and Tent Sites, Camping Cabins, Deluxe Cabins, Vacation Rentals**

▷ **Water, Electric, Sewer**

There is little to no shade at this oceanfront campground, and the RV and tent sites are small and lack privacy. But if you can get past those things, you are in for a magical stay if the weather is good. The Wright brothers came here for good reason—it can be windy at any time of year, and we come back here again and again for good reason too. The beaches are beautiful and great for fishing or surfing. In fact, some of the best surfing on the East Coast happens right in front of this campground. The pool complex is also one of the best pool campgrounds in the country. Kids love the zero-entry side, and adults love the lap lanes and spacious hot tub. When camping here, we spend our days going back and forth between the beach and the pool.

Our evenings are spent grilling back at our site and playing Wiffle ball in the sand. This KOA has been our first pick when visiting Cape Hatteras over the last decade. But nearby Camp Hatteras is every bit as good, just somewhat less geared toward families that travel with young kids. When our kids fly the coop we will probably choose Camp Hatteras instead for a bit more peace and quiet.

## Camp Hatteras

▷ **Rodanthe, North Carolina**

▷ **camphatteras.com**

▷ **RV and Tent Sites, Park Model Rentals**

▷ **Water, Electric, Sewer**

Camp Hatteras is less than half a mile north of the KOA, and it is also an excellent choice for those who want to camp with hookups and amenities. With sites on both sides of NC 12, you can choose to camp steps away from the Atlantic Ocean or the Pamlico Sound—both are terrific choices. The outdoor pool and hot tub at the KOA is nicer than the outdoor pool and hot tub here, but Camp Hatteras also has an indoor pool, which is a really nice option for days with inclement weather. Camp Hatteras does win when it comes to the RV sites. Generally speaking, they are bigger than the sites at the KOA, and they have nice concrete pads that come in very clutch on rainy days. We have experienced flooded sites at the KOA on numerous occasions. The clubhouse at Camp Hatteras is also a warm and cozy spot on windy or rainy days. There is a communal kitchen if you need a little more space than your RV offers, and there are also board games, books, and magazines. Of course we all hope for great weather when we visit the Outer Banks. The beaches right in front of these excellent private campgrounds are among the best on the East Coast for surfing, swimming, fishing, and just kicking back and relaxing with sand between your toes.

## Ocean Waves Campground

▷ Waves, North Carolina

▷ oceanwavescampground.com

▷ RV and Tent Sites

▷ Water, Electric, Sewer

Just a bit farther south on NC 12 is this quiet and comfortable oceanfront campground with just under seventy full hook-up sites. The amenities here are very limited compared to the campgrounds mentioned earlier, but the price is also more budget friendly, and you still get direct access to the beach. So if you aren't camping with kids, and want to save a few bucks, this may be a perfect choice for you. Ocean Waves is family owned and operated, and its customer service is widely known to be excellent.

## Frisco Campground

▷ Frisco, NC

▷ thefriscowoodscampground.com

▷ RV and Tent Sites, Cabins

▷ Water, Electric, Sewer

If you take NC 12 south past the Cape Hatteras Lighthouse section of the national seashore, you will end up in the sleepy little village of Frisco. If you want to get away from it all, and really get away from the crowds, then the Frisco Campground might be a great option for you. Its location on the Pamlico Sound is gorgeous and excellent for those who love to kayak or stand-up paddleboard. Uncrowded beaches are also nearby. This campground is simple and somewhat rustic, but it is also affordable and clean.

---------------------------- **Free Camping** ----------------------------

Up for a tent camping adventure under a sky full of stars? Head farther south to Cape Lookout National Seashore for free camping on the beach. But come prepared with food and water! There are no camp stores within the national seashore.

# Cape Hatteras Highlights

**The Cape Hatteras Lighthouse**, which is still in operation, towers over "the graveyard of the Atlantic" and serves as its most iconic structure without rival. If Climbing its 257 steps doesn't take your breath away, the views from the top certainly will. Kids must be 42 inches tall to make the climb, so plan accordingly.

**Gear Up at Natural Art Surf Shop:** Whether you need a new surfboard and surf trunks, or just a new beach towel and flip flops, the Natural Art Surf Shop is the place to plunk down your bucks. This is a legitimate local institution that has been serving the surfers and beachgoers since 1977.

**Catch a Wave:** The surfing in and around Cape Hatteras National Seashore is the best on the East Coast. Conditions can vary from beginner friendly to full on victory-at-sea insanity. We've surfed in both type of conditions there. Always take caution if you are an amateur—and even if you're not.

**Kiteboarding on the Sound:** Have you ever seen a kiteboarder flying through the sky and leaving the earth's gravitational pull far behind? Ever want to become one of them? Then grab a lesson with Kite Club Hatteras in Avon. Its instructors are known to do excellent work with beginners. Your flight will be departing in no time at all!

**Lazy Days on the Beach:** This is one of the rare NPS trips where we suggest doing as little as you possibly can. Relaxing on the beach is the order of the day on the Outer Banks, so make sure you bring a good book and plenty of sunscreen.

**Good Eats at Buxton Munch:** This self-proclaimed "Groovy Little Place with a Whole Lot of Taste" is one of our favorite places for grub in the Outer Banks. Skip the more expansive and stuffy seafood restaurants nearby and grab some epic (and affordable) fish tacos here!

**A Day Trip to Ocracoke Island:** Taking a ferry ride to Ocracoke Island is a great way to spend a day in the Outer Banks. Quirky restaurants and shopping line the streets of this little village, but the real adventure is just getting there and getting back.

# Gulf Islands National Seashore

Gulf Islands National Seashore was created to protect the barrier islands along the coast of Florida and Mississippi in the Gulf of Mexico. The 160 miles of white sand beaches meet crystal clear waters and offer plenty of historical and natural attractions in the country's largest national seashore.

The layout of this national seashore is unique and important to take into consideration when making your campground plans. There are two distinct units of the park—one in Mississippi and one in Florida—and the areas are not geographically connected. In fact, there's about a 100-mile driving distance between the two. Each state unit has one developed campground that we detail in this section, but make sure you consider where you want to be and what activities you want to do before picking a base camp.

The most crowded time of year in this region is from early spring through August. The campgrounds and beaches are packed starting with spring break vacationers until kids return to school. October and November can be a lovely time of year, once peak hurricane season has passed, the crowds have diminished, and the water and air temperatures are still warm. Some northerners are surprised by how chilly it can be in the winter months.

# CAMPGROUNDS INSIDE THE PARK

## Davis Bayou Campground

▷ Ocean Springs, Mississippi

▷ nps.gov

▷ RV and Tent Sites

The Davis Bayou Campground is an absolute delight. It is clean and well-kept and has spacious, shady sites surrounded by live oaks and pine trees. This is one of the rare NPS campgrounds in the country to offer water and electric hookups at every site. RV owners who camp here in the heat of the summer love being able to run their air conditioning at night. The campground is adjacent to a saltwater marsh and is in a great spot for those who love bird-watching. RV and tent sites here are angled and easy to get into, and offer lots of shade for a coastal camping environment. Kids will also love riding their bikes here. The bathrooms here are clean but on the older side. Downtown Ocean Springs is a short bike ride away and has good eats and funky coastal shopping.

## Fort Pickens Campground

▷ Pensacola Beach, Florida

▷ nps.gov

▷ RV and Tent Sites

Fort Pickens Campground is a coastal gem in the NPS system. The drive to the campground is even beautiful—with sand and water surrounding the road on each side. While it may fly under the radar nationally, it is still one of the busiest and most visited public campgrounds in the country. This is partly because it is open all year. The campground itself is not directly on the beach, but sand and warm water are just a short walk away. Even though the beach is close, you will want to make sure you have a cart to schlep all your stuff to and from your site. The roads are a bit tight for larger RVs, and some of the tent sites lack privacy, but you are camping in paradise—so don't nit-pick the small stuff.

# CAMPGROUND OUTSIDE THE PARK

### Pensacola Beach RV Resort

▷ **Pensacola Beach, Florida**

▷ **pensacolarvresorts.com**

▷ **RV Sites, RV Rentals**

If you are an RV owner looking to glamp it up during your visit to Gulf Islands National Seashore, then book a premium site with a view of the Santa Rosa Sound at this posh RV resort. Once your RV is set up, head over to the Sneaky Tiki Bar for a drink or walk right into town for dinner or live entertainment. The white sand beaches of the Gulf of Mexico are directly across the street. There is so much to do in and around this resort that you might even forget to make the drive into the nearby national seashore.

--------- **Boat-in Backcountry Camping Locations** ---------

There are not many national park units that have multiple options for boat-in backcountry camping, so if you've always wanted to try it, this is the place! There are strict guidelines around where visitors are allowed to set up camp, and stays are limited to fourteen days. Make sure to read all rules and regulations on the national park website before venturing out.

**Florida**

▷ Perdido Key Area

**Mississippi**

▷ Petit Bois

▷ West Petit Bois

▷ Horn Islands

▷ Cat Islands
(NPS-owned portion)

# The Twelve Areas of Gulf Islands National Seashore

## Florida

▷ **Fort Pickens** is one of the most developed areas of the Gulf Islands National Seashore. There is a discovery center with wildlife exhibits, historical displays, and educational programs. There's also a swim beach and picnic pavilion. Historic Fort Pickens can be explored independently or by guided ranger tour.

▷ **Naval Live Oaks** does not offer the facilities found at some of the other areas, but visitors come for the hiking and biking trails, along with horseback riding trails. There is a picnic pavilion with restrooms, and pets are allowed on the trails, but not on the beaches.

▷ **Okaloosa** is a favorite destination for a quiet, calm, peaceful beach experience. There are restrooms and outdoor showers, plus a boat launch.

▷ **Perdido Key** is a bustling Gulf Islands destination, with swim beaches, restroom facilities, and picnic pavilions. There's also an accessible loop trail for birding enthusiasts. The area often closes for maximum capacity during the summer months, so arrive early to ensure entrance.

▷ **Santa Rosa** hosts the Opal Beach Complex, a fully developed swim beach area with restrooms, outdoor showers, picnic areas, and seasonal lifeguards. The waters can be rough here, and pets are not allowed.

▷ **Fort Barrancas** has been closed to the general public since 2019, but current military ID holders and their families, along with veterans, can still access the visitor center. See the NPS website for updates.

## Mississippi

▷ **Cat Island** is only accessible by private boat, and some of the island is privately owned. Visitors enjoy the gorgeous sandy beaches and interior live oaks and swamps. The island got its name from early explorers who thought the raccoons were cats. These bold raccoons are still a major attraction for visitors.

▷ **Davis Bayou** has a visitor center with robust educational exhibits and regularly scheduled ranger programs. There's a fishing pier, boat launch, and Nature's Way Loop Trail—a 0.5-mile path through the bayous.

▷ **Ship Island** has a developed swimming beach area with a snack bar, pier, and seasonal lifeguards. Historic Fort Massachusetts offers regularly scheduled tours and programs.

▷ **Horn Island, Petit Bois Island, and West Petit Bois Island** are completely undeveloped barrier islands that are only accessible by private boat. There are no facilities on any of these islands, but boat-in camping is allowed in certain areas.

# Everglades National Park & Big Cypress National Preserve

Just an hour's drive from Miami, the Everglades brings visitors back in time to a pre-development Floridian landscape—a tropical coastal swamp protecting alligators, manatees, bobcats, and even panthers. Neighboring the Everglades to the north is our nation's first national preserve, Big Cypress National Preserve, with 700,000 acres of protected swampland. Both national park units see more than one million visitors every year.

When planning your visit, understand that the dry season runs from December through April, and the wet season runs from May through November. As with all weather patterns, these are variable time frames, but the ideal time to tour the Everglades is in the dry season, when the region sees lower humidity and mild temperatures. This is when the majority of tours and ranger programming will run as well. During the wet season, temperatures will often soar above 90°F with very high humidity levels. The bugs can be unbearable during this time, so it is not ideal for camping, hiking, biking, birding, or any of the other outdoor activities popular with visitors to this national park and preserve.

# CAMPGROUNDS INSIDE THE PARK

## The Flamingo Campground

▷   Homestead, Florida

▷   nps.gov

▷   RV and Tent Sites, Eco-Tents, Houseboats, Lodge Rooms

The Flamingo Campground is popular among tent campers and RV owners for a variety of reasons, and it is the most obvious place to park your rig or pitch your tent inside Everglades National Park. The sites here are large but offer almost no shade. Thankfully, the campground is located directly on Florida Bay, and there is often a nice breeze that cools things off a bit. Outdoor enthusiasts will love the nearby hiking and kayaking trails, and the saltwater fishing is world class. With almost 300 sites, the campground is quite large, but the bathrooms and facilities are kept clean, and the customer service from the concessionaire is relatively good. Those who are not tent camping or RVing will want to check out a variety of other unique accommodations including eco-tents, lodge rooms, and even houseboats! The restaurant and bar are open every day and serve breakfast, lunch, and dinner. Mosquitoes can be ferocious, so come prepared.

## Long Pine Key Campground

▷   Homestead, Florida

▷   nps.gov

▷   RV and Tent Sites

Long Pine Key Campground is a bit smaller and simpler than the Flamingo Campground, but it may be even more lovely. The sites are angled and easy for RVs to get into, and most tent campers will feel comfortable with the amount of privacy they offer. Tall and skinny pine and palmetto trees dot the skyline and provide dappled shade for most sites. When the wind blows through these trees, the sound is soothing and enchanting. Plan on walking through the campground with a cup of coffee in the early morning hours before heading out to explore the park.

# CAMPGROUNDS OUTSIDE THE PARK

## Midway Campground at Big Cypress National Preserve

▷　Ochopee, Florida

▷　nps.gov

▷　RV and Tent Sites

There are eight developed campgrounds in Big Cypress National Preserve, and Midway Campground is probably the best option for most campers. The campground is beautiful, and the back-in sites are paved and level. Some of the sites are downright magical with sun coverage from palm trees and lots of room to relax. Electric hookups are available for RVs. The tent sites are very close to the road, so tent campers who want more privacy might check out one of the other campgrounds in the preserve.

---

------------ **Wildlife Safety in the Everglades:** ------------
**Florida Alligators and Crocodiles**

Many visitors come to the Everglades hoping to catch sight of Florida's many alligators and crocodiles. Remember: these are wild and protected animals, so follow park guidelines when spotting these creatures.

1. Always remain at least 15 feet from alligators and crocodiles.
2. Never feed any wild animals.
3. If an alligator or crocodile is hissing, it feels threatened, and you need to move away immediately.
4. Never allow pets or children to approach these animals.
5. Do not swim in any body of water where there are posted alligator or crocodile warnings. Avoid swimming at dawn or dusk, as this is their regular feeding time.

# Wilderness Camping in Everglades National Park

This national park offers extensive opportunities for backcountry camping in the Marjory Stoneman Douglas Wilderness area, but there are reservation and permitting guidelines and restrictions.

▷ Permits are required for all overnight stays in the backcountry areas of the park.

▷ Reservations can be made on recreation.gov and are available three months in advance of the stay.

▷ Permits are also available on a first-come, first-served basis at the Gulf Coast or Flamingo visitor centers.

▷ Permit fees and per-night fees will be collected.

▷ There are limits on camping days allowed in this national park: no person may camp more than thirty days in a calendar year, or more than fourteen consecutive days between November 1 and April 30.

There are three types of backcountry camping sites in the Marjory Stoneman Douglas Wilderness area.

▷ **Chikee Sites:** Ten-by-twelve-foot elevated platforms in areas without accessible dry land for pitching tents.

▷ **Ground Sites:** Elevated mounds of dirt in mangrove areas along rivers and bays.

▷ **Beach Sites:** Situated along the coast. Campers are encouraged to beware of nesting wildlife and sea oats, which stabilize the beaches.

## Scenic Drives

Everglades Loop Road runs 24 miles through a cypress swamp and offers views of a sawgrass prairie and plenty of opportunities for wildlife spotting.

Turner River, Wagonwheel, and Birdon Road Loop Drive meanders 17 miles through wet prairies, making this a popular drive for birders.

## Find a Ranger Tour!

Guided ranger tours will bring the elusive, wild Everglades to life. Find unique, regularly scheduled programs in these locations, including guided tram tours, birding excursions, and biking tours.

▷ Flamingo District

▷ Gulf Coast District

▷ Royal Palm District

▷ Shark Valley District

## Read and Watch

▷ *The Swamp: The Everglades, Florida, and the Politics of Paradise* by Michael Grunwald

▷ "The Swamp," episode on *American Experience* by PBS

# MIDWEST REGION

# Sleeping Bear Dunes National Lakeshore

We think the Midwest gets short shrift when it comes to travel coverage of all kinds. Michigan is truly one of America's most underrated states for camping, and Sleeping Bear Dunes—while hardly a well-kept secret—flies under the radar of most RV owners and tent campers who do not live in the region. The park can still feel crowded for many visitors, but that's only because there are limited camping options and reserving a good campsite can be challenging. The park itself is quite manageable in terms of avoiding crowds, even during the peak summer months.

Many campers work hard to get sites inside the park at Platte River and DH Day Campgrounds, and for good reason. Both of these campgrounds are gorgeous and offer up a classic NPS camping experience at a bargain basement price. If you want to camp in either of these locations, then get on it early—like the very day and hour your site becomes available to reserve at recreation.gov.

Can't get a site at Platte River or DH Day? Camping in the Traverse City area is not really a compromise at all. Popular sections of Sleeping Bear are only about forty minutes away—and Traverse City and Grand Traverse Bay are not-to-be-missed destinations in their own right. The charming downtown area is an absolute gem with great coffee shops, independent bookstores, breweries, restaurants, and a cool, understated, outdoorsy vibe.

# CAMPGROUNDS INSIDE THE PARK

### Platte River Campground

▷ **Honor, Michigan**

▷ **nps.gov**

▷ **RV and Tent Sites**

The Platte River Campground is open all year—but summer is when the big magic happens. Tubing or kayaking in the clear, warm waters of the Platte River and ending up in the crisp, cool waters of Lake Michigan is a transcendent NPS experience. Booking a site at Platte River can be difficult, so know your booking window, wake up early with a huge cup of coffee, and pray to the camping gods for help. We booked six months in advance and recommend you do the same. The stress of booking your site will be a distant memory once you pull into Platte River. The campground is cozy and shaded, and sites are mostly large and private. Some sites even offer electric hookups, but there is no water or sewer at the sites so plan accordingly. Many of the sites are back-in and have a large area behind them with a picnic table and fire ring. Pull-through (or pull-off ) sites are also available, but we liked the back-in sites much better. We liked loops 2 and 3 best (but take whatever you can get!), and don't forget to catch a ranger program at the amphitheater.

# DH Day Campground

▷ Glen Arbor, Michigan

▷ nps.gov

▷ RV and Tent Sites

The DH Day Campground is one of the most beloved places to camp in all of Michigan. It's more rustic than Platte River, with pit toilets instead of full bathroom facilities. Nevertheless, many campers love DH Day even more than Platte River. Why? Location, location, location. This place is smack dab in the middle of wonderland. The epic Dune Climb is nearby, and so is Pierce Stocking Scenic Drive. When we camped here we spent an entire day at the beach at Glen Haven, a charming historic village nearby, and another day shopping and eating in Glen Arbor. Cherry Republic is one of our favorite stores in the country. We dream of eating dark chocolate covered cherries again and dipping our chips in its original cherry salsa!

# North and South Manitou Island Camping

▷ North and South Manitou Island, Michigan

▷ nps.gov

▷ Tent Sites

More adventurous tent campers will love the remote camping vibe on North Manitou Island (with one campground) and South Manitou Island (with three campgrounds). Catch the ferry in the wee little fishing village of Leland and bring water filtration equipment, because there is no purified source of drinking water on either island.

# CAMPGROUNDS OUTSIDE THE PARK

### Holiday Park Campground

▷ Traverse City, Michigan

▷ holidayparktc.com

▷ RV and Tent Sites

Holiday Park Campground is fifteen minutes from downtown Traverse City and has a hipster charm that is all its own. The setting is quiet and bucolic, and the waters of Silver Lake are crystal clear and warm for swimming. This used to be a seasonal campground for Airstream owners only—with a few rental sites for transient campers. The restriction was lifted many years ago, but there are still dozens of sites occupied by classic Airstreams, which makes for some serious RV eye candy for folks with wandering eyes like us. The campground actually functions a bit like a co-op because the seasonal campers own their sites. But when they leave to take their RVs elsewhere, many rent out their sites to the public—whether you live riveted or not. These sites are beautiful—particularly the sites that ring the lake. We kayaked from our site over to the swimming beach and then kayaked back for dinner. The fishing was also good, and Moomers ice cream is sold in the camp store.

### Traverse City State Park

▷ Traverse City, Michigan

▷ www2.dnr.state.mi.us

▷ RV and Tent Sites, Lodge and Mini-cabins

Camping at the creatively named Traverse City-Modern Campground (better known by its unofficial moniker Traverse City State Park) is also an option for those looking to visit Sleeping Bear Dunes. Your trip may feel more Traverse City centric, but that is not a bad thing at all. This campground is wooded and rustic, but also a short bike ride away from downtown. There is also a day-use area right across U.S. 31 with a quarter mile of Grand Traverse

Bay shoreline. This campground is busy and bustling all summer long, so if you are looking for peace and quiet, it probably is not for you. But if you love the sound of campfires, laughter, children playing, and music straying from other sites—then this could be your place.

## Traverse City KOA

▷ Buckley, Michigan

▷ koa.com

▷ RV and Tent Sites, Deluxe Cabins, Camping Cabins

The Traverse City KOA serves as a great backup plan if you can't get a site inside of Sleeping Bear Dunes National Lakeshore, or if you are just looking for full hook-up sites and a campground with a robust list of kid-friendly amenities. Kids will love cooling off in the pool and jumping on the bouncy pillow after spending a day exploring the national seashore.

-------------------- **A Day in Traverse City** --------------------

Traverse City is a great American city. We love walking the streets of downtown, hopping from one brewery to another, and paddling around the lake. The fifteen-minute drive to Moomers Ice Cream is worth every mile. Don't miss out on tasting what some folks claim is America's best ice cream. Here are our favorite things to do, eat, and drink in Traverse City.

▷ Higher Grounds for a cup of coffee

▷ Brilliant Books for the perfect independent bookstore experience

▷ The River Traverse City for kayak and SUP rentals

▷ The Filling Station MicroBrewery for pizza and a pint

▷ Mission Point Lighthouse for a tour and splashing in the lake

▷ Jolly Pumpkin Brewery for dinner and a brew

▷ Moomers Ice Cream for a sweet treat

# A Quick Guide to Sleeping Bear Dunes National Lakeshore

Sleeping Bear Dunes is the perfect place for a family national park adventure. There is something for every age and ability level from swimming to hiking, tubing, and sightseeing. Visit in July or August to find out what a magical Michigan summer is all about.

## Where to Stock Up

Empire is considered the gateway town to Sleeping Bear Dunes, and that's where you'll find the main visitors center. You'll also find a small grocery and some dining options. Glen Arbor is another small town near the dunes with more dining and shopping options, including the famous Cherry Republic. Then there's Traverse City, a forty-minute drive, which has all of the big-box stores plus plenty of local mom-and-pop options as well.

## Your First Day in Sleeping Bear Dunes

### Visit the Philip A. Hart Visitor Center in Empire

There are daily ranger programs here along with an interpretative exhibit. Make sure to pick up your Junior Ranger book at the beginning of your visit if you plan on completing the program: many of the activities are location specific, and things are very spread out in Sleeping Bear Dunes, so you'll want to have a plan of attack.

### Drive the Pierce Stocking Scenic Drive

This 7.4-mile loop is a fantastic introduction to the park. There are twelve official "stops" on the national park map, and some of the best dune and lake overlooks are on this loop. Plan on returning to many of these locations for more extensive hiking or exploration later on your trip.

### Head to the Dune Climb

These dunes top out at more than 400 feet above the Lake Michigan shoreline. Although physically strenuous, it's a blast to climb the dune and then race back down to the bottom. Our kids enjoyed doing this over and over again, begging to return later during our trip. Make sure to visit in the morning or late afternoon when the sand is not so hot. Also avoid going during windy weather.

## Hikes in Sleeping Bear Dunes

### Empire Bluff Trail

This 1.5-mile, out-and-back trail runs through a beech and maple forest and then emerges along a dune ridge with stunning views of Lake Michigan and an observation deck that sits 450 feet above the shoreline. Bring the camera.

### Alligator Hill Trail

This 4.7-mile loop trail has great shade for much of the hike, and then emerges to offer beautiful views of Glen Lake.

### Pyramid Point Loop

This 2.8-mile loop trail has a steep elevation gain, but the lookout point hundreds of feet above Lake Michigan is worth the effort. You can shorten the hike to just over a mile by going to the lookout and then heading back to the trailhead.

## Swimming in Sleeping Bear Dunes

### Platte River Point

This is where Platte River meets Lake Michigan, and you could happily spend your entire vacation at this spot. Folks bring their tubes to float down the river into the lake and then walk back up and do it all over again. There are ever-changing sandbars created by the tides, and plenty of fun tidal pools to play in.

### Glen Haven Beach

This dog-friendly beach is located right next to the Cannery Boat Museum and offers beautiful views of the Manitou Islands.

### North Bar Lake

This is a very popular beach in the park on account of the warmer shallow water. At times the tides connect this lake with Lake Michigan, and visitors have a blast floating along with the current. We rented paddleboards from a nearby shop and spent the whole day at this beach, swimming and paddling our hearts out.

## Pets in the Park

Some national parks are pet friendly and some are not. Sleeping Bear Dunes is a bit of a hybrid, restricting dogs in a range of places mostly on account of the endangered bird population. Luckily, the park offers very clear guidance on where you can bring your furry friend: nps.gov/slbe/planyourvisit/pets

# Pictured Rocks National Lakeshore

The Pictured Rocks at this national lakeshore get their name—and their stunning colors—from minerals in the water seeping through the cracks of the cliffs that rise above the water's edge. The vivid stains have led to this destination winning accolades for being the most beautiful place in Michigan. Visit both Pictured Rocks and Sleeping Bear Dunes and decide for yourself.

One of the oldest national lakeshores in the country, this destination is nothing if not remote, spread out over 40 miles of lakefront along Lake Superior in Michigan's Upper Peninsula, just across the water from our Canadian neighbors. The journey is worth the payoff, though, as more than one million annual visitors will attest.

All the campgrounds in the park are open from May 15 through October 15 and require a reservation, which can be made up to six months in advance. The three rustic park campgrounds are small and less than manicured, with vault toilets and well water and no reliable cell signal. If you are looking for more creature comforts, or have a larger RV, check out the great municipal campground options located right outside the park boundaries. Book in advance to land a site directly on shores of Lake Superior.

# CAMPGROUNDS INSIDE THE PARK

## Twelvemile Beach Campground

▷ **Grand Marais, Michigan**

▷ **nps.gov**

▷ **RV and Tent Sites**

Located 15 miles west of Grand Marais, Twelvemile Beach Campground is the largest of the three NPS campgrounds in Pictured Rocks National Lakeshore. It is simple, rustic, and majestic. You can hear the sounds of Lake Superior from every site, and some of those sites have views of the water and offer direct access down to the beach. This campground is excellent for tent camping and suitable for small- to medium-sized RV setups. The NPS does not allow single vehicles longer than 36 feet, or vehicle trailer combinations beyond 42 feet. Campsites are shaded and spacious, and all are located on a sandy plateau above the beach. This is a heavenly spot for beach lovers, photographers, kayakers, and anyone who loves to feel the sand between their toes. The White Birch Trail and North Country Trail are both excellent easy rambles and can be accessed directly from the campground.

## Hurricane River Campground

▷ **Seney, Michigan**

▷ **nps.gov**

▷ **RV and Tent Sites**

Choosing a "top pick" between Hurricane River and Twelvemile Beach is a difficult task because they both share some excellent qualities. Both have spacious and shaded sites within earshot of Lake Superior, and they both have sites that are just steps away from the beach. At Hurricane River, the lower section is more desirable than the upper section because it is located directly on the lakefront. This is an absolute gem of a campground, and the lake and the river that spills into it are lovely. But be forewarned: there are no services nearby and there is no ranger station nearby either. If a group of rowdy campers show up, they could easily ruin your night. It doesn't happen often, but it is known to happen. So avoiding summer weekends here might be a wise plan.

## Little Beaver Lake Campground

▷ **Shingleton, Michigan**

▷ **nps.gov**

▷ **RV and Tent Sites**

Little Beaver Lake Campground is aptly named. It is quite little, with only eight sites, and it is situated right on a beautiful lake. Camping here is a quiet and delightful treat if you can get a site. It is a near perfect spot for those with small boats (with electric motors only) because there is a small boat ramp. Like Twelvemile Beach Campground, this is a great spot for tent camping or for those with small- to medium-sized RVs. Single vehicles over 36 feet are not permitted, nor are combined vehicle/trailer lengths that are over 42 feet. We recommend keeping RVs even smaller than recommended because the road into the campground is tight and windy with low hanging branches.

# CAMPGROUNDS OUTSIDE THE PARK

## Munising Tourist Park Campground

▷ **Munising, Michigan**

▷ **munisingtouristpark.com**

▷ **RV and Tent Sites**

Munising Tourist Park Campground is an absolute delight, especially if you can score one of the sites directly on Lake Superior. You can see the Great Lake from most of the sites, but the large back-in sites directly on the water are spacious and have spectacular views. They also have direct access to their own little beach areas, so you can launch a kayak or dip your toes in the water a few feet away from your RV. Grand Island is located nearby, and more adventurous kayakers paddle over there to explore if the lake is calm enough for the journey.

The campground also has two rustic tent camping areas tucked away in the front corners of the property right on the lake. The bathhouses here are also very clean, making this an excellent option for tent campers who can't find a site in the park. The dirt roads in the campground can get a little sloppy after a hard rain, but they are not hard to navigate, even when wet. This campground is owned by the city of Munising and has been in operation for almost one hundred years. We wish more cities and municipalities would open campgrounds like this. Munising Tourist Park Campground is a boon to the local economy and an absolute treasure for those wishing to explore Pictured Rocks and all that Michigan's Upper Peninsula has to offer.

## Woodland Park Campground

▷ **Grand Marais, Michigan**

▷ **burttownship.com/recreation/woodland-park-campground**

▷ **RV and Tent Sites**

Woodland Park Campground is run by Burt Township, and much like Munising Tourist Park Campground, it is a source of pride for the local community. Located directly on the shores of Lake Superior, it offers thirty-six reservable sites, and 132 first-come, first-served sites. This is the only downside here. If you are traveling from far away (and the Upper Peninsula is far away for most people!), then banking on getting a site on the night of arrival is certainly risky—especially during peak months. The sites here are nice and most are shaded, and this stretch of the Lake Superior shoreline is spectacular. Plan on kicking off your shoes (if it's not too chilly!) and spending hours strolling on the beach or hunting for a wide variety of gorgeous multicolored rocks like agate, basalt, and sandstone.

# Otter Lake Campground

▷ Munising, Michigan

▷ otterlakemichigan.com

▷ RV and Tent Sites, Cabin Rentals

Otter Lake Campground is a very solid option for those who cannot find a site inside the national lakeshore or those who simply want to camp with hookups and amenities. Otter Lake earns high marks for having great customer service from the owners who are almost always on-site and for sites that are fairly spacious and easy to navigate. The lake is pretty and peaceful, and it serves as a great spot for kayaking or canoeing. Boat rentals are available. There is a playground for the kids, and a basketball court, tetherball court, and ga-ga ball court so the kids can unwind after a long day of exploring the national seashore. Otter Lake is not fancy, but it's a friendly and reliable base camp for a Pictured Rocks National Lakeshore adventure.

---

### Plan Ahead

Mosquitoes and black flies have been known to ruin the Pictured Rocks experience for many a camper, especially in the spring months and through the end of June. If you are visiting during this season, it is especially important to be prepared with bug spray and other insect deterrents. Invest in lightweight hiking pants, long-sleeved shirts, and perhaps even a wide-brim hat with neck flap.

## Views from the Water

Many of the most stunning natural sights at Pictured Rocks are best seen—and photographed—while on the water. Pictured Rock Cruises is the authorized concessionaire providing guided boat rides on Lake Superior. There are a few different cruises to choose from, and all of them last two and a half to three hours. Two-hour guided kayak tours are also available.

## Five Favorite Photo Ops at Pictured Rocks

▷ Spray Falls

▷ Pictured Rocks Cliffs

▷ Miners Castle

▷ Bridalveil Falls

▷ Grant Portal Point

## Cuyahoga Valley National Park

Cuyahoga Valley flies under the radar for many folks, but Cleveland and Akron locals treasure the national park that borders their urban neighborhoods. While there isn't one amazing attraction that visitors flock to see—although Brandywine Falls is quite the popular photo op—there are many opportunities for hiking, biking, paddling, and nature photography.

Cuyahoga Valley is a unique example of the National Park Service stepping in to restore and protect an area ravaged by human industry. By the mid-1900s, the Cuyahoga River was one of the most polluted waterways in America and repeatedly caught on fire in the 1960s. A visit to Cuyahoga Valley is an opportunity to reflect on our own capacity to either ravage or protect not just remote, beautiful places, but our very own backyards. Its close proximity to urban centers provides greater access to national park programs and activities, and more than two million people visit every year.

If you live in the region, this national park provides the perfect centerpiece for a long weekend getaway paired with some activities in nearby Cleveland. If you are traveling cross-country on an epic RV trip, make this a stop along your journey, especially if you are taking Route 80. Late spring and summer are good times to plan a camping trip, since biking, hiking, and paddling are the main activities for many visitors. The fall, however, may be the best season, offering mild temperatures and beautiful foliage displays.

There are no designated campgrounds or boondocking areas in Cuyahoga Valley National Park, so our featured campgrounds in this chapter are all in state parks or privately owned.

## CAMPGROUNDS OUTSIDE THE PARK

### Punderson State Park

▷ Newbury, Ohio

▷ ohiodnr.gov

▷ RV and Tent Sites, Cabin Rentals, Lodge Rooms

Ohio State Park campgrounds are woefully underrated, and native Ohioans couldn't be happier about it. Punderson State Park is about thirty to forty minutes from Cuyahoga Valley National Park, but it is a destination in its own right, so we think it makes a great base camp for exploring the entire region—including downtown Cleveland. Punderson also appeals to all kinds of campers. Whether you are tent camping or road-tripping in a larger RV, it will have something for you. Cabin campers and those seeking out lodge rooms will also want to check out Punderson Manor Lodge located near the campground. It offers comfortable lodging options at budget prices. Back at the campground the lakefront sites are excellent, and the roads in and around the loops are great for riding bikes or taking a stroll. Kayak rentals are available at the camp office, and it also loans out games for free—a nice touch that you rarely see at a public campground. We love the family-friendly vibe at Punderson and know that you will too. The campground is also great for those without kids because the sites are spacious and private. Staying at Punderson is a win, no matter who you are and no matter how you camp.

## Woodside Lake Park

▷ Streetsboro, Ohio

▷ woodsidelake.com

▷ RV and Tent Sites, Cabin Rentals

The sites here are relatively small with little privacy, but the location, which is just 12 miles away from Cuyahoga Valley National Park, is attractive and fun for families. Swimming and fishing in the lake are quite nice, and the huge inflatable obstacle course will keep tweens and teens occupied for hours. There is also a huge game room with arcade games and pool tables that could help salvage a rainy day. The cabins here are cute and clean, but you must bring your own bedding, towels, and cooking utensils.

## Streetsboro, Cleveland KOA Holiday

▷ Streetsboro, Ohio

▷ koa.com

▷ Glamping Tent, Camping Cabins, Deluxe Cabins, RV and Tent Sites

This KOA is a solid choice for RV owners and cabin campers who want to explore Cuyahoga Valley National Park, downtown Cleveland, and the world's largest annual gathering of twins at nearby Twinsburg. Tent campers will probably be happier at the campgrounds listed earlier. Make sure you buy some homemade fudge from the general store while you are here—and bring your fishing poles. The lake is well stocked!

---------------------------- **Watch** ----------------------------
*Generations: Cuyahoga Valley National Park*, produced by Western Reserve, PBS

# Six Things to Do in Cuyahoga National Park

1. Start at the Boston Mill Visitor Center to learn about the park, pick up maps, and get itinerary advice from rangers.
2. Hike to Brandywine Falls via the 1.4-mile Brandywine Gorge Trail.
3. Take a ranger-led hike around the Ledges, and learn about the geology of the sandstone cliffs.
4. Visit Beaver Marsh early in the morning for wildlife viewing and bird photography.
5. Learn how canals operate at the Canal Exploration Center, complete with a functioning lock and live demonstrations.
6. Bring your own kayaks and paddle the Cuyahoga River.

## Bikes and Trains

Two main attractions at Cuyahoga National Park are the Ohio and Erie Towpath Trail and the Cuyahoga Valley Scenic Railroad. The Ohio and Erie Towpath Trail is a gravel path that runs alongside the Cuyahoga River tracing the route that mules walked to tow canal boats many decades ago. If you don't have your own bikes, you can rent them at concessionaires like Century Cycles conveniently located right off the trail. The scenic railroad also runs along the river, and riders can purchase roundtrip tickets with a variety of seating options. A great way to enjoy both experiences is to participate in the bike shuttle options. Cyclists can ride the tow trail one way, then hop on the train for the return trip.

## Day Out in Cleveland

Don't miss out on the opportunity to explore this fun, underappreciated U.S. city when visiting Cuyahoga Valley National Park. Stop by the Rock & Roll Hall of Fame and pay your respects to the legends of rock. Watch a Cleveland Guardians game at Progressive Field, situated in the downtown area and surrounded by a vibrant restaurant and bar scene. Visit the Christmas Story house for a unique photo op. Eat your way through the West Side Market and bring back fresh produce and baked goods to the campsite. Visit the largest collection of primates in the U.S. at Cleveland Metroparks Zoo. End the day enjoying a flight at one of the many brewpubs sprinkled throughout the city.

# Indiana Dunes National Park

Indiana Dunes National Lakeshore became Indiana Dunes National Park on February 15, 2019, and made national news in the process. Its transformation into our sixty-first national park gives campers one more great reason to consider taking an epic road trip to America's Midwest—and staying for a while. Blowing past Indiana Dunes on a trip out west, or a trip back east, would be a foolish mistake.

Camping options are not abundant, but two of them are very good. Indiana Dunes National Park offers a rustic little gem in Dunewood Campground. Nearby Indiana Dunes State Park also has an excellent campground that is loved and adored by those who live in the region. We suspect—and hope—that the economic boom associated with this new national park will give birth to a handful of good private campgrounds with full hookups just outside of the park. Until then, do your best to book a site at Dunewood or the state park campground. You can't go wrong in either place.

When planning a camping trip to this national park, consider all that the state park offers as well. The parks are right next door to each other, and much like Redwoods National Park and state parks in California, they can often seem indistinguishable.

# CAMPGROUND INSIDE THE PARK

### Dunewood Campground

▷ Indiana Dunes National Park

▷ nps.gov

▷ RV and Tent Sites

Dunewood Campground has long played second fiddle to Indiana Dunes State Park Campground, which offers more services and amenities and direct access to the beach. Dunewood is rustic, and there are no hookups at the sites, but that shouldn't stop you from considering it as your base camp for all that Indiana Dunes has to offer. If you are tent camping or have a solar setup, then the lack of electricity at your site might not matter much to you anyway. The sites here are lovely, wooded, and shady, and many offer privacy and ample space. We camped here in the fall when foliage was at its peak, and this lovely little campground was lit up with kaleidoscopic colors. It was also as peaceful and quiet as any campground we have ever visited. Bigger rigs may struggle getting into a few of the sites, so choose wisely. Don't forget to catch an evening ranger program at the amphitheater—even if you decide to stay at the state park.

# CAMPGROUNDS OUTSIDE THE PARK

### Indiana Dunes State Park Campground

▷ Chesterton, Indiana

▷ in.gov/dnr/parklake

▷ RV and Tent Sites

Indiana Dunes State Park campground has direct access to the beach and electrical hookups at each site, which is probably why it tends to be more beloved by most locals than Dunewood, its national park neighbor. This classic state park campground is delightful and has a well-stocked camp store—which is open in the summer—and a playground, heated restrooms, paved roads, spacious sites, and ample opportunities to enjoy ranger-led programs. The park regularly hosts themed weekends, including vintage camper rallies and birding festivals. Its nature center is excellent and has exhibits about the ecology of the area that are enjoyable for kids and adults. But for us, camping at Indiana Dunes is all about the beach. A short and easy hike from the campground on trail 4 leads you to the top of Mount Tom and then down onto the beach—which is the real star of the show here. We love swimming in the clear, warm waters of Lake Michigan in August and spending an entire summer day playing in the sand.

## Sand Creek Campground

▷ Chesterton, Indiana

▷ sandcreekcampground.org

▷ RV and Tent Sites

Can't get a site at Dunewood or the state park campground during the busy summer months? Don't fret. Sand Creek Campground is a short drive from the dunes and has been under new management since 2021. The new owners are investing in upgrades at the park, but for now it is a simple, affordable private campground that offers easy access to the main attraction: the national park. Cabins are available, and there are sites for tents and RVs—some shaded and some full sun—so make your preference clear when booking.

---

### ------------------ Accept the Challenge ------------------

The Three Dune Challenge is a 1.5-mile loop that begins and ends at the Indiana Dune State Park Nature Center. Complete the 552-vertical-feet climb, post a selfie with #3DuneChallenge, and then pick up your free bumper sticker at the Indiana Dunes Visitor Center.

# Outdoor Activities at Indiana Dunes National Park

## Swimming and Sunbathing

There are many options for beachgoing at Indiana Dunes National Park, but if you want lifeguards and showers, head to West Beach. Just make sure to get there early on summer weekends if you don't want to circle endlessly for a parking spot.

## Bird-watching

This is a delightful spot for bird-watching, so make sure you bring your binoculars. Indiana Dunes National Park also features prominently in the annual Indiana Dunes Birding Festival every May.

## Biking

Indiana Dunes National Park has a robust biking trail system that spans over 37 miles. We also love its progressive e-bike policy—bikes with less than 750 watts of horsepower are allowed anywhere that regular bikes are allowed.

## Hiking

There are more than 50 miles of trails in Indiana Dunes National Park, and to be honest, you will more likely find us on the beach on a hot summer day. In fall or spring we definitely recommend filling up your water bottles and lacing up your hiking boots. The coastal landscape is surprisingly diverse.

## Gearing Up

Forget a bathing suit or need an extra set of binoculars for bird-watching in the park? Head to the Bass Pro Shops store in Portage to get properly outfitted for your trip. This store is big enough to keep you busy for a few hours on a rainy day. Just don't blow your entire vacation budget on camping gear and new fishing poles, okay?

**Gateway Arch National Park**

A visit to Gateway Arch National Park is also a visit to one of America's greatest cities. The arch was built to celebrate the pioneers who settled the American West, but also to revive St. Louis's moribund economy during the Great Depression. Four million Americans visit this park every year. Those who are not claustrophobic can head into the five-seat trams that will take you to the top for stunning views that can stretch for 30 miles in every direction. There is a sample tram at the bottom, so visitors can take a seat and see if they want to ride a real one to the top.

When it comes to food, culture, history, and sports, St. Louis has so much to offer—and like most cities in our country, you can camp within striking distance of its most iconic spots. The three recommended campgrounds below are all about thirty minutes from downtown, and they offer good sites at a variety of price points. Serious travelers and national park lovers do not consider the Midwest to be flyover country. It is the home of a wide variety of terrific NPS sites that should be on every camper's bucket list. Many of these NPS sites in the Midwest are also significantly less crowded than their brethren in the American West, and that is certainly something worth celebrating.

# CAMPGROUNDS OUTSIDE THE PARK

## St. Louis West/Historic Route 66 KOA

▷ Eureka, Missouri

▷ koa.com

▷ RV and Tent Sites, Caboose Camping Cabin, Deluxe Cabins

This KOA serves as a great base camp for exploring St. Louis—which is about thirty minutes away. Six Flags St. Louis is also only a mile away. But the real cherry on top is that this campground is located directly on historic Route 66 and makes for a more than comfortable overnight stop for those exploring the mother road. Overall, this midwestern gem could easily serve as a terrific base camp for a week's vacation. The long pull-through sites here make parking a big rig easy, and they are situated under attractive shady trees. Tent camping here is also a solid option, and there are water and electric hookups at each of the level and tidy sites. But the tent sites do lack privacy. The Kozy Caboose rental is cute, and you can fall asleep inside of a piece of Route 66 history. Kids will also enjoy the organized activities and the pool area on warm afternoons after visiting the city. Mom and Dad will appreciate great customer service and reasonable prices in a kid-friendly environment. This campground feels like a throwback to simpler, easier days, before screens took over and the world went crazy.

## Lakeside Park

▷ St. Peters, Missouri

▷ tpetersmo.net

▷ RV Sites, Group Camping

Lakeside Park is owned and operated by the city of St. Peters, and it offers an affordable RV park with seventy-five full hook-up sites in a clean and comfortable setting. Depending on traffic, the drive into St. Louis isn't bad either and is plus or minus thirty minutes. The park features a 140-acre lake that offers boating and fishing galore that feels a world away from the hustle and bustle of the city.

## Yogi Bear's Jellystone Park Camp-Resort Eureka

▷   Pacific, Missouri

▷   eurekajellystone.com

▷   RV and Tent Sites, Cottages and Cabins

Yogi Bear and friends like to hang out and help kids make magical family memories at this Jellystone Park just thirty minutes west of St. Louis. Excellent customer service rules the day here, and the managers and camp staff will make sure that your family has a terrific stay. The cottages and cabins here are cute, but the RV sites are a bit tight. But if you don't mind camping close to your neighbor, there is a lot to love about this Jellystone.

### ----------------- Visit One of the Wildest, ----------------- Wackiest Museums in the World

City Museum of St. Louis is a must stop in our book. The building it inhabits used to be a shoe warehouse filled with spiral chutes that were used for conveyance. Artists have now repurposed those slides, and one of them can be found in almost every installation. Make sure you try the ten-story slide and the Ferris wheel before you go. They are both every bit as memorable as the Gateway Arch.

### --------- Who Makes the Best BBQ in St. Louis? ---------

That simple question can lead to a fistfight in St. Louis, so be careful if you ask. We recommend Pappy's Smokehouse on Olive Street. The ribs are ridiculously good, but the burned ends and pulled pork are even better.

# Five Interesting Facts about Gateway Arch

1. Gateway Arch National Park was originally called Jefferson National Expansion Memorial. It was renamed in 2018.

2. The Gateway Arch is the Tallest Arch in the world, and it is just as tall (630 feet) as it is wide.

3. The idea for the arch originated in 1933 as a way to jump-start

4. the city's stagnant economy during the Great Depression. However, construction on the arch did not begin until 1961.

5. The Gateway Arch has a gigantic 70,000-square-foot underground visitor center located between its two legs that is filled with exhibits about American expansion.

6. Around four million tourists visit Gateway Arch every year, bringing a massive injection of cash in the economy each year, just as predicted back in 1933.

### Big Bend National Park

If you really want to get away from it all, there is no better camping destination than Big Bend National Park, which the NPS website describes as "splendid isolation." It has been designated as an International Dark Sky Park—the International Dark Sky Association claims that the skies here are among the darkest in North America—so if sleeping under the stars is your camping jam, put this place on your bucket list.

A visit to Big Bend National Park takes planning and commitment. This park is far from any of the major cities in Texas—it will take you between seven to ten hours to drive from Austin, Dallas, or Houston. All four campgrounds in the park require reservations, which can be made up to six months in advance for up to fourteen consecutive nights. No boondocking or dispersed camping is allowed in the park. However, there are sixty-four primitive roadside campsites spread throughout some of the most remote areas of the park. Permits are required for all of these backcountry campsites, and about half of them can be obtained up to six months in advance at recreation.gov. For the other half of these campsites, permits can only be obtained in person at the Panther Junction or Chisos Visitor Centers. The park service claims that these campsites are fully reserved throughout most of the year, so again—plan ahead.

The busy season for Big Bend does not align with typical national park tourism trends. The park sees most of its visitors between January and April and also fills up during Thanksgiving, Christmas, and spring break weeks. Big Bend can be brutally hot in the summer, with temperatures above 100°F in the desert. Some relief from the heat can be found in the Chisos Mountains where elevations keep temperatures ten to twenty degrees cooler on average.

In general, campers will want to be prepared with everything they need when they enter the park. Fuel, food, water, and supplies are often not available without driving many miles. The effort will be worth it when you soak in the views of the desert landscape, mountains, rivers, and endless skies.

# CAMPGROUNDS INSIDE THE PARK

### Chisos Basin Campground

▷ **Big Bend National Park, Texas**

▷ nps.gov

▷ **RV and Tent Sites**

Chisos Basin Campground is deeply loved by tent campers, van lifers, and those with tiny trailers that are actually allowed on the road into the campground—motor homes over 24 feet are not allowed on this road, and neither are trailers over 20 feet. The campground is nestled in a nook surrounded by stunning mountains and more than any other option, gives visitors a Big Bend camping experience that they will never forget. Roadrunners, coyotes, rabbits, and bears can visit the campground and its immediate environs, so please secure your food and pay attention to the park's animal safety guidelines. There are only sixty campsites here, and they go quickly during the cooler months, so book one immediately when they become available. Also make sure to bring comfortable hiking boots. Many of the best trailheads in the park are close to Chisos Basin.

## Cottonwood Campground

▷ Big Bend National Park, Texas

▷ nps.gov

▷ RV and Tent Sites

Cottonwood is a small and simple campground that is very close to Santa Elena Canyon (which is an epic location for hiking and kayaking within the park), and it is also close to the Rio Grande. So just about everything about this little campground's location is epic. There is only one loop here with twenty-four sites, and not every site has shade, so do your homework and try to grab one with some tree coverage if you can. This is a delightful campground for those who love to bird-watch or simply kick back and listen to birdsong. Bring binoculars and a hammock—depending on your level of ambition.

## Rio Grande Village Campground

▷ Big Bend National Park, Texas

▷ nps.gov

▷ RV and Tent Sites

The Rio Grande Village Campground is a concessionaire-managed campground within Big Bend National Park that is situated on the banks of the Rio Grande. Mexico's Sierra del Carmen Mountains can be viewed to the east and are spectacular at sunset. The campground has one hundred sites and some can handle RVs up to 40 feet. There are no hookups at the sites, but the Rio Grande Village Store has supplies and is right outside of the campground. The Rio Grande Village Nature Trail starts in the campground next to site #18 and ends at a gorgeous bluff overlooking the Rio Grande. The Rio Grande

Village RV Campground is located directly across from its big brother and offers twenty-four RV sites with full hookups. It is basically a parking lot, but the location is great for those who are not equipped for dry camping.

# CAMPGROUNDS OUTSIDE THE PARK

## Maverick's Ranch RV Resort

▷  Lajitas, Texas

▷  lajitasgolfresort.com

▷  RV Sites (adjacent to hotel rooms, cabins, suites, condos)

Maverick's Ranch RV Resort is a terrific base camp for those who are traveling with friends and family who do not have an RV, because its golf club (which is adjacent to the campground) offers a wide variety of comfortable accommodations for noncampers. This RV resort actually lives up to its name by offering clean and comfortable facilities and a pool area that is very much like an oasis in the desert. The clubhouse area is also excellent and provides a cool place to lounge or play a game of Ping-Pong on a hot day. Dogs seem to love Maverick's just as much as humans do—the dog park is huge and the entire vibe is pet friendly. The sites here are level and spacious, and the views are spectacular in all directions. Staying inside Big Bend is clearly an epic option, but Maverick's makes staying outside of the park every bit as good.

## RoadRunner Traveler's RV Park

▷  Terlingua, Texas

▷  roadrunnertravelers.com

▷  RV Sites

RoadRunner Traveler's RV Park is relatively new, but it is already earning high marks for customer service, reasonable pricing, and spacious full hook-up sites within close proximity to Big Bend National Park. The Wi-Fi here is strong, so if you need to work during your trip to Big Bend, then RoadRunner's makes an excellent choice for that reason alone. Dog owners also like the large fenced-in dog park area, and everyone loves when the owners bring in local musicians for concerts under the stars. All of the sites here are flat and level, and the campground is in a desert setting without much shade, but the views of the mountains are lovely, and the sunsets are showstoppers. As of this writing, the owners are adding amenities to the campground on a regular basis. Please call first for an update if you need particular services for your stay.

### Bring Your Passport!

Enjoy the unique experience of crossing the border within the park and visiting the village of Boquillas del Carmen, Mexico. The Boquillas Port of Entry is staffed by park rangers who work in cooperation with U.S. Customs and Border Protection officers. Once you've shown your documentation and passed through the port of entry, take a small rowboat across the river or wade across if the water is not too high. From there it is a half-mile walk to the village where visitors can enjoy a handful of restaurants and a variety of souvenir shops.

### Pet Friendly?

Although dogs are allowed in Big Bend National Park, they can only go where your car can go and are not allowed on any trails, off road, or on the river. Carefully consider these restrictions before bringing your furry friend to the park!

### Soak It Up

Drive down a 2-mile gravel road to arrive at the Hot Springs Historic District where a short quarter-mile hike will bring you to the foundation remains of a long-gone bathhouse. You can still take a soak in the water that geothermal magic keeps heated to about 105°F.

## Get on the Road

Ross Maxwell Scenic Drive is a 30-mile road that offers a taste of virtually everything people love about Big Bend National Park with overlooks, short walking trails, and interpretive exhibits. Some favorite stops along the road include:

- Old Sam Nail Ranch
- Blue Creek Ranch
- Sotol Vista
- Tuff Canyon
- Castolon Historic District

## Get off the Road

If you have a four-by-four and a healthy sense of adventure, head for the 8.5-mile Black Gap Road, which has earned the Jeep Badge of Honor Trail designation. For even more off-road detours, check out the *Road Guide to Backcountry Roads of Big Bend National Park*, published by Big Bend Natural History Association and available to purchase through its online store.

## Where to Watch the Sunset

Big Bend is known for its dark skies but also for its stunning sunsets. Here are some favorite spots for magic hour.

1. Sotol Vista along Ross Maxwell Scenic Drive
2. Mules Ear Overlook
3. Window View Trail in the Chisos Basin
4. Fossil Discovery Exhibit overlooking the hoodoos to the west

# Epic Hikes for the First-Time Visitor

There are so many amazing easy, moderate, and challenging hikes in Big Bend National Park that it can be a challenge for first-time visitors to choose. Here are some that offer plenty of bang for your buck.

## Lost Mine Trail (4.8 miles round trip)

Located in the Chisos Basin area of the park, you'll find the trailhead at mile 5 of Basin Road. Get your camera ready for all the amazing photo opportunities along the trail.

## Santa Elena Canyon Trail (2.6 miles round trip)

This easy trail can be accessed right off the Ross Maxwell Scenic Drive, west of Castolon. The path runs along the Rio Grande, gradually leading up to a stunning view of the canyon and then back down to the water's edge. Hikers love cooling down in the water at the end.

## The Window Trail (5.6 miles round trip)

The trailhead for this hike is near the Chisos Basin Visitor Center, but you can shave a mile off the hike by starting from the Chisos Basin Campground. The hike takes you to what is called the window pour-off, where a natural notch in the mountain forms a window to the beautiful desert landscape.

## The Chimneys Trail (4.8 miles round trip)

The trailhead for this hike is at mile 13 of the Ross Maxwell Scenic Drive. The mostly flat trail winds through the desert and leads to ancient volcanic formations. Look for petroglyphs along the way.

## Emory Peak Trail (11 miles round trip)

This is a strenuous, 7-hour hike leading to the highest elevation in the park. There are rock scrambles and the descent can be challenging.

## Mule Ears (3.8 miles round trip)

This desert hike can be accessed at mile 15 on the Ross Maxwell Scenic Road. The mule ears are two large volcanic formations rising up in the distance. The trail leads to a small spring where the brown landscape suddenly turns green.

# Hot Springs National Park

Hot Springs National Park is home to one of the most unique NPS sites in the country. Where else can you find a visitor center housed in a historic bathhouse? This delightful and popular national park includes a historic town, a delightful campground, and miles of hiking trails filled with creeks and mountain views. The star of the show is Bathhouse Row, which consists of eight historic bathhouses. Two of them still entice visitors to soak in their healing waters and partake in their spa services just like tourists did over one hundred years ago. Hot Springs National Park may be our smallest national park—but it still offers up an epic adventure. If you don't believe us, just ask one of the over two million visitors who stop by every year.

## CAMPGROUND INSIDE THE PARK

### Gulpha Gorge Campground

▷    Garland County, Arkansas

▷    nps.gov

▷    RV and Tent Sites

Gulpha Gorge Campground is the only campground inside of Hot Springs National Park, and it is an absolute gem. This park is particularly great for RV owners, because every site offers full hook-up, and most of them can accommodate larger rigs. How many NPS campgrounds can you say that about? Many of the sites are also located on Gulpha Creek, and those are the best and hardest to get. Tent campers may feel a distinct lack of privacy here, but for the price—and considering there are no other campground options inside the park—we still think it is a very good option. There is good hiking and strolling in and around the park, so bring comfortable shoes. Also make sure to check the schedule for ranger-led programs. The amphitheater is lovely and the talks are always fun and informative. Gulpha Gorge only has forty sites, so book ahead if you want to camp here next.

# CAMPGROUND OUTSIDE THE PARK

### Hot Springs National Park KOA Holiday

  ▹   Hot Springs, Arkansas

  ▹   koa.com/campgrounds/hot-springs-national-park

  ▹   RV and Tent Sites, Cabin Rentals

This KOA has a great location near Hot Springs National Park, though some of the sites are close to the road and have some road noise at night. We recommend calling and asking for a quiet site instead of booking online. Some of the RV sites are also a bit on the tight side, but other than that, this clean and comfortable KOA makes a great base camp for a visit to the region. Kids will love the pool and fishing right at the campground. They will also love grabbing a pancake breakfast at Grandpa's Griddle on summer weekends.

## ----------- The Gangster Museum of America -----------

Hot Springs, Arkansas, was an absolute hot spot for gangsters back in the 1920s, '30s, and '40s. The hot springs themselves were a major draw for infamous folks like Al Capone, but so were gambling, boozing, and philandering—all things for which Hot Springs was also famous. This museum documents those wild years and the wild men and women who recreated next to the likes of presidents, evangelists, and movie stars. Admission for children is free.

Padre Island
National Seashore

With 66 miles of protected coastline off the southeast coast of Texas, Padre Island National Seashore is the longest undeveloped barrier island in the world. Visitors come to enjoy the beautiful beaches and calm gulf waters but also to spot some of the 380 bird species that pass through the area and to visit the nesting beach for the Kemp's ridley sea turtle—the most endangered sea turtle in the world.

The park has been participating in sea turtle preservation efforts for decades, and one of the most popular times to visit the seashore is during the summer when hatchlings are released. If you wish to schedule a camping trip that coincides with a release, that will take some planning and some luck. Releases are not scheduled daily; they occur at nature's discretion. Rangers recommend looking closely at the current nesting season page on the park website and picking dates that align with the predicted hatching dates of multiple nests for the best chance at witnessing a sea turtle release.

All the campgrounds in the park are open year-round, and all camping sites are first-come, first-served. There are no RV hookups, and no provisions (except ice) are sold within the boundaries of the national sea-shore, so campers need to be prepared and self-sufficient. Winters are generally mild, but the weather is temperamental in this region, so visitors should watch for strong wind conditions, thunderstorms, and hurricanes and tropical storms between June and October.

First-time visitors sometimes expect to visit South Padre Island when camping at the Padre National Seashore since it looks like they are relatively close as the bird flies. Note that you will have to drive inland back through Corpus Christi and down the coast more than three hours to go from the seashore to the island, so plan accordingly.

# CAMPGROUNDS INSIDE THE PARK

## Malaquite Campground

▷ Corpus Christi, Texas

▷ nps.gov

▷ RV and Tent Sites

The sites on the ocean side of the road at Malaquite Campground are sandy and sit right at the edge of a dune that is not tall enough to block magnificent ocean views. The sites on the other side of the road look just like large parking spots with picnic tables. Either way, you have incredible views of the water, and you can hear the waves crashing right on the beach. Tent campers are also welcome to pitch their tents directly on the beach or at one of these campsites. Malaquite feels like it is in the middle of nowhere, and it offers a peaceful beach camping experience that is among the best in Texas, but the NPS visitor center and a variety of shops are just a half mile away. The beach in front of Malaquite is large and lovely with plenty of room to spread out and relax or go for a long stroll at the edge of the water.

## Bird Island Basin Campground

▷ Corpus Christi, Texas

▷ nps.gov

▷ RV and Tent Sites

Bird Island Basin Campground isn't far from Malaquite, but it offers up a different camping experience. This campground is located directly on the Laguna Madre Bay and is excellent for fishing, kayaking, and windsurfing. Most campers will choose Malaquite for its ocean views and sandy beaches, but Bird Island Basin is a great choice for those who want to paddle in much calmer water. It also makes a great second choice if Malaquite is full.

## South Beach Primitive Camping and North Beach Primitive Camping

▷ Corpus Christi, Texas

▷ nps.gov

▷ RV and Tent Sites

When many Texans think of beach camping in Padre Island National Seashore, they think of camping right next to the ocean in the north and south primitive beach camping areas. There are no amenities here whatsoever, and all driving is on the beach. Tent campers and properly equipped RV owners who pay for a park entry pass and camping permit can overnight just steps away from crashing waves. South Beach has 60 miles of pristine beach for camping, and North Beach has a single mile where camping is available.

## Other Campgrounds Inside the Park

↦ **Yarborough Pass Primitive Camping**

# CAMPGROUND OUTSIDE THE PARK

## Mustang Island State Park

▷   Corpus Christi, Texas

▷   tpwd.texas.gov

▷   RV and Tent Sites

Less than thirty minutes north of Padre Island National Seashore is the equally wonderful Mustang Island State Park. Bird-watcher and beach lovers delight at the miles of wide-open beaches here as well. Fishing and boating opportunities are also ample both in the Gulf of Mexico and in the calmer waters of Corpus Christi Bay. The section of the campground with water and electric sites isn't much more than a parking lot, but tent camping sites are directly on the beach. Both RV and tent campers love falling asleep to the sounds of the surf crashing on the shore.

### Laguna Madre

At only 3 feet deep, this hypersaline lagoon is one of only six in the world. It's also one of the best windsurfing destinations in the country. Take a lesson with Worldwinds Windsurfing, a concessionaire that operates inside the national seashore. If you want something a bit lower key, it also rents kayaks and stand-up paddleboards.

### A Birder's Playground

Between November and April, volunteers lead guided birding tours around the national seashore, exploring the grasslands, shoreline, and lagoon. Many of these tours include areas otherwise inaccessible to park visitors. Print out a checklist of common winter birds of the national seashore from the website before you arrive and conduct your own birding scavenger hunt.

## Driving on the Beach

Driving on the beach is permitted along most of the Padre Island National Seashore beaches. However, you do so at your own risk, and plenty of visitors each year find themselves surprised by deep sand or rising tides. Two-wheel drive vehicles are allowed on the first 5 miles of South Beach, conditions permitting. Beyond that, a four-wheel vehicle is required to navigate the pockets of deep sand. Park officials will not tow vehicles, so getting stuck will come with an expensive price tag from a private tow service, often costing thousands of dollars.

# Carlsbad Caverns National Park & Guadalupe Mountains National Park

It may throw readers for a loop seeing a national park in New Mexico paired with a national park in Texas. Carlsbad Caverns National Park and Guadalupe Mountains National Park are smaller, less visited park units that are less than an hour from each other, so they provide the perfect opportunity for a multistop trip. Visitors can combine a visit to the largest accessible cave chamber in the country at Carlsbad with a hike to the highest elevation in Texas at Guadalupe Peak.

There is no established campground in Carlsbad Caverns National Park, and overnight RV parking is not permitted in any of the lots—there is only the option for primitive camping in the backcountry, and permits for that must be obtained from the visitor center. The national park is surrounded by BLM land where camping is allowed without a permit, but most of those boondocking spots resemble large dirt parking lots. We recommend camping outside the national park at a private campground or staying at one of the campgrounds in Guadalupe Mountains and driving to the caverns for the day.

Both national parks are open year-round, but you'll want to schedule a visit according to your personal interests. Late spring and early fall are the most pleasant weather wise, but the autumn months offer the vibrant foliage displays in McKittrick Canyon. For those interested in the bats at Carlsbad, the best flights are in August and September, when baby bats born over the summer leave to join the northern migrations. A September visit could bring the best of both foliage and bat viewing.

---

### Pet Alert!

Neither of these national parks is pet friendly, so make sure to have a plan in place if you are traveling with your furry companions. Dogs are not allowed in the cavern or on unpaved park trails in Carlsbad Caverns. In the Guadalupe Mountains, dogs are restricted from all but two trails.

---

# CAMPGROUNDS OUTSIDE CARLSBAD CAVERNS NATIONAL PARK

### Carlsbad KOA Holiday

▷  Carlsbad, New Mexico

▷  koa.com

▷  RV and Tent Sites, Camping Cabins and Deluxe Cabins

This KOA is about forty-five minutes away from Carlsbad Caverns National Park, which has no campground options within its borders. So this is our base camp pick if you want to explore the caverns while enjoying a campground with rock-solid amenities. This KOA has an on-site smoker and owners who love to cook and deliver BBQ right to guest sites. You might have a tough time choosing between the pecan and mesquite wood-smoked combo brisket with pork and sausage or the BBQ baby back pork ribs—but it is all good. Bobby Flay even featured their grub on his show, *BBQ with Bobby Flay*. The BBQ may be the star of the show, but other amenities also shine. The laundry facilities and bathrooms are immaculate here, and so are the pool and playground areas. Tent campers also love the hexagonal tent village that offers shade, privacy, a storage locker, and water and electric hookups. Many KOAs have invested in their tent camping sites over the last ten years, and this is a great example of that trend.

## Carlsbad RV Park

▷ **Carlsbad, New Mexico**

▷ **carlsbadrvpark.com**

▷ **RV and Tent Sites, Cabin Rentals**

The Carlsbad RV Park provides another rock-solid option for travelers who want hookups and amenities while visiting the national park. The gravel sites are all level, and some have trees and shade while others do not. Large RVs are welcome here, as are tent campers, but as the name implies, the property is more RV-centric. Kids will love the indoor pool, and adults will love the friendly owners and staff who know the area well and are more than willing to help you plan your trip. Recent upgrades to the park include refurbished bathrooms and a Tesla and smart-car charging site.

# Ten Things to Do at Carlsbad Cavern National Park

1. Book your timed entry reservation for the cavern in advance at rec-reation.gov.

2. Wear closed-toed shoes with good traction to avoid slipping on cave paths. Also wear layered clothes, as the temperature in the caverns will be in the midfifties even if the temperatures outside are in the eighties. Bring a flashlight or headlight.

3. To prevent the spread of white-nose syndrome, never wear gear, shoes, or clothes that have been in one cave system into another one.

4. Rent audio guides at the visitor center or take a ranger-guided tour.

5. Take time to explore the educational exhibits in the visitor center, which cover the geology of the cave and the history of the park.

6. Watch the park film *Hidden World*, which plays every thirty minutes in the visitor center.

7. If you are able, take the 1.25-mile Natural Entrance Trail to access the Big Room. The path is steep and equivalent to climbing up a seventy-five-story building. There is a shorter, accessible path to the Big Room, if needed.

8. Attend a night sky program between May and October, which includes a ranger talk and demonstration.

9. Go on a 1.5-mile roundtrip desert night hike led by a park ranger.

10. Attend the evening Bat Flight Program at the Bat Flight Amphitheater, which takes place every night from Memorial Day through October.

# CAMPGROUNDS INSIDE GUADALUPE MOUNTAINS NATIONAL PARK

## Pine Springs Campground

▷ Salt Flat, Texas

▷ nps.gov

▷ RV and Tent Sites

Pine Springs Campground is small and charming (in a rough and rugged kind of way) with only twenty tent sites and thirteen RV sites, so it can be hard to find a spot here, but please try to get one if you can—especially if you are a tent camper. The tent sites are close together for an NPS campground, but there is natural landscaping between them that creates some privacy. RV sites are in a separate section that is basically a parking lot. There is little to no shade there and no privacy between sites. Several good hikes are nearby, and your kids will enjoy looking for little lizards around the campground and on the trail. Mountain views are excellent, and the night skies are dark and perfect for stargazing.

## Other Campgrounds Inside Guadalupe Mountains National Park

→ **Dog Canyon Campground**

→ **Frijole Horse Corral Campground**

# Ten Things to Do at Guadalupe Mountains National Park

1. Start at the Pine Springs Visitor Center and tour the museum.

2. Pick a trail in the Pine Springs area that suits your hiking ability, from the easy, paved 1-mile Pinery Trail to the more challenging 3.8-mile Devil's Hall Trail featuring a natural rock staircase.

3. Hike to the highest elevation in Texas on the Guadalupe Peak Trail, a very difficult 8.5-mile roundtrip hike with a 3,000-foot elevation gain. Leave early in the morning to give yourself plenty of time to complete the hike, which takes folks on average between six and eight hours.

4. Drive to the Salt Basin Dunes for amazing views of El Capitan and the Guadalupe Mountains.

5. If you have four-wheel drive, head to Williams Ranch on a primitive dirt road that offers great views of the western escarpment of the Guadalupe Mountains.

6. Head to McKittrick Canyon to enjoy the foliage if visiting in the fall, or just take in the scenery any other time. The McKittrick Canyon Nature Trail is a 1-mile loop hike with a wide variety of desert plants.

7. Hike to Pratt Cabin, the former summer vacation home of Wallace Pratt, at the heart of McKittrick Canyon (4.8 miles round trip), and bring a picnic lunch to eat on the cabin porch or surrounding picnic tables.

8. Print the free checklist from the national park website, pack your binoculars, and head to Frijole Ranch to spot some of the many species of birds that rely on the Frijole Spring for a water supply and the large, shady trees for shelter.

9. Visit Dog Canyon, a remote and secluded area of the park, and hike the Indian Meadow Nature Trail.

10. Pack plenty of groceries for this national park visit and be prepared to bring a cooler and lots of water for your days of exploring. Picnic lunches work best with limited options to purchase prepared food.

# White Sands National Park

One of our newest national parks, White Sands is home to the world's largest gypsum dunefield, with huge white sand dunes that are like nothing most visitors have ever seen in their lives. As with most large dunes, this area is completely exposed to the elements, so you'll want to be thoughtful when you visit.

The summer months—June through August—bring scorching hot temperatures with daily highs from 90°F to 105°F. At night the temperatures drop to between 50°F and 65°F. The summer will see the highest chance of rain as well, and morning and late afternoon thunderstorms are common from early July through late September. Spring temperatures are more moderate, but strong winds up to 50 miles per hour are common. If you can visit between September and November, you'll have the greatest chance for warm, sunny days with light winds and cool nights.

White Sands is only a few hours from Carlsbad Caverns National Park and Guadalupe Mountains National Park, so make sure to check out that chapter for additional camping information and tips on planning a trip to this area.

# CAMPGROUNDS OUTSIDE THE PARK

## Oliver Lee Memorial State Park

▷ Alamogordo, New Mexico

▷ emnrd.state.nm.us

▷ RV and Tent Sites

The rugged landscape and ravishing views of the Sacramento Mountains on one side and a sweeping desert landscape on the other will make you fall in love with Oliver Lee Memorial State Park the second you back into your spacious and private site. New Mexico natives love this park and often use it as a base camp when visiting White Sands National Park, which is about thirty minutes away. However, plenty of folks also like to just kick back here and enjoy all that Oliver Lee has to offer. Enjoy a leisurely stroll on the Riparian Nature Trail or challenge yourself with a strenuous hike up the Dog Canyon Trail for stunning views on all sides. Sunrise and sunset are typically beautiful here, so plan on bringing an extra SD card! Jackrabbits run through the park, and a wide variety of birds, such as owls, hummingbirds, and mockingbirds, also pass through depending on the season. The exhibits at the visitor center are also worth checking out, and the rangers and camp hosts are friendly and helpful.

## Aguirre Spring Recreation Area and Campground

▷ Organ, New Mexico

▷ blm.gov

▷ RV and Tent Sites

Aguirre Spring Campground is forty-five minutes away from White Sands National Park, but it is still an excellent choice for many campers. The campsites are surrounded by cliffs, and many look like they were ripped out of the pages of *Sunset Magazine*. The views and natural landscaping are ravishing. This gem in the BLM system of developed campgrounds is best for tent campers because the drive up (which is breathtaking!) is narrow and winding with several sharp turns. Van lifers and those in tiny trailers may feel comfortable making the drive, but RVs over 23 feet are advised to camp elsewhere. All sites have sun shelters and picnic tables under them, so you can still relax and eat inside, even in the heat. Those who do make the drive up will discover terrific sites and a rugged Wild West landscape that feels like something out of an old cowboy movie.

## Alamogordo/White Sands KOA Journey

▷  **Alamogordo, New Mexico**

▷  **koa.com**

▷  **RV and Tent Sites, Cabin Rentals**

This cute and friendly KOA puts you about twenty minutes away from White Sands National Park and serves as a comfortable base camp for those who enjoy parking their rigs or pitching their tents in an urban setting. The rec room has ping-pong and foosball to entertain the kids, and the breakfast area is a great place to grab coffee and a local newspaper in the morning. The pool was recently restored and is a great place to cool off on a hot summer afternoon.

------------- **Four Popular Ranger Programs** -------------
**at White Sands National Park**

Ranger programs at a park like White Sands can turn a great photo opportunity into an unforgettable learning experience. Here are some popular programs to put on your itinerary.

1.  **Sunset Strolls** are offered most Fridays, Saturdays, and Sundays. These one-hour sand walks explore the flora, fauna, and wildlife of the dunes.

2.  **Full Moon Hikes** take place April through December on the evening before a full moon.

3.  **Lake Lucera Tours,** available from November through March, focus on the geology of the dunes and how they were formed.

4.  The park stays open late for **Full Moon Night** from May through October.

# A Nearly New National Park!

White Sands was a national monument from 1933 to 2019, when it was redesignated as a national park. You'll want to do a bit of planning before you visit this otherworldly destination. Here's what you need to know:

1. Pay attention to the weather. Windstorms, dust storms, and thunderstorms are common at various times throughout the year. Plus, temperatures can exceed 100°F in the summer months.
2. Check for closings due to testing at the White Sands Missile Range. These closures usually last a few hours, so make sure you plan ahead.
3. Make sure you have the right sled for the dunes. Bring your own or buy one from the visitor's center. Just make sure it has a waxed bottom for the best sledding experience.
4. Bring your furry family members. White Sand Dunes is one of the most pet-friendly national parks in the country, allowing dogs on every one of the trails. Make sure that you explore the sand before it gets too hot for their paws in the summer months.
5. Be prepared for strenuous hiking. People who haven't hiked on sandy trails before are often surprised by how much more difficult it is. Be prepared with plenty of water and appropriate clothing.
6. Look into the ranger-led walks. From sunset strolls to full moon hikes, these ranger programs are a great way to learn more about a remarkable ecosystem.

## Photography at White Sands

Many visitors hope to capture Instagram gold when visiting this unique and beautiful landscape. It's actually not unusual for folks to schedule family portrait sessions with local photographers for once-in-a-lifetime shots. If you are going the DIY route, here are some tips to remember.

1. Treasure the golden hours. Photos taken during the middle of day will most likely look washed out and overexposed. Plan to take your pictures in the early morning or evening, two hours after sunrise or before sunset.
2. Beware of the sand. The fine gypsum sand will wreak havoc on your lenses. Protect cameras and smartphones from blowing sand and bring lens wipes or a microfiber cloth for regular cleaning.
3. Try to get pictures of undisturbed sand before a day's worth of footprints have removed the waves of lines created by wind.
4. Even though you'll have a ton of fun on the biggest dunes, the smaller dunes can offer more private photo opportunities away from the crowds.
5. Do a bit of Instagram research in advance of your visit and use hashtags like #whitesandsdunes to get some inspiration for your photos.

## Dune Trails for Every Hiker

First-time visitors are often surprised at how strenuous sand hiking is, so be prepared with plenty of water and plan to explore during cooler parts of the day.

Playa Trail: Short, easy half-mile roundtrip hike to a playa that is a dry lake bed for most of the year, but fills with water during the rainy season.

Dune Life Nature Trail: Another short trail clocking in at 1 mile, this interpretative hike is a bit more difficult because it requires folks to climb two steep dunes.

Alkali Flat Trail: A strenuous 5-mile trail that runs along the edge of Lake Otero and requires adventurers to climb up and down dunes throughout the hike. There is no shade.

# Yellowstone National Park

One of the top five most visited national parks in the country, Yellowstone sees millions of visitors every year and many of them are campers. The campsites inside the park are available to reserve six months in advance. The reservation window opens at 8:00 a.m. (MST) and sites go fast, so if you have your heart set on camping inside the national park, set a reminder on your calendar and be ready to nab a spot quickly. The most popular campgrounds like Fishing Bridge can book up within minutes for popular summer dates. Even if you are planning on staying outside the park, make your reservations as early as possible. This area sees a lot of tourism traffic in a few short months every year, and it's risky to wing it if visiting between the beginning of June and the end of August.

If you can visit during the shoulder seasons, May and September are ideal, since you still can enjoy the wildlife but with fewer crowds. Make sure to be prepared for wildly fluctuating temperatures and even snow. If you must visit during the peak summer months, try to be Zen about the crowds and not let it ruin your experience. Visit popular locations in the early morning or evening hours and challenge yourself to explore some of the more remote places in the park, of which there are many. You can visit during the winter—and many claim it is an absolutely magical experience—but only the north entrance is open, and many roads are closed to vehicles.

One of the keys to enjoying your Yellowstone trip is having a general plan...and then being flexible with it. You'll definitely want to do your research in advance and narrow down your must-see list. Yellowstone is huge, and popular points of interest can be hours away from each other. Without a plan of attack, first-time visitors often report being overwhelmed and disappointed. Be open to gathering intel from park rangers and other campers—where and when the wildlife is putting on a show changes by the day. Also check in daily for park alerts and road closures.

# CAMPGROUNDS INSIDE THE PARK

## Madison Campground

▷   **Near West Yellowstone, Wyoming**

▷   **nps.gov**

▷   **RV and Tent Sites**

If you are a tent camper or own a small- to medium-sized RV and want to be close to Yellowstone National Park's most popular and iconic locations, then Madison Campground will serve as a terrific base camp. The campground is situated near the Madison River under a canopy of fragrant lodgepole pine trees. West Yellowstone is 14 miles away if you want a nice dinner after exploring the park, or if you need to make a run for supplies. The campground is also perfectly situated for exploring the wonderland that is Yellowstone's lower loop. Magical locations like Grand Prismatic Springs, Old Faithful, and dozens of others are a short drive away from Madison. Most campsites are spacious and offer a bit of privacy, but many sites are not level—so if you have an RV, be prepared. The back-in sites tend to be preferable to the pull-off sites because your tent or RV will be farther from the road and more tucked into the trees. But Madison Campground is extremely popular because of its epic location in the park, so you should take what you can get and not get upset. With almost 300 sites, Madison tends to get jam-packed in the summer months. But it holds a crowd incredibly well and still manages to serve as a peaceful, rustic retreat.

## Fishing Bridge RV Park

▷ **Near Lake, Wyoming**

▷ **nps.gov**

▷ **Self-Enclosed RVs Only**

RV owners who want full hook-up sites inside Yellowstone have one option—and this is it. Thankfully, Fishing Bridge RV Park recently underwent a major renovation that forced its complete closure for the 2020 and 2021 camping seasons. This disappointed many RV owners who visited Yellowstone during that time period, but the improvements were desperately needed, and the end result is absolutely terrific. The park added a variety of new sites, including larger pull-through sites to accommodate today's larger RVs and a new dump station that is easier to navigate. The registration building was also completely renovated and is now twice the size. More showers and bathrooms (for men, women, and families) were also added. We hope that funding provided by the Great American Outdoors Act will allow the NPS to make improvements like this at dozens of other campgrounds in the system that are desperately in need of repair—just like Fishing Bridge was before this complete overhaul. The nearby Fishing Bridge General Store is also one of the best places in the park to grab a book or a souvenir—or a scoop of ice cream after a long day spent exploring the park.

## Bridge Bay Campground

▷ **Near Lake, Wyoming**

▷ **nps.gov**

▷ **RV and Tent Sites**

Much like Madison Campground, Bridge Bay Campground is quite large, and it can feel like a bustling camping village in June, July, and August. Madison Campground is prettier, and in a general sense, the campsites there are better as well. Many of the tent sites, and a good number of the RV sites at Bridge Bay feel like they are situated right next to the road or in open field-like areas that offer no privacy. So if you don't want to step out of your RV or tent in the morning and feel like you are in a fishbowl, you will need to choose your site wisely. Overall, Bridge Bay is in an excellent location right next to Yellowstone Lake. We think it makes an excellent second choice for those who can't get a site at Madison Campground but still want a campground located near the most popular spots in the park.

## Mammoth Campground

▷  **Near Gardiner, Montana**

▷  **nps.gov**

▷  **RV and Tent Sites**

The only campground in the park with first-come, first-served campsites from October through April, Mammoth Campground is a terrific option for exploring North Yellowstone and all that the Upper Loop has to offer. It is an appealing location to those making multiple stops in the park, or for those who want to escape the summertime crowds in the Lower Loop. Views of Lava Valley are rugged and stunning from every site, and the location near Mammoth Hot Springs is excellent for exploring this magnificent and under-rated section of the park. There is a wide range of campsite sizes at Mammoth Campground. There are several tiny tent sites and a handful of huge sites that will accommodate combined truck/trailer lengths of 75 feet—and everything in between those two extremes. This campground also serves as an excellent jumping-off point for exploring Lamar Valley, which is, to many Yellowstone wildlife lovers, the heart and soul of America's first national park. Hanging out and relaxing at the Mammoth Campground can also be a divine experience—especially when elk and bison wander by to say hello.

## Other Campgrounds Inside the Park

- ⇢ **Canyon Campground**
- ⇢ **Grant Village Campground**
- ⇢ **Indian Creek Campground**
- ⇢ **Lewis Lake Campground**
- ⇢ **Norris Campground**
- ⇢ **Pebble Creek Campground**
- ⇢ **Slough Creek Campground**
- ⇢ **Tower Fall Campground**

# CAMPGROUNDS OUTSIDE THE PARK

*Author's*
☆☆☆
**CHOICE**

## Under Canvas Yellowstone

- ▷ West Yellowstone, Montana
- ▷ undercanvas.com
- ▷ Glamping Tents

There are plenty of options for roughing it in and around America's first national park, but when it comes to a real high-end glamping experience, Under Canvas Yellowstone is absolutely magnificent. It also offers an excellent location near the park. Located just ten minutes from the west gate, this peaceful and attractive property gives you land (lots of land) and a starry sky above. This particular Under Canvas also manages to be a terrific place for a family with multiple kids, or for a couple trying to get away from it all. If you want to end a long day of adventuring in Yellowstone tucked in under luxurious linens with a wood-burning stove keeping your tent toasty warm, then this is where you should camp next. The sounds of live music fill the air at night in the summertime, and cocktails, s'mores kits, and hot chocolate are readily available. The coffee in the morning is included and is excellent. Grab a magazine inside the gorgeous community tent and spend some time alone, or set up a board game and enjoy time together with your family. Evenings are magical here. Watching falling stars shoot across the sky on the deck of your tent will be one of your favorite Yellowstone memories. When you wake up make sure you grab breakfast at the on-site restaurant. The French toast and the breakfast bowl with eggs, hash browns, and veggies are both hearty and amazing.

## Yellowstone Grizzly RV Park

▷ **West Yellowstone, Montana**

▷ **grizzlyrv.com**

▷ **RV Sites, Cabins**

The west entrance to Yellowstone National Park is only four blocks away from Yellowstone Grizzly RV Park, and a wide variety of shopping and dining options are also located nearby. So this is a perfect base camp for RV owners and cabin renters who want to explore the park from its western side. The entire park is clean and nicely landscaped—but the star of the show here are the back-in sites along the edge of the campground with national forest land directly behind them. Non-RV owners should take note—the cabins are cute, but tent camping is no longer allowed. Activities and amenities are somewhat limited at Yellowstone Grizzly, but the camp store offers free coffee in the morning and the camp workers are kind and knowledgeable about the area. When you are this close to Yellowstone, do you really need a pool or bounce pillow anyway? Make sure that you grab breakfast at Ernie's Bakery and Deli before heading into the park. After a long day of hiking and exploring, grab a cup or cone of huckleberry ice cream at The City Creamery. You won't regret it. There is also a tasty Taco Bus in town. Nuff said.

## West Yellowstone KOA

▷ **West Yellowstone, Montana**

▷ **koa.com**

▷ **Deluxe Cabins, Camping Cabins, RV and Tent Sites**

This KOA, which is right next door to the Under Canvas listed above, is a bit close to the road and can be noisy at night—so tent campers and those in pop-up campers might look elsewhere first. But those in hard-sided RVs and those renting cabins will have no trouble with noise here. The amenities and activities for kids are very good here, and so is the proximity to the west gate of the park. They are just 6 miles away. Some campers complain about the size of the sites here, but most don't go to Yellowstone to relax at their sites. If you are planning on spending the entire day in the park and are just looking for a clean and convenient place to stay, this is a very good option.

## Cody KOA Holiday

▷ Cody, Wyoming

▷ koa.com

▷ Deluxe Cabins, Camping Cabins, Teepees, RV and Tent Sites

This KOA is located an hour away from the eastern gate of Yellowstone National Park—but Cody is a vacation-worthy destination in its own right. The Buffalo Bill Center of the West and the Cody Night Rodeo are full-day itineraries. And so is downtown Cody, which is filled with good food, good coffee, and wonderful outfitters who have everything you need to explore the great outdoors. Grab free pancakes in the morning at the KOA before heading out to explore the region, then plan on spending some time relaxing in the hot tub when you get back each night. The drive into Yellowstone National Park on the Buffalo Bill Cody Scenic Byway is so gorgeous that it makes the hour-long drive to the east gate of Yellowstone worthwhile.

# Cody and the Wild West

Cody tends to fly under the radar, being surrounded by so many natural wonders. But it ends up being a memorable and favorite destination for many families who camp there. Here are some of the highlights:

## Buffalo Bill Center of the West

The center has five distinct museums under one roof, and there is a reason the entrance ticket is good for two days. You'll need that amount of time to explore the Buffalo Bill Museum, Plains Indian Museum, Whitney Western Art Museum, Draper Natural History Museum, and the New Cody Firearms Museum.

## The Cody Nite Rodeo

Cody is the self-proclaimed rodeo capital of the world, and this one runs nightly from June through August.

## Buffalo Bill Dam and Visitors Center

This dam was completed in 1910 and was the highest dam in the world at the time. You can walk all the way across the top of the dam and look down 325 feet to the Shoshone River.

## Shoshone National Forest

This was our country's first national forest, and it has hiking trails, campgrounds, and picnic areas. There are also snowmobiling trails and cross-country skiing trails for hearty adventurers.

## Buffalo Bill State Park

There's boating, fishing, paddleboarding, and plenty of other water recreation activities on the reservoir.

# Conquering Yellowstone National Park

Yellowstone National Park might be one of the more overwhelming parks to navigate, clocking in at 2.2 million acres. The Grand Loop runs for 142 miles, connecting northern attractions like Mammoth Hot Springs with popular spots in the south such as Old Faithful. You'll want to plan this trip out in advance and think through a flexible itinerary at the bare minimum. Here are some tips:

▷ Allow plenty of time to see the park. There are NPS sites that can be enjoyed in a single day, but Yellowstone is not one of them. Driving times will be slower on account of traffic and wildlife.

▷ Do your research before deciding where to camp. There are five entrances to the park, and there are beautiful campgrounds near each one, depending on the area you would most like to explore. Certain park highlights might be one to two hours from a particular base camp. Many visitors pick two locations (one on the east side and one on the west) and split up their stay.

▷ Pack a lunch and plenty of snacks every day. Navigating the roads and crowds in Yellowstone often means that you are nowhere near a restaurant when you are dying to eat. Ward off the "hangry" attacks by being prepared with your own food.

▷ Plan for a wide variety of weather conditions. Temperatures can vary greatly throughout the course of the day, so wear layers and pack rain gear. Nights can get below freezing, even in the summer. Bring plenty of warm clothing.

▷ Respect the wildlife and make sure you and your children understand park guidelines. It seems that many of the ridiculous videos of tourists acting inappropriately with wildlife come out of Yellowstone each year. Be a good steward of our national parks and leave no trace.

# The Yellowstone Top Five

## Old Faithful, Observation Point Trail, and the Upper Basin

Just because it's crowded, doesn't mean you shouldn't go. You have to see Old Faithful during your visit—maybe even more than once. Hike up the Observation Point Trail to watch the eruption with a bird's-eye view.

## Old Faithful Inn

This is just everything a national park lodge is supposed to be. Even if you don't stay here, visit the lobby to see the huge stone fireplace and enjoy live music in the evenings.

## Grand Canyon of the Yellowstone

Hike the Brink of the Lower Falls Trail to look down over the edge of a waterfall. When you've had your fill of steaming vents and geysers, this is where you should go.

## Mammoth Hot Springs & Historic District

This is like stepping onto another planet with boardwalks built over steaming, sulfuric hydrothermal features. The history of Yellowstone comes to life in this area of the park as well, housing the original visitors center and Fort Yellowstone.

## Yellowstone Lake

This lake sits 7,000 feet above sea level and is full of native cutthroat trout and surrounded by towering pines. Drop your kayak in for a paddle but be aware of safety warnings from the national park: water temperatures are low even in the summer and sudden strong winds take even seasoned paddlers by surprise.

# Three Days in Yellowstone

Here's a sample itinerary for seeing many of the park highlights in three days, entering each day from the West Yellowstone gate.

## Day One

▷ The Boardwalk Hike at the Fountain Paint Pot Trail
▷ Grand Prismatic Spring
▷ Biscuit Basin to the Mystic Falls Hike
▷ Old Faithful Geyser with cold drinks and snacks from the cafeteria
▷ Firehole Canyon Drive

## Day Two

▷ Gibbons Falls
▷ Canyon Village
▷ Brink of the Lower Falls, Lookout Point, Grand View, Inspiration Point on the North Rim Drive
▷ Upper Falls View, Uncle Tom's Trail, Artist Point on the South Rim Drive
▷ Hayden Valley Drive
▷ A boat ride at Yellowstone Lake
▷ Boardwalk trail at West Thumb Geyser Basin

## Day Three

▷ Mammoth Hot Springs
▷ Upper Terrace Drive
▷ Mammoth Hot Springs Hotel
▷ Historic Fort Yellowstone
▷ Roosevelt Lodge
▷ Lamar Valley in the evening for wildlife viewing

Conservationist George Bird Grinnell played a pivotal role in the creation of Glacier National Park and also coined its appropriately grand nickname, "The Crown of the Continent." Glacier was founded in 1910 and now welcomes between two and three million guests each year. The area that the park sits in today contained over 150 glaciers in 1850, but today only 25 of them are active.

Glacier offers excellent dry camping inside the park in a variety of locations, and there is an incredible KOA on the west side and a decent one on the east side—both just outside of park boundaries. Glamping near Glacier is also an option. NPS campsites are always affordable, but as soon as you start looking outside of the park, prices for sites skyrocket. The season is short, and campground owners need to make most of their profits in just a few short months.

Many visitors start by choosing a "side"—east or west—as a base camp, depending on which bucket-list items are on their Glacier National Park itinerary. The park is huge, and it can take hours to get from a west-side campground to an east-side glacier trailhead. Another popular option is to split camping days between each side of the park.

More than other famous national parks, Glacier truly is a hiking park. While there are beautiful sites to see on and off Going-to-the-Sun Road, many of the park's magnificent locations can only be seen by strapping on your hiking boots and moving your legs. Want to spot black bears at the edge of Avalanche Lake and mountain goats at Logan Pass? Excited to dip your feet into the frigid waters of Grinnell Glacier? Pack your bear spray and bells, and come prepared for some of the longest, most rewarding hikes of your life. Visiting the "Crown of the Continent" should be somewhere near the very top of every camper's bucket list.

# CAMPGROUNDS INSIDE THE PARK

### St. Mary Campground

▷    Browning, Montana

▷    nps.gov

▷    RV and Tent Sites

▷    No Hookups

While other Glacier National Park campgrounds may offer more of a remote and wild camping experience, the St. Mary Campground has easy access to Going-to-the-Sun Road, great wildlife viewing opportunities, and otherworldly mountain views. Plus, it is close to the St. Mary visitor center and shuttle service. The interior roads and the campsites themselves are not super friendly for larger RVs, so take a look at the nearby KOA if you are in a big rig. But those in smaller RVs with dry camping capacity will be delighted. Restrooms are clean and potable water is available, but other amenities are sparse. Tent campers and those with soft-sided RVs beware—when there is bear activity in the campground, you may be reassigned to the Two Medicine Campground or end up with no place to sleep in a somewhat remote section of the park. The town of St. Mary is nearby, but hotel rooms are expensive and inventory is limited.

## Many Glacier Campground

▷ **Browning, Montana**

▷ **nps.gov**

▷ **RV and Tent Sites**

▷ **No Hookups**

One of the most popular campgrounds within Glacier National Park, Many Glacier is located on the east side of the park near famous hikes such as the Grinnell Glacier and Iceberg Lake trails. It is also close to Many Glacier Lodge, which offers access to restaurants, boat tours, Red Bus tours, horseback riding, and other amenities and activities. Other than that, campers should know that this is a remote campground in a remote national park. There is no cell coverage, and the St. Mary park entrance and access to Going-to-the-Sun Road is a solid forty-minute drive. While most campsites can accommodate small RVs under 20 feet, only thirteen sites will fit RVs up to 35 feet in length. Check site size closely when booking.

## Fish Creek Campground

▷ **Near West Glacier, Montana**

▷ **nps.gov**

▷ **RV and Tent Sites**

▷ **No Hookups**

Fish Creek is one of four reservable campgrounds in Glacier and the second largest next to Apgar. Located on the western side of the park, it sits next to Lake McDonald, one of the most photographable lakes in the world. Some sites have direct access and views of the water through the fragrant spruce, fir, and hemlock trees. Those trees provide ample shade in the summer months but also make recharging solar panels difficult, if not impossible.

Head over to Lake McDonald Lodge to rent kayaks or for a casual lunch at Jammer Joe's Grill and Pizzeria.

## Two Medicine Campground

▷ **East Glacier Park, Montana**

▷ **RV and Tent Sites**

▷ **No Hookups**

Love viewing mountain goats by day and stargazing by night? Then put Two Medicine Campground on your bucket list. Sites here are first-come, first-served. This campground is often used as an overflow site when St. Mary Campground is full, but it is every bit as beautiful. Part of the campground wraps around Pray Lake, and mountain views are abundant. The nearby hike to Running Eagle Falls is one of two handicap-accessible hikes in the park, Trail of the Cedars in west Glacier being the other. Reservations are not accepted at Two Medicine Campground.

## Apgar Campground

▷ **West Glacier, Montana**

▷ **nps.gov**

▷ **RV and Tent Sites**

▷ **No Hookups**

This bustling campground is just steps away from Apgar Village and the busiest section of the Lake McDonald shoreline. If you want to camp inside the national park, and also have food, shopping, and kayak and SUP rentals nearby, then this is the perfect spot. Glacier's free shuttle service stops at this campground, making it ideal for those who don't want to search for parking at popular trailheads in the early morning hours. Eddie's Cafe and Mercantile in Apgar Village has been serving visitors for more than sixty years. The grub is good and you can also grab some ice cream after a long day of hiking in the park.

## Avalanche Campground

▷ West Glacier, Montana

▷ RV and Tent Sites

▷ No Hookups

Large shaded sites make this a popular choice for tent campers and those with smaller RVs. The campground is located just steps away from Trail of the Cedars, which serves as the starting point for the hike to Avalanche Lake. Reservations are not accepted at Avalanche Campground.

## Rising Sun Campground

▷ East, Browning, Montana

▷ RV and Tent Sites

▷ No Hookups

Located at the halfway point of St. Mary Lake, Rising Sun Campground may be best suited for those in smaller, hard-sided RVs up to 25 feet since bears are commonly spotted here. Reservations are not accepted at Rising Sun Campground.

# CAMPGROUNDS OUTSIDE THE PARK

## West Glacier KOA Resort

▷ West Glacier, Montana

▷ koa.com

▷ Camping Cabins, Deluxe Cabins, Multifamily Lodge Rental, RV and Tent Sites

▷ Water, Electric, Sewer

This West Glacier KOA is one of the most beautiful campgrounds in the country. Period. The smell of pine trees and the mountain views are ravishing—and so is the hand-dipped ice cream at Scoops. Breakfast at the Lazy Bear Cafe is also excellent. We ate there just about every morning before heading out for another epic hike in Glacier National Park. We stayed in a charming deluxe cabin (with loft for the boys) with an outdoor firepit and seating area that seemed like it had been ripped from the pages of a landscape design magazine. Our boys loved the large basketball and ga-ga ball courts, and they spent hours there each night making fast friends with the rest of the campground kids. We appreciated the "adults only" pool and hot tub area and took turns relaxing and chatting with other adults each night. The RV sites at this campground, particularly those at the bottom of the mountain, are among the most beautifully manicured sites we have ever seen. The West Glacier KOA Resort charges top dollar and deserves it. Proximity to the west side of the park is also excellent.

## Under Canvas Glacier

▷ Coram, Montana

▷ undercanvas.com

▷ Glamping Tents

After spending a long day hiking in one of America's most spectacular national parks, you will be thrilled to kick up your heels in one of Under Canvas's luxurious safari glamping tents. Tents have sinks, showers, bathrooms, and some have wood-burning stoves. Wrap a blanket around your shoulders and head out onto your own private deck and gaze at the night stars.

## St. Mary/East Glacier KOA Holiday

▷ St. Mary, Montana

▷ koa.com

▷ RV and Tent Sites, Camping Cabins, Deluxe Cabins, Four-Bedroom Home

▷ Water, Electric, Sewer

The location of this campground is just about perfect—and so are the views. The large pool, hot tub, and bocce ball courts are also excellent. We *loved* it here, and would go back in a Montana minute, but some folks are less than impressed. Why? Because this KOA is expensive and the landscaping is shaggy around the edges. Those things didn't bother us. Ice cream and coffee in the camp store were excellent—and so was the customer service.

## Glacier Campground

▷ **West Glacier, Montana**

▷ **glaciercampground.com**

▷ **RV and Tent Sites**

▷ **Water and Electric, Dump Station**

Located just 1 mile from the west entrance to Glacier, this campground is a more budget-friendly option than the West Glacier KOA. Many sites are close together, but thick trees provide privacy. Customer service is usually good, and sometimes great. Some sites are tough to back into, and some of them are unlevel—so bring some extra blocks. The bathrooms and showers are somewhat older and limited in scope, but they are serviceable and clean. Despite a few shortcomings, most folks say they would come back and leave as happy campers.

## Mountain Meadow RV Park and Cabins

▷ **Hungry Horse, Montana**

▷ **mountainmeadowrv.com**

▷ **RV Sites, Cabins, Rental RVs**

▷ **Water, Electric, Sewer**

This family-owned park is a bit farther away from the west entrance to the park, but it is also affordable and attractive. Call this your backup plan if you can't get rezzies anywhere else.

# Six Favorite Hikes in Glacier National Park

### Sunrift Gorge to St. Mary Falls Trail

The St. Mary Falls trail is a popular, easy 3-mile hike, but by a happy accident we did a longer version that started at the Sunrift Gorge parking lot. We are so glad we ended up experiencing this 5.5-mile roundtrip hike instead. The first mile runs along a ridge that gives hikers stunning views of St. Mary Lake. We enjoyed watching three moose through our binoculars. Some people do swim at the base of St. Mary Falls, so bring a suit if you'd like to take a dip.

### Grinnell Glacier

There are only twenty-five active glaciers left in Glacier National Park, and this is one of the easiest to get to. But it's still going to take a 12-mile roundtrip hike over very difficult terrain. We did it. We were exhausted. And it was worth every step for that amazing payoff experience. You will need to be at the Many Glacier Hotel before 8:00 a.m. to snag a parking spot.

### Hidden Lake Trail at Logan Pass

Logan Pass is definitely one of the most crowded places in the park, and this is probably the most crowded trail. Hike it anyway. You won't care about all the people when you see the mountain streams bordered by brilliant wild-flowers. The wildlife viewing is phenomenal. We watched families of mountain goats wander alongside the trail and a half a dozen hoary marmots play in a field. A note about Logan Pass: this is the single most difficult place to park in all of Glacier. Get there early or take a shuttle.

### Iceberg Lake

If you aren't up for the Grinnell Glacier hike, this might be a great alternative. It's a bit shorter at just 9 miles, and the hike is not as strenuous. The payoff is just as good, though. Many people swear this is their favorite hike in the entire park.

## Avalanche Lake via the Trail of Cedars

This is one of the easier hikes in all of Glacier, yet the payoff views at Avalanche Lake are as stunning as anything in the park. It's a 5-mile roundtrip hike without a lot of elevation gain. The first part of the hike is the Trail of Cedars, an accessible boardwalk hike. Get to the trailhead early to find parking, or take a shuttle from the St. Mary, Apgar, or Logan Pass Visitor Center.

## The Highline Trail

The Highline Trail is one of the most beautiful hikes in North America. It rises above Going-to-the-Sun Road and provides spectacular mountain views and breathtaking drop-offs. The path is narrow for many stretches, so pick another hike if you are afraid of heights. There are several ways to approach the hike, but the 11.6-mile one-way stretch from Logan Pass to the Loop is probably the most popular. Plan on taking the shuttle back to your starting point, or turn around halfway and return to your car.

# Other Great Activities at Glacier National Park

## Take the Red Bus Tour

These classic car tours allow you to take in the beauty of the landscape without the stress of navigating Going-to-the-Sun Road. The guides are brilliant at bringing to life the history and geology of the park, along with injecting campy, local humor. We highly recommend the half-day Eastern Alpine tour if you are having difficulty deciding between all the options.

## Enjoy a Ranger Program at the St. Mary Campground

The topics vary greatly from bear safety to glaciers, but the beautiful setting with mountain views is breathtaking no matter the subject.

### Have Dinner and Drinks at the Many Glacier Hotel

Even if you aren't staying at the hotel, make time to enjoy the epic views in this iconic national park lodge.

### Go Horseback Riding with Swan Mountain Outfitters

Swan Mountain Outfitters is the concessionaire that runs all the stables in Glacier National Park. It has a wide variety of hour-long, half-day, and full-day rides. If you are ready for a break from hiking, this is a great way to see the park.

### Take a Boat Ride on Lake McDonald or St. Mary Lake

The Glacier Park Boat Company has been operating Glacier National Park since 1938. The classic boats are a wonderful part of this national park's history. A few of the daily boat rides include an on-board park ranger talk. All other tours host an on-board naturalist who will interpret the land around the lakes.

## Read Before You Go

### *Night of the Grizzlies* by Jack Olson

Based on a series that first ran in *Sports Illustrated*, Olson's page-turning account documents events that led to the savage killing of two young women by grizzly bears in Glacier National Park in 1967. Think this book will scare you out of your wits? Think again. Reading *Night of the Grizzlies* before visiting Glacier is oddly reassuring. The NPS's negligent management practices at that time are a thing of the past. Though Glacier may be safer to visit today, hikers should still take every precaution before tackling its magnificent trails.

### *Where the Deer and the Antelope Play:*
### *The Pastoral Observations of One Ignorant*
### *American Who Loves to Walk Outside* by Nick Offerman

The first ninety-seven pages of this quirky book by the *Parks and Recreation* star recounts a hilarious and action-packed trip to Glacier National Park with Wilco's lead singer Jeff Tweedy and author George Saunders of *New Yorker* fame. These three middle-aged dudes are best buddies and their trip to Glacier was legit. They hiked the Highline Trail and made the trek to Grinnell Glacier—their ruminations, hijinks, and mishaps along the way make the first long section of this book an absolute pleasure to read.

### --- What to Bring: Packing for Glacier National Park ---

We've been to a lot of national parks, but the remote location of Glacier National Park did require us to pack a bit differently. Be aware that there is little to no cell reception or Wi-Fi in most of the park and plan accordingly.

- Bear spray
- Bear bells
- Prepaid phone cards
- Printed out confirmations and reservations
- Good-quality binoculars
- AllTrails App, Pro Version
- Layers of clothing
- Quality hiking gear

# Theodore Roosevelt National Park

North Dakota might be one of the most under-the-radar camping destinations in America, but the folks who do visit will tell you that it was worth the detour. Many visitors are drawn to the state by a desire to visit one of the more remote NPS sites in the United States, Theodore Roosevelt National Park. Roosevelt came to North Dakota to hunt bison and to grieve the death of both his mother and wife. As it turns out, his time spent in this state impacted decades of conservation policy in our country, and North Dakota is dotted with historical sites that speak to this legacy.

The national park that bears his name is excellent and a great place to get away from the crowds that plague other NPS sites. It has a stark and muted beauty that takes many visitors by surprise—and the camping options here are limited but exceptional. The two campgrounds inside of the park are beautiful and much loved by tent campers and RV owners who are equipped for dry camping. Those who want hookups can find them in nearby Sully Creek State Park, which is not as immediately beautiful as Cottonwood and Juniper but still boasts huge sites and excellent views of North Dakota's Badlands.

# CAMPGROUNDS INSIDE THE PARK

### Cottonwood Campground

▷ Medora, North Dakota

▷ nps.gov

▷ RV and Tent Sites

The campgrounds in Theodore Roosevelt National Park are underrated gems. World-class wildlife viewing and hiking opportunities can be found near the park's campgrounds without the crowds that are often associated with Yellowstone, Badlands, and Glacier. Cottonwood Campground—which is partially situated along the banks of the Little Missouri River in the park's South Unit—is our favorite option. Half of the sites here are reservable, and half are first-come first-served—but all of them are simple, quiet, and beautiful. Book as early as possible because Cottonwood does fill up despite the generally uncrowded nature of the park—and bring your own soap to the bathhouse because it often runs out. If you are just a little bit lucky, you will see bison wandering through the campground and maybe even onto your campsite. Keep your distance and get ready to be in awe of these mighty and magnificent creatures.

## Juniper Campground

▷ Grassy Butte, North Dakota

▷ nps.gov

▷ RV and Tent Sites

Campsites here are first-come, first-served, and while it may be hard to imagine driving all the way to North Dakota without reservations, you will probably do just fine at Juniper—which rarely fills up. Everything about this North Unit's campground location is lovely. You can hear the rushing sound of the Missouri River right from your huge site, and there is lots of grassy, open space for a game of tag or catch. Your kids will absolutely love the "Cannonball Concretions" pullout area right outside of the campground. These large, round, pearl-like stones are great for climbing, and relatively safe for explorers of all ages.

# CAMPGROUND OUTSIDE THE PARK

## Sully Creek State Park

▷ Medora, North Dakota

▷ parkrec.nd.gov

▷ RV and Tent Sites

North Dakota may have the most underrated state park system in the entire country. Thirteen of its state parks also have great campgrounds. Sully Creek State Park is one of them. The sites here are huge and sit in a wide-open field surrounded by North Dakota's Badlands. Ten of the sites here offer water and electric hookups at a bargain basement price. Theodore Roosevelt National Park and its charming (and very small!) gateway town of Medora are both just minutes away.

---- **What to Do in Theodore Roosevelt National Park** ----

▷ Soak in the North Dakota Badlands at Painted Canyon Visitor's Center.

▷ Drive the 36-mile scenic loop drive in the morning or evening for best wildlife viewing.

▷ Visit the Maltese Ranch Cabin, built from 1883 to 1884 at the request of Theodore Roosevelt.

▷ Track down the isolated Elkhorn Ranch Site deep in the North Dakota Badlands.

▷ Drive the 14-mile Theodore Roosevelt North Unit Scenic Byway.

▷ Stop at the Oxbow Overlook for a sweeping view of the Little Missouri River.

▷ Watch (but don't feed!) the prairie dogs.

## -- Popular Hikes in Theodore Roosevelt National Park --

**South Unit**

▷ Ridgeline Nature Trail (0.6 mile)

▷ Coal Vein Trail (0.8 mile)

▷ Wind Canyon Trail (0.4 mile)

**North Unit**

▷ Little Mo Trail (0.7 mile)

▷ Caprock Coulee Nature Trail (1.5 miles)

▷ Sperati Point via the Achenbach Trail (1.5 miles)

## ---------------- Must See: *Medora Musical* ----------------

The *Medora Musical* is a live musical attraction that has been performed in Medora for over fifty years. Get the dinner and a show package to enjoy an outdoor buffet before the musical extravaganza. This is the perfect way to end a day at Theodore Roosevelt National Park.

## ---------------- Sweet Treats in Medora ----------------

Cowboy Lyle's Candy Barn is a must stop for families with kids. Named after Cowboy Lyle Glass, who performed in the *Medora Musical* for almost half a century, this candy shop has all the old-timey classics and delicious handmade chocolates and truffles.

The Medora Fudge & Ice Cream Depot offers up homemade fudge and ice cream that people line up to eat in the summertime. Try the juneberry ice cream for a regional treat that you will never forget.

## Read Before You Go

▷ For Kids: *The Camping Trip That Changed America: Theodore Roosevelt, John Muir, and our National Parks* by Barb Rosenstock

▷ For Older Kids: *Who Was Theodore Roosevelt?* By Michael Burgan

▷ For Adults: *The Rise of Theodore Roosevelt* by Edmund Morris

## While You Are in North Dakota!

You may only get to North Dakota once in your life, so make sure to drive the Enchanted Highway during your trip to Theodore Roosevelt National Park. This 32-mile drive stretches from Gladstone, North Dakota, and features large metal sculptures along the road. The art installations include *Geese in Flight*, *Deer Crossing*, and *Grasshoppers*. You can purchase a souvenir of your favorite sculpture at the small gift shop in Regent.

## Join the Best for Last Club!

If you are on a quest to visit all fifty states, and you save North Dakota for last, you may join the prestigious Best for Last Club sponsored by the Fargo-Moorehead Visitors Center. Club members get a T-shirt and an official certificate. The club has over 4,000 members. Will you be the next to join its ranks?

# Badlands National Park, Mount Rushmore National Memorial & Wind Cave National Park

The western side of South Dakota is an NPS lover's dream. Unfortunately, many visitors blast through the state too quickly as they hurry toward more famous points farther west—looking at you, Yellowstone and Grand Teton. We have always recommended slowing down and enjoying the rugged and varied landscape of South Dakota. Or even better, make a dedicated visit to the region and save Yellowstone and Grand Teton for another day.

Badlands National Park takes most visitors by surprise, and many are awed by its otherworldly beauty. Just minutes away from Badlands National Park is the Minuteman Missile National Historic Site, which offers a rare chance to get up close and personal with a nuclear missile. Advance reservations are required for all guided tours at the site, but even if you can't nab those, the self-guided museum is still worth a visit.

Many cynical and world-weary travelers claim that Mount Rushmore is overrated—nothing more than a cheesy tourist trap with a tainted background. We beg to differ. A visit to Mount Rushmore can be a compelling, thought-provoking, and inspirational trip. Whose hills are these anyway? A visit to the national monument and the nearby Crazy Horse Memorial will force you to think hard about the answer to that question.

Wind Cave National Park and Jewel Cave National Monument are both nearby and make for excellent day trips. Custer State Park is also just as magnificent as many of our great national parks—and just a stone's throw away from Mount Rushmore. South Dakota is a magnificent state for those of us passionate about America's best idea.

A wide variety of amazing camping options is available throughout this NPS-rich region, bolstering its case for a dedicated trip as opposed to a quick stop on the way to another location. There is a campground for every type of camper in western South Dakota. Whether you love full-fledged RV resorts, National Park campgrounds with stunning views, or glamping tents with luxurious tents—this is an unforgettable part of the country.

# CAMPGROUNDS INSIDE BADLANDS NATIONAL PARK

### Cedar Pass Campground and Cedar Pass Lodge

▷  Interior, South Dakota

▷  cedarpasslodge.com/campground

▷  RV and Tent Sites, Cabin Rentals

When it comes to campgrounds, sometimes it is all about location, location, location. There is absolutely nothing spectacular about the Cedar Pass Campground. The RV sites are unlevel, the bathrooms are less than sparkling, and the amenities are spartan at best. But the campground is in a spectacular location in Badlands National Park that is surrounded by astonishing beauty. Camping at Cedar Pass is a visually spectacular experience, particularly when a blood-red sunset colors the mountains that are just steps away. The best hikes in the park are nearby, and when you come back to your site, just sitting in a camp chair and having a cold drink is a magical and profoundly relaxing experience. The Lodge is a short walk away from the campground and has an excellent camp store and a surprisingly good restaurant if you don't feel like grilling back at your site. The cozy and comfortable cabins at the Lodge (which were built by local craftsmen) are climate controlled and conveniently located. The open-air amphitheater is located between the campground and the lodge, and we highly recommend that you attend a ranger talk or night sky program.

### Sage Creek Campground

▷ **Wall, South Dakota**

▷ **nps.gov**

▷ **Tent and RV sites**

If you are willing to camp without reservations and without hookups, the Sage Creek Campground may be a good fit. RVs greater than 18 feet in length are not allowed. Sites here are free, and getting one on a busy summer weekend may be competitive—but the campground rarely reaches capacity. It offers pit toilets that are surprisingly clean, but water is not available at the campground. This section of the park can also get very windy—so take precautions with tents and RV awnings!

# CAMPGROUNDS OUTSIDE BADLANDS NATIONAL PARK

### Badlands/White River KOA Holiday

▷ **Interior, South Dakota**

▷ **koa.com**

▷ **RV and Tent Sites, Cabins, Teepee, Yurt**

▷ **Water, Electric, Sewer**

Located just 4 miles from Badlands National Park, this campground lacks Cedar Pass's panoramic views, but it has amenities like a small pool, mini-golf, bike rentals, a snack area, and even a motorcycle care area. The sites here are not large, but most are shaded and have full hookups. The dog park is large for those traveling with pups, and the pancake breakfast at the Cook Shack is very good. Bird-watching in and around the campground is excellent, so pack a pair of binoculars. They will also come in handy in the park, especially on the Wildlife Loop Road, which often offers up more wildlife viewing than any one spot in Yellowstone. This KOA also boasts a clean laundry room and clean bathroom facilities—which you won't find at Cedar Pass, where the showers are dirty and you have to pay to use them.

## Nomad View Dispersed Camping

▷  **Buffalo Gap National Grasslands**

▷  **Wall, South Dakota**

▷  **fs.usda.gov**

▷  **RV and Tent Camping, Car Camping**

Adventurous souls might consider setting up camp in an area of Buffalo Gap National Grasslands that boasts spectacular views of Badlands National Park and the wild landscape surrounding it. Parking your rig or pitching your tent at Nomad View is completely free, but there are (obviously) no hookups or facilities of any kind. Be advised—the road in can be bumpy. Many RVers like to set up their rigs close to a sharp drop-off known as "the Wall." Take precautions if you do this, and consider a more traditional camping experience if you are traveling with young kids. The wind is consistently high in this area, and it can get very hot in the summer months, so while you might be tempted to pull your awning out it might not be a very bright idea.

## Sleepy Hollow Campground

▷ **Wall, South Dakota**

▷ **Sleepyhollowcampgroundsd.com**

▷ **RV and Tent Camping Sites**

▷ **Water, Electric, Sewer**

Located just a short walk from Wall Drug, Sleepy Hollow Campground gets solid reviews for cleanliness and customer service. The Badlands KOA has better amenities, and Cedar Pass is far more beautiful, but this campground serves as a more than adequate backup plan if neither of those is available.

# CAMPGROUNDS OUTSIDE MOUNT RUSHMORE NATIONAL MEMORIAL

## Rafter J Bar Ranch

▷ **Hill City, South Dakota**

▷ **rafterj.com**

▷ **RV and Tent Sites, Cabin Rentals**

Many seasoned RVers will argue that Rafter J Bar Ranch is one of the best campgrounds in the country. The sites are incredibly spacious for a private campground, and the views of the Black Hills that rim the campground are inspiring. This private campground combines the natural beauty of a state park with the amenities of a true RV resort. Rafter J is located about fifteen minutes away from Mount Rushmore and serves as a near perfect base camp for exploring the entire region. The large heated pool and hot tub are perfect after a long day of exploring Crazy Horse and Mount Rushmore, and there is a gas fire pit for warming up right after a swim.

## Horse Thief Lake Campground

▷ **Black Hills National Forest**

▷ **Hill City, South Dakota**

▷ **fs.usda.gov**

▷ **RV and Tent Sites**

Horse Thief Lake Campground has four major things going for it besides its amazing name. First, it's only 2 miles from Mount Rushmore and is the closest campground to the historic landmark. Second, it's beautiful and peaceful, though close to the road. Third, the lake is small but delightful, so bring kayaks or SUPs if you have them. Last, the affordable price point is attractive to those on a budget. Be forewarned, Horsethief only has thirty-six sites and is far more accommodating to smaller RVs. Book early, campers.

## Mount Rushmore KOA at Palmer Gulch

▷ **Hill City, South Dakota**

▷ **koa.com**

▷ **RV and Tent Sites, Camping Cabins and Deluxe Cabins**

Folks almost come to blows over which campground is better for a trip to Mount Rushmore—Rafter J or Palmer Gulch. They are both awesome—so don't torture yourself over the decision. The KOA offers a true resort camping experience with amenities like a pool, climbing wall, on-site restaurant, and chuckwagon dinner. The RV sites are not as big as Rafter J's, but there are definitely more scheduled activities for those who like to go go go.

## Under Canvas Mount Rushmore

▷ **Keystone, South Dakota**

▷ **undercanvas.com**

▷ **Safari-Style Glamping Tents**

We are unabashed fans of the Under Canvas glamping experience—and this location, just 4 miles from Mount Rushmore, is nothing short of excellent. The safari-style tents are sumptuously outfitted, and the communal lobby tents are filled with charming West Elm furniture. After a day of exploring in the Black Hills, come back to Under Canvas for an evening filled with stars, s'mores, and live music. On-site food options are delicious, and wine, beer, and cocktails are available for a drink before and after dinner. Plan on spending your South Dakota evenings here. You will never want to leave.

# CAMPGROUNDS INSIDE WIND CAVE NATIONAL PARK

### Elk Mountain Campground

▷ Hot Springs, South Dakota

▷ nps.gov

▷ RV and Tent Sites

Elk Mountain does not accept reservations, so have a backup plan if you decide to try to nap a spot here. The campground has a modest sixty-one sites, and RV sites have a max length of 40 feet. Even with these limitations, we can't help but recommend this beautiful campground for an immersive Black Hills camping experience. Make sure to catch one of the ranger programs at the amphitheater, which are scheduled every night in the summer.

---

**YouTube Watch**

Check out an excellent vlog by an adorable couple named Adam and Kathryn from *Adventures of A+K* called "One Day at Badlands National Park: Notch Trail, Badlands Loop Road, & visiting Wall Drug Adventures." They grabbed some great footage of many of the spots mentioned in this chapter—and we agree, the climb down on the Notch Trail is harder than the climb up!

# Hiking in Badlands National Park

There's a variety of options when it comes to hiking in the Badlands. We have a few tips before diving into the specific trails, though. During the summer, temperatures can soar to over 100°F by midday. We did all our hiking in the early morning or late afternoon. We filled the middle of the day with ranger programs and other indoor activities. You'll want to carry plenty of water, and wear hats and sunglasses. Last, wear sturdy shoes that can get very, very dirty. The clay soil here gets on, and it just won't come off.

The **Door Trail** (0.75 mile), **Window Trail** (0.25 mile), and **Notch Trail** (1.5 miles) are all clustered together near the northeast entrance. This is a great place to start your Badlands hiking adventure.

The Door Trail is a quick hike, but our boys loved following the trail markers across the barren landscape. This hike also offers some classic Badlands photo opportunities. It's important to remember that this landscape looks completely different at different times of the day because of lighting.

The Window Trail is more of a fun scramble than a hike. Adults and kids alike have a blast climbing on the rock structures and peering out through the "windows" to the hills in the distance.

The Notch Trail is challenging, but it was a family highlight for all of us. There's a fairly steep ladder that you'll have to climb to complete the hike. Folks with a fear of heights might struggle a bit coming down the ladder as well. If you are physically and mentally able, do not miss this amazing hiking experience!

# Tips for Visiting Mount Rushmore

## Tip #1: Mount Rushmore is not just a "pass-through" destination.

Many folks treat Mount Rushmore as a quick stopover on their way out to visit the "more exciting" destinations of Yellowstone, Grand Teton, or Glacier National Park. We have heard from so many listeners over the years that they wished they had spent more time in the Black Hills region. Take your time and enjoy the Black Hills. It's truly a national treasure.

## Tip #2: Visit early or later in the summer to avoid the crowds.

Another common complaint from people is how crowded the Mount Rushmore Memorial and surrounding area can get during the peak summer season. Crowds and heat can conquer even the most intrepid travelers. Consider visiting toward the end of August, when many kids in the South are back to school. Or you might try visiting in early June, when most East Coast schools are still in session. Avoid the Fourth of July and Sturgis Bike Rally if you want a more peaceful experience.

## Tip #3: Attend the Evening Lighting Ceremony first.

Attend the Evening Lighting Ceremony on the very first day you arrive in the Mount Rushmore area, and then return the following day for all the ranger talks and tours. The Evening Lighting Ceremony is grand and inspiring, and you will be pumped up and ready to return for more the next day.

## Tip #4: Attend a park ranger talk or walk.

There is a wide variety of ranger walks and talks every day at this national park. The tricky part is that the schedule is not advertised online, but rather displayed at the ranger stations on-site. Try talking to the rangers when you arrive for the Evening Lighting Ceremony and plan out the following day. The Junior Ranger program is excellent, offering separate booklets for kids up to five years old and kids over five years old.

## Tip #5: Avoid the gift shops if rampant consumerism is not your thing.

Some visitors say that Mount Rushmore felt overly consumeristic. The main gift shop is gigantic with an almost Disney-esque vibe. However, you don't have to go to the gift shop. Stick to the visitor's center, memorial, and walking paths for a noncommercial experience.

## Tip #6: Try the TJ's Ice Cream.

It seems pretty gimmicky, but TJ's Ice Cream is surprisingly yummy. Apparently, President Jefferson is credited for bringing the first written ice cream recipe to the United States back in 1780. The vanilla ice cream really is rich, sweet, and super vanilla-y. Try not to cringe at the price when you make your purchase.

# Get Your Cave Fix!

Both Wind Cave National Park and Jewel Cave National Monument are in South Dakota, just a short drive from Custer State Park. There are some quirks to visiting these caves, though. Please read all cave alerts in advance of your visit.

## Wind Cave National Park

A percentage of tour tickets are available to purchase in advance from recreation.gov. The remaining tickets are first-come, first-served at the visitor center. Candlelit and Wild Cave tour tickets are only available through advance reservations. Arrive early to purchase timed tickets for the popular Natural Entrance Tour, suitable for all ages.

## Jewel Cave National Monument

This cave site does allow for advanced reservations for a limited number of guided tours, and purchasing tickets in advance is highly recommended. There are quite a few rules about the reservations, so make sure to check out the NPS site for details.

Lastly, the temperature in these caves is in the midfifties no matter the season, so dress in layers and always bring a light jacket.

Wind Cave Park Ranger tip: Pets are not allowed in any of the caves, but they can explore with you on two trails—the Prairie Vista Trail and the Elk Mountain Campground Trail.

## ------------ Come One, Come All to Wall Drug ------------

If you can tolerate a whole lot of kitsch, just up the road from Badlands National Park, you will find one of our nation's most popular roadside attractions, Wall Drug. Made famous by the hundreds of signs that line Interstate 90 from one side of the state to the other, Wall Drug is an awe-inspiring conglomeration of shops, restaurants, and attractions.

Our kids couldn't get enough of the Little Britches Toy Store, the Shooting Gallery Arcade, and the Mining Company Rock Shop. If you're traveling with little ones, bring in a change of clothes since the back patio even has water sprinklers amid the humorous array of photo ops, including an iconic giant jackrabbit. If you stop at Wall Drug, you need to come hungry. From the famous five-cent coffee to the homemade donuts, you'll find some seriously good grub. The Western Art Gallery Restaurant is a feast for the eyes and your stomach.

# Grand Teton National Park

Grand Teton National Park is under an hour's drive from the southern boundary of Yellowstone National Park, and many campers combine a visit to both bucket-list locations in a single trip. Grand Teton is smaller and more manageable, and three to four days will enable you to experience many of the highlights—hiking, wildlife viewing, driving, and boating.

This national park is a bit of a campground outlier compared to the other popular national parks in the west like Glacier, Yellowstone, Grand Canyon, or any of Utah's big five. Those parks offer some great campground options in the park and some top-notch private campground options outside of the park. Grand Teton National Park is just miles from Jackson, Wyoming, one of the most expensive real estate markets in the entire country. This has squeezed out the private campground market, and there are really none that we would recommend in the immediate region.

If you are camping in or near Grand Teton, this is the moment to embrace public campgrounds and stretch your rustic camping muscles. There's a range of amazing options, from Colter Bay Campground with electric hookups to hundreds of dispersed camping areas in nearby Bridger-Teton National Forest.

# CAMPGROUNDS INSIDE THE PARK

### Colter Bay Village

▷   Moran, Wyoming

▷   nps.gov

▷   RV and Tent Sites, Cabin Rentals, Tent Cabin Rentals

Colter Bay Village is the most developed and bustling place inside of Grand Teton National Park. It includes Colter Bay Campground, Colter Bay RV Park, Colter Bay Tent Village, and Colter Bay Cabins. So if you want to camp under the stars and get away from the madness of the crowd, then the variety of camping options here is probably not for you. But if you want to wake up and walk to a rustic but well-stocked general store for a hot cup of Starbucks coffee and fresh baked donuts in the morning—then this is your place. There is so much else to do within the village as well. It has restaurants, a visitor center, an amphitheater, a marina, a swimming beach, and more. There are no electric sites at Colter Bay Campground, so it is better for tent campers and those RV owners who are well equipped for dry camping. Colter Bay RV Park offers full hook-up sites.

Both of these options are located in a densely wooded lodgepole pine forest with nicely shaded sites. Neither of these two campgrounds is located on Jackson Lake, but you can easily walk down to the water for spectacular views of Mount Moran. The Colter Bay Tent Village and the log cabin rentals offer excellent and fairly affordable options for those who want a comfortable camping experience without having to pitch a tent or bring an RV into the park. The cabins are borderline glampy. Make sure to do the Lakeshore Trail located just behind the visitor center. It will take you around two interconnected loops that meander around Colter Bay and into a small stretch of delightful forest. The highlight is reaching the tip of the peninsula, walking to the edge of the water, and looking out across the water at some of the most magnificent mountains in the world.

## Jenny Lake Campground

▷ Moose, Wyoming

▷ nps.gov

▷ Tent Sites

The sites at Jenny Lake Campground that have direct views of the Teton Range must be among the most beautiful tent camping sites in the world. Jenny Lake is a short walk away from the campground, and you can pick up a trail just steps from your site that will lead you directly to its shores. There are only sixty-one sites here, and they are very hard to get. Once you dip your toes into the cold, clear, and reflective waters of this magical lake, you will understand why. Take caution! The rocks beneath the water are colorful and mesmerizing to look at, but they are slippery and wobbly. The hike around the lake and the hikes in and around Cascade Canyon are filled with streams, waterfalls, and fragrant trees that will delight your senses.

## Signal Mountain Campground

▷ Moran, Wyoming

▷ nps.gov

▷ RV and Tent Sites

Signal Mountain Campground is situated in a gorgeous lodgepole pine forest with breathtaking views of Mount Moran. It has the added benefit of being close to Signal Mountain Lodge, which has a bar and several decent dining options plus other amenities like an ATM and gift shop. Sites are located just steps away from the scenic waters of Jackson Lake, so get your cameras ready for a workout.

## Gros Ventre Campground

▷ Kelly, Wyoming

▷ nps.gov

▷ RV and Tent Sites

With almost 300 sites, Gros Ventre Campground (pronounced *grow-vont*), is the largest campground in Grand Teton National Park, and it might be the most beloved. This is egalitarian national park camping at its best. You will see everything from solo campers pitching tents to veteran RV owners pulling in with massive motor homes. The crowd may vary, but everyone loves Gros Ventre. Why? Because of its level sites, magnificent views, great location in the southeastern section of the park, and abundant opportunities for spotting wildlife. Moose wander in and around the campground almost every day. Anglers also love walking from their campsites to the Gros Ventre River where they can catch whitefish and trout...and plenty of 'em.

## Other Campground Inside the Park

⇢⇢ **Lizard Creek Campground**

# CAMPGROUNDS OUTSIDE THE PARK

### Granite Creek Campground

▷    Teton County, Wyoming

▷    fs.usda.gov

▷    RV and Tent Sites

The campgrounds in Bridger-Teton National Forest do not take reservations, so they are most appealing to those adventurous souls who scoff at making reservations in the first place. Granite Creek Campground is located about 8 miles down a dirt road, and it can accommodate RVs up to 30 feet, but this is a much more friendly place for tent campers, van lifers, and those with small travel trailers that are equipped to go off-road. The NPS provides RV length restrictions for every single campsite on its website—but just remember, your RV may fit in a site, but you've got to get it there first! The road into this gem of a campground can be a bit bumpy. But its location along Granite Creek is a slice of near wild heaven. Mountain views abound, and the fishing is good. Granite Falls is nearby, as is the Granite Hot Springs Pool, which was built by the Civilian Conservation Corps in 1935. Visitors pay a small fee to soak for up to one hour.

## Headwaters Campground and RV Park

▷ Moran, Wyoming

▷ nps.gov

▷ RV and Tent Sites, Cabin Rentals

Headwaters Campground at Flagg Ranch is located in the John D. Rockefeller, Jr. Memorial Parkway, just 2.5 miles from the bottom of Yellowstone and 5 miles from the top of Grand Teton National Park. This campground is a bit off-the-radar, and it provides an excellent base camp for visiting both national parks without having to pack up and camp in two different places. The sites here are nicely shaded and semiprivate, and almost 100 of them have water, electric, and sewer hookups. Tent sites and cabins rentals are also available—though RVs seem to dominate the landscape. Overall, this is a really good option if you can't get a site in Yellowstone or Grand Teton and want to visit both.

## Curtis Canyon Campground

▷ Teton County, Wyoming

▷ fs.usda.gov

▷ RV and Tent Sites

Curtis Canyon Campground is about 8 miles from Jackson (above the National Elk Refuge) and serves as a great base camp for exploring Grand Teton National Park. Much like Granite Creek, this is not a spot for medium or larger sized RVs, but those with tents, rooftop tents, and off-road campers will do just fine if they are properly equipped and well prepared. The campground is wooded and shaded, but blue-sky views of the Teton Range are just steps away from most sites.

# Camping in Bridger-Teton National Forest

To the east of Grand Teton National Park lies the 3.4-million-acre Bridger-Teton National Forest, beloved by adventurers chasing remote, scenic, dispersed camping. There are almost 200 designated camping areas in the national forest, including cabin rentals, established campgrounds, dispersed camping, and group camping areas. If you are interested in trying your hand at boondocking in this area, here is what you need to know:

▷ All campgrounds in the national forest operate on a first-come, first-served basis. There are no reservable sites except for some of the larger group camping areas.

▷ Stay limits are generally fourteen days for camping in the national forest. After fourteen days, campers must move at least 5 miles from where they were camping. You can return after seven days.

▷ In the summer season, many of the most popular national forest campgrounds fill up by mid-morning. It is best to have a few backup camping options.

▷ The national forest is organized into ranger districts. The best way to learn about individual campgrounds is to visit the individual ranger district pages on the Bridger-Teton National Forest site. There you will find any safety alerts and closures, recreation opportunities, and maps of campgrounds and dispersed camping areas.

▷ Be prepared. This is a wild, remote area with virtually no cell or Wi-Fi service. Have access to GPS and make sure all necessary information is either downloaded to devices or printed. Have plenty of food and water. Know and follow proper wildlife safety precautions.

## ----------- Five More Amazing Camping Spots -----------
## in Bridger-Teton National Forest

▷ Toppings Lake Dispersed Campsites, Upper and Lower Teton View

▷ Spread Creek Dispersed Campsites

▷ Atherton Creek Campground

▷ Shadow Mountain Designated Dispersed Campsites

▷ Porter Reservoir

## --------------------- Scenic Drives ---------------------

Many visitors spend a lot of their time driving in Grand Teton, taking in the breathtaking mountain landscape and world-class wildlife viewing.

### John D. Rockefeller, Jr. Memorial Parkway

This 27-mile scenic drive connects the northern end of Grand Teton National Park with the West Thumb Geyser Basin in Yellowstone National Park.

### Jenny Lake Scenic Drive

Running along the eastern shore of Jenny Lake, this road is about 5 miles long and offers plenty of Grand Teton photo opportunities along the route.

### Signal Mountain Summit Road

This is a favorite road to drive at dawn or dusk for spotting elk, moose, and bear. An added bonus is that cell service is very strong at the top of the mountain—unlike in the rest of the park—so you can check in on your texts and voicemails while up there.

### Moose-Wilson Road

The marsh and forest habitats along this 7-mile drive offer a great opportunity to spot a wide variety of wildlife like beaver, fox, great blue herons, and sandhill cranes.

## A Day at Jenny Lake

Jenny Lake is one of the most visited areas of the park, but don't let the crowds keep you away from this awe-inspiring location. Schedule your visit during the early morning or late afternoon hours, especially during peak summer months.

1. Walk the accessible Discovery Trail and read the interpretative panels that bring the history and geology of the region to life.
2. Take the shuttle boat from the East Boat Dock to the Cascade Canyon Trailhead across the lake. The boat departs every fifteen to twenty minutes and will shave 2 miles off the hike while offering stunning views of Mount Teewinot.
3. Debark from the shuttle boat and hike to Hidden Falls (1 mile round trip), Inspiration Point (2 miles round trip), or venture farther into Cascade Canyon. Just be sure to get back to the dock for the last boat of the day.
4. If you wish to spend more time on the lake, book a one-hour scenic cruise with expert guides. You can also rent canoes or kayaks for an independent paddle.
5. Eat at the Jenny Lake Lodge Dining Room, offering a five-course prix fixe dinner menu with locally sourced, sustainable ingredients.

## Floating the Snake River

For many visitors, spending time on the Snake River is the highlight of a Grand Teton National Park experience. The Grand Teton Lodge Company offers 10-mile scenic floats that depart from the Jackson Lake Lodge from late May to late September. The trips are three to five hours long and run throughout the day. If you want something a bit more adrenaline inducing, try white water rafting with one of the local Jackson Hole outfitters, like Teton Whitewater.

## Gateway Town: Jackson, Wyoming

Jackson is just a short drive south of Grand Teton National Park, and you don't want to miss visiting this legendary resort town. The town square has arches of antler sheds that are Instagram-worthy, plus it hosts a vibrant farmers market on the weekends. The downtown art galleries and boutiques make for great window shopping even if your souvenir budget is tight. The National Museum of Wildlife Art features work from Georgia O'Keefe, John James Audubon, Andy Warhol, and other well-known artists. And the local restaurant scene offers something for every palette and every budget—Snake River Brewing, Gather, and Cultivate café are a few favorites.

# Bryce Canyon National Park & Capitol Reef National Park

As with all the mighty five national parks in Utah, Bryce Canyon and Capitol Reef have been impacted by surging numbers of visitors over the last decade. However, these parks still do see fewer guests than parks like Arches and Zion, so many folks claim to enjoy their time here even more than at the more popular Utah locations. Since it is a short two-hour drive between the parks, it's easy to find a centrally located base camp and day trip into each one. Other campers choose to stay near one and drive to the other for a day or two. A third option is to spend just two or three nights in both parks, enjoying the short—and shockingly beautiful—drive between campgrounds.

May through September are the most popular months to visit these parks in southern Utah when the daytime temperatures are warm and the nights are cool. There are also more programs and activities available during this peak tourism window. April and late September can be great opportunities to enjoy lovely weather with fewer crowds if that is a priority. Note that both Bryce Canyon and Capitol Reef are open year-round, and visitors enjoy snowshoeing on the trails and viewing the stunning display of white snow against the vibrant, red rock hoodoos in the winter. Some of the campgrounds featured in this chapter—such as North Campground in Bryce Canyon and Fruita Campground in Capitol Reef—are also open year-round and would make great base camps for an adventurous winter camping trip.

# CAMPGROUNDS INSIDE THE PARKS

## North Campground

▷ Bryce Canyon City, Utah

▷ nps.gov

▷ RV and Tent Sites

North Campground is far from the prettiest or best maintained national park campground in Utah, but it is still your best option for camping inside of Bryce Canyon National Park because of its terrific location across the road from the visitor center. Your exploration of Bryce Canyon National Park can start right from your campsite, and there is little need to drive your car around in the park once you are settled in here. Incredible views on the Rim Trail are just steps away, and that is just one spectacular hike out of many that are nearby. You can even walk to the general store for supplies if you are feeling energetic. The sites in loops A and B are paved and are primarily for RVs, though tent campers can reserve sites here. The sites in loops C and D are not paved and are for tent campers only. The sites here are shaded and most are fairly large. But some are not level—so bring leveling blocks if you are an RV owner. The campground does get crowded in the summer and cars driving through can kick up a lot of dust, so plan on spending your days exploring the park and not hanging out at your site.

## Sunset Campground

▷ **Bryce Canyon City, Utah**

▷ **nps.gov**

▷ **RV and Tent Sites**

The sites at Sunset Campground offer more privacy and shade than those at North Campground, but generally speaking they are a bit smaller and tighter to navigate. Sunset is a great option if you can't get into North Campground, but most campers will prefer the proximity to the visitor center and general store that North offers. Amazing hiking trails surround both campgrounds, and you can pick up a park shuttle at either location.

## Fruita Campground

▷ **Torrey, Utah**

▷ **nps.gov**

▷ **RV and Tent Sites**

Fruita Campground is the only developed campground in Capitol Reef National Park, and it is an absolute gem. Campers can pick fresh fruit from historic orchards during the day when park rangers and staffers put up "U-Pick" signs—and at night, the stargazing is spectacular. This campground is small with only seventy-one sites, but every inch is lush and lovely, making it feel like a little camping oasis for those who are lucky enough to grab a site.

# CAMPGROUNDS OUTSIDE THE PARKS

## Singletree Campground

▷ Near Torrey, Utah

▷ fs.usda.gov

▷ RV and Tent Sites

Singletree Campground is a bit of a hidden gem in Fishlake National Forest. There are only thirty-one sites here, but some of them can accommodate larger RVs. The campground sits at a high elevation, providing much cooler temperatures than those in nearby Capitol Reef National Park. The campsites here are lovely, and there is a lot of wide-open space for roaming around and exploring. Ponderosa pine and aspen trees provide some shade, and the views of Capitol Reef are magical. A small creek runs right past some of the sites, and several family-friendly hikes start right from the campground. There are no hookups at the sites (no surprise in a NPS campground), but clean toilets are available, along with drinking water and a dump station for RVs. This is one of the best campgrounds in any of our national forests. If you want to visit Capitol Reef in the summer and stay cool and comfortable, this is where you should camp next.

## Ruby's Inn RV Park and Campground

▷ Bryce Canyon, Utah

▷ brycecanyoncampgrounds.com

▷ RV and Tent Sites, Cabin and Tipi Rentals

Ruby's Inn RV Park and Campground scores huge points for providing full hook-up sites and convenient amenities right up the road from the main entrance to Bryce Canyon National Park. The RV sites are not huge, but who is traveling to Bryce to hang out at the campground all day, anyway? The tent camping sites here are excellent. They offer shade, some privacy, and a good amount of space in between sites. Cabin and tipi rentals are clean but sparse—so make sure you bring your own bedding and creature comforts. ATV rentals are available, and campers have access to the pool and hot tub at the inn.

## Under Canvas Bryce Canyon

▷ **Widstoe, Utah**

▷ **undercanvas.com**

▷ **Glamping Tents**

Brand new in 2022, Under Canvas's fourth property in Utah is in an epic location with views of red rocks all around. Bryce Canyon National Park is also just fifteen minutes away. If you are looking for a romantic getaway, then book the Stargazer Tent with a large window over the bed for viewing the night sky. If you are traveling with a family, then book the Hoodoo Suite with a private deck and firepit that connects mom and dad's luxurious sleeping and lounge area with a separate kids tent with twin beds. Both of those accommodations come with a full private bath stocked with organic bath products, of course!

# Utah Scenic Byway 12

In between Bryce Canyon National Park and Capitol Reef National Park lies the 124-mile Scenic Byway 12 that routinely gets hailed as one of America's most beautiful drives. Here are some must-see stops along the route.

## Red Canyon

Here you'll see about 4 miles of striking geographical features formed from erosion. If you have your bikes, Thunder Mountain Trail is a popular 5-mile path. Stop in at the Red Canyon Visitor Center for interpretive exhibits. Snap pictures of the red rocks juxtaposed against the green pines.

## Dixie National Forest

Scenic Byway 12 enters and exits the national forest a few times along the drive. Stop at Blue Bell Knoll on Boulder Mountain, the highest point on the scenic route.

## Grand Staircase-Escalante National Monument

This 1.9-million-acre national monument is one of the largest pieces of publicly managed land in the continental United States. Stop in at the visitor center to learn more about the history of dinosaurs and humans in the region.

## Kodachrome Basin State Park

Hike the 2.9-mile Panorama Trail and see the upright cylinders called sand pipes, some stretching as high as 170 feet in the air.

## Head of the Rock Overlook

At this stop you can get a bird's-eye view of the Escalante Canyons and see Boulder Mountain in the distance.

## Homestead Overlook

This stop provides a view of the five peaks of the Henry Mountains.

# Arches National Park & Canyonlands National Park

Located in southeastern Utah, Arches and Canyonlands National Parks are under an hour's drive from one another, but Arches is much smaller and more accessible and welcomes almost double the visitors each year. The gateway town of Moab is just 5 miles away from the entrance to Arches, so many campers may choose to pick a base camp near there and then day trip into the most accessible area of Canyonlands—Island in the Sky.

If you want to explore both of these parks more fully, then choose a base camp near Arches and then one inside of Canyonlands. Folks looking for a more remote camping experience can explore all the backcountry camping options available in the over 300,000-acre park. Understand that Canyonlands offers some of the most remote and rugged national park experiences in the country, so preparation and good survival skills are key if venturing beyond the more accessible visitor center areas.

It can be scorching hot in the summer months with daytime temperatures above 100°F, so if you can visit in spring or fall, you will most likely enjoy the experience much more. Moab is a hub for adventure outfitters, so if you've been wanting to try river rafting, off-roading, rock climbing, or mountain biking, this is the place to do it.

# CAMPGROUNDS INSIDE THE PARKS

### Devil's Garden

- ▷ Moab, Utah
- ▷ nps.gov
- ▷ RV and Tent Sites

Devil's Garden is the only campground in Arches National Park, and it is spectacular. It has no hookups, no activities, and no amenities, but its wild beauty and its location in one of our most iconic national parks more than make up for its lack of services. The views of the slickrock outcroppings give this campground an otherworldly look, and there is direct access to bouldering and rock scrambling just steps away from the campground. The rock formations within the campground are also endlessly interesting, and there is plenty to explore right by your site. Most RV owners like the back-in sites better than the pull-off sites, so book one if you can. Several amazing hikes are nearby. Strap on your hiking boots and head to the Sand Dune Arch to Broken Arch Loop Trail for a relatively short hike that you will never forget.

## The Needles Campground

- ▷ San Juan County, Utah
- ▷ nps.gov
- ▷ RV and Tent Sites

The Needles Campground is the larger of the two campgrounds located in Canyonlands National Park—but it still only offers twenty-six sites and three group sites. The sites here are large and level, and many of them offer a fair amount of shade on those hot summer days. There are also cool rock formations on or near most of the sites, which make Needles feel like a natural playground for those who love to explore. If you are looking for solitude and awe-inspiring beauty, then this is your place. The location on the east side of the park is quiet, peaceful, and wonderful.

## Island in the Sky (Willow Flat) Campground

▷　San Juan County, Utah

▷　nps.gov

▷　RV and Tent Sites

Located in the Northern district of Canyonlands National Park, Island in the Sky campground (a.k.a. Willow Flats) is aptly named. If you can manage to grab one of the twelve sites here, you will feel like you are camping among the clouds, especially if you head over to the Green River Overlook, which is close by. The sites here are large and have some shade and natural desert-like landscaping that makes them semiprivate and entirely beautiful. Rustic sun shelters are also provided at each site, and water is available outside of the visitor center during part of the year depending on weather.

# CAMPGROUNDS OUTSIDE THE PARKS

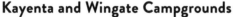

## Kayenta and Wingate Campgrounds

▷　Moab, Utah

▷　stateparks.utah.gov

▷　RV and Tent Sites, Yurt Rentals

These two campgrounds at Dead Horse Point State Park are among the most desirable in the entire Utah State Park system. Why? Because this state park is drop-dead gorgeous and a destination in its own right, and it is located about fifteen minutes from Canyonlands and forty minutes from Arches. Kayenta Campground has twenty-one superb campsites, and each of them comes with a sun shelter, tent pads, and electrical hookups for RVs. Spectacular hiking starts right from the campground. The East Rim Trail leads to the popular and oft-photographed Dead Horse Point Overlook. The West Rim Trail is more rugged but also boasts breathtaking views.

Wingate Campground was built in 2018 and offers thirty-one excellent campsites. Twenty of those sites have electrical hookups for RVs. These sites can also accommodate big rigs. Each site also has a sun shelter with a picnic table underneath that makes eating outside much more comfortable in the summer heat. The roads here are paved and easy to navigate, both for RV owners on big rigs and kids on bikes. Spacious and well-equipped yurt rentals are also available at Wingate—just make sure to bring your own bedding. As you can imagine, Kayenta and Wingate are both incredibly popular, so booking sites is difficult at both. Get up early on the morning sites become available and pray to the camping gods for help. Divine interventions may be required to get a site.

## ACT Campground

▷ Moab, Utah

▷ actcampground.com

▷ RV and Tent Sites, Yurt Rental, Room Rentals

The ACT Campground has more in common with the holiday parks of New Zealand than the typical private campgrounds in America. ACT offers a robust community kitchen where guests can cook meals, relax, and socialize with other campers. Those with large RVs may not find the appeal, but van lifers and those in tiny trailers will appreciate the usable kitchen space. The community center was built using environmentally friendly materials, and solar power is used throughout the property. The location in between Arches and Canyonlands is very good, and the mountain views from the campsites are excellent. There is road noise here—so tent campers be forewarned. Those in self-enclosed RVs will be fine.

# Sun Outdoors Arches Gateway

▷ Moab, Utah

▷ sunrvresorts.com

▷ RV and Tent Sites, Cabin Rentals, Airstream Rentals

Clean as a whistle and cute as a button, the Moab Valley RV Resort wins points for its proximity to Arches National Park (it's less than 3 miles away) and its friendly and helpful customer service. The red rock mountains of the Moab Valley surround the campground and provide views from every site. The pool and the hot tub are nice after a long day of hiking in the park, and the bicycle wash and repair station is absolutely clutch for those who love to mountain bike.

## ──────── Five Great Hikes in Arches National Park ────────

**Balanced Rock**

Easy 0.3-mile loop trail with fantastic views of one of the most iconic rock features in Arches National Park.

**Double Arch**

Easy 0.6-mile out-and-back hike leading to a rock scramble at the end that takes hikers to the base of the arches.

**Sand Dune Arch**

Easy 0.3-mile out-and-back trail with lots of sand and small rock scrambles along the way.

**Delicate Arch Trail**

Moderate 3.2-mile out-and-back trail brings you to the famous arch featured on Utah's license plates. The rock colors come alive in the morning and evening hours.

**Fiery Furnace**

Strenuous ranger-led hike, this 2-mile hike requires a permit, and children five years old and under are not allowed on the trail.

# Districts of Canyonlands National Park

Canyonlands National Park is divided into five districts. Here are some high-lights in each one.

## Island in the Sky

If you are driving through Canyonlands—or have just one day to explore—you'll probably want to spend your time in this district. Head to the visitor center and take in one of the best views in the park from the overlook there. Take in the view of Mountain Basin from Grand View Point. Pick one of the many trails to hike, from easy to strenuous. Favorites include Mesa Arch (easy, 0.5 mile), Upheaval Dome (moderate, 1 mile), and Gooseberry Canyon (strenuous, 5.4 miles).

## The Needles

It takes a bit of time and effort to get to the Needles district, but that means visitors are rewarded with fewer crowds and a shockingly beautiful, remote landscape. The Visitor Center is about 75 miles from Moab. Sandstone spires are what are referred to as the "needles," and many of the trails in this district wind through these towers of rock. Hike the Roadside Ruin Trail (easy, 0.3 mile), Pothill Point (moderate, 0.6 mile), and Cave Spring (moderate, 0.6 mile).

## Horseshoe Canyon Unit

This district features some of the most well-preserved rock art in the United States, and most visitors will want to see the Great Gallery featuring life-size figures on rock panels. This will require a 7-mile roundtrip hike that takes on average more than five hours. Park officials warn folks about extreme heat in the summer months and always bringing at least one gallon of water per person. The best bet may be taking one of the ranger-led hikes to the Great Gallery that are available in the spring and fall.

## The Rivers

The Colorado and Green Rivers have formed much of the landscape of this national park, but they are now largely hidden and difficult to access from the most visited areas of the park. The best way to experience the rivers is on a guided rafting trip. The NPS has a list of authorized concessionaires that run river trips from one to seven days in length.

## The Maze

This district is remote and only accessible by 4x4 vehicles. If you tow a Jeep behind your RV, or are into overlanding, don't miss the opportunity to explore The Maze. This type of adventure requires planning and backcountry expertise, so do your research in advance.

Zion
National Park

About a decade ago, Utah's tourism board launched The Mighty Five marketing campaign in an effort to advertise the wonders of the state's underappreciated national parks. The campaign perhaps worked a little too well, and now millions of visitors are flocking to these destinations every year. Zion's annual number of guests has jumped more than 60 percent over the last ten years.

The influx of tourists has strained park resources, and Zion has been experimenting with ways to manage crowds for the past few years with the expansion of shuttle services and permitting, along with testing timed-entry passes. All of this to say—if you go during peak summer months, expect crowds. And if you wish to avoid the crowds, visit during the shoulder seasons.

If visiting in the spring, summer, or fall, reservations are a must, whether camping in or outside of the park. Campgrounds in the park will immerse you in the wonder and beauty of Zion's breathtaking scenery. Campgrounds outside of the park will offer electric hookups for RV air conditioning and a

pool to cool off in after long hikes. Some campers spend a few nights rough-ing it inside the park, then move to a resort campground to enjoy more comfortable accommodations.

Wherever you are staying, research the shuttle system, permits, and temporary alerts and closures in advance of your arrival. Planning ahead is one of the best ways to have a successful visit to one of the most popular national parks in the country.

# CAMPGROUNDS INSIDE THE PARK

### South Campground

▷  Virgin, Utah

▷  nps.gov

▷  RV and Tent Sites

Many seasoned Zion National Park campers love Watchman Campground more than South Campground because it is quieter and perhaps even more beautiful. But South Campground earns our top pick because you can walk to the shuttle and Zion Canyon Visitor Center and not have to worry about snagging a parking spot. Considering the overcrowding issues that Zion is facing, this convenience is no small thing. Many of the sites at South Campground are partially shaded, and many of the tent sites are rocky, so you may have to do a little maneuvering to get set up. Most of the sites have great views, but a few are almost completely surrounded by trees. But don't fret if you get one of these sites—spectacular canyon wall views are probably just steps away. The crystal clear Virgin River runs along the outer edge of the campground, so if you can book a site along its banks, then you certainly should. After a hot day of hiking, you can cool off right here before making dinner at your site.

## Watchman Campground

▷ Springdale, Utah

▷ nps.gov

▷ RV and Tent Sites

Beautiful canyon and mountain views abound as the Virgin River rolls by this delightful NPS campground. There are, quite literally, epic views from every single site. The location inside the park is also excellent, and the visitor center and Zion Canyon shuttle stop are within walking distance. Generators are not allowed, but loops A and B have electric sites. The B loop has gorgeous river view sites. Good luck trying to book there—they are in high demand.

## Lava Point Campground

▷ Springdale, Utah

▷ nps.gov

▷ Tent Sites

Lava Point Campground only has six primitive camping sites, and its location, at the top of Zion National Park, is pretty far off the beaten track. No vehicles over 19 feet are allowed, but the campground and location are beautiful for those who want to get away from it all. You can walk to the Lava Point Overlook from the campground and take in spectacular views of the park with few others around.

# CAMPGROUNDS OUTSIDE THE PARK

### Zion River Resort

▷   Virgin, Utah

▷   zionriverresort.com

▷   RV and Tent Sites, Cabins and Two-Bedroom Suites

Zion River Resort may be the nicest resort-style campground in all of Utah. Unlike some private RV resorts that can look like parking lots, this one is absolutely beautiful in every way. The Virgin River runs alongside the campground, and you can hear it from many of the sites, though views can be somewhat limited due to a protective berm. But mountain views encircle the campground, and the sight of red rock and blue skies will fill your heart with joy. The amenities here are also excellent. The heated pool and hot tub are excellent for a relaxing post-hike dip, and the communal camp kitchen with charcoal grills is a great place to stretch your legs and meet your neighbors. There is also a spa for guests who are fourteen years old and up. During the spring and summer months, the on-site take-out grill offers up hot and cold sandwiches, salads, and ice cream. The resort also offers a fourteen-person shuttle bus that will, for a fee, drop you off and pick you up directly in front of the entrance to Zion. This service could be clutch for those renting motor homes and traveling without a car.

## Under Canvas Zion

▷   Virgin, Utah

▷   undercanvas.com

▷   Glamping Tents

Under Canvas Zion offers one of the most stunning and magnificent glamping experiences in our entire country. When it comes to glamping, Under Canvas is not just dialed in, it is a trendsetter and industry leader in the outdoor hospitality category—and this is one of its best properties. The red, pink, tan, and green colors from the surrounding canyon walls are spectacular and make guests feel like they are camping inside the national park, even though they are outside of its boundaries. Start your day with a delicious cup of coffee in the main tent, and then grab a yoga mat for a morning session that will refresh your spirit. When you get back from exploring the park in the evening, expect live music under the stars and s'mores around a community campfire. Before you drift off to sleep, take a hot shower in your tent and light the wood-burning stove so you stay warm and cozy all night long.

## Zion Canyon Campground

▷ Springdale, Utah

▷ zioncamp.com

▷ RV and Tent Sites

This family-owned campground is an excellent option for RV owners who want to camp close (really, really close!) to the park with full hook-up sites or for tent campers who cannot get a site inside of the park. The views are gorgeous, and the customer service is friendly and knowledgeable. Most sites are also shaded by lovely trees. Riverside sites are the best, and they only cost a few bucks more, so grab one if you can. The only downside here is that many of the sites are small and packed together somewhat tightly. But the prices are reasonable, so don't hesitate to make this your base camp for an epic Zion National Park adventure.

# A Quick Guide to Zion National Park

## When to Go
Zion National Park is open year-round. April through October are the busiest months. Spring and fall are the best times to visit if looking to avoid high temperatures. However, if you visit in the spring, the famous Narrows Hike may not be open on account of high water levels.

## Before You Go
Read: *The Complete Guide to National Parks of the West* and *Utah's Big Five National Parks: Adventuring with Kids*, both by Fodor's Travel.

## Where to Stock Up
▷ **Springdale:** This small town is just outside the south entrance and has groceries, camping supplies, and dining options.
▷ **Virgin:** A bit farther afield, this town has lots of outfitter options for biking, tubing, horseback riding, and other outdoor adventures.

## How to Get Around
Zion is notoriously crowded during the summer months, and it is wise to make use of the park shuttle during your visit. The shuttle runs to all the major park attractions and has stops in Springdale. When the shuttle is running, visitors may not drive their own vehicles on Zion Canyon Scenic Drive.

## First Stop: Visitor Center
Weather conditions are always changing in Zion, so stop at the visitor center to check on trail closures, water flow, and rockslide updates. You can also pick up a Junior Ranger packet for the kids there.

## Permits and Reservations
In an effort to manage the growing number of visitors who arrive at this park every year, the park service is always expanding and experimenting

with its permits and reservations system. Check the national park website for up-to-date information on what is required. If a hike requires a permit, you will need to apply for the lottery drawing in advance and then print or download the permit before arriving in the park.

## Biking

If you bring your bikes camping, enjoy the Pa'rus Trail bike path that starts at the visitor center and runs along the Virgin River. You can also rent bikes from Zion Outfitter—right outside the pedestrian entrance to the park—and cycle in. E-bike rentals are now available as well.

## Hiking

### Angels Landing

One of the most notorious hikes in the park, this trail features a series of switchbacks before leading you high up to a narrow ridge of rocks. The narrow trail offers only a chain to help you stay anchored on the steep incline. This hike is not for the faint of heart, and currently requires a permit.

### The Narrows

Another one of the most popular hikes, the Narrows takes you through Zion Canyon where the rim walls rise over 1,000 feet above the ground. Flash flooding is an ever-present danger on this hike, so consult rangers before heading out.

## Riverside Walk

This 1-mile paved, accessible trail runs along the edge of the river and offers a taste of the Narrows without the potential danger.

## Canyon Overlook Trail

This hike is another 1-mile roundtrip hike that gives visitors great views without a whole lot of strenuous labor.

## Watchman Trail

A relatively easy 3.3-mile roundtrip, this trail is located near the Zion Canyon Visitor Center and is easily accessible from the Watchman Campground.

# Great Sand Dunes National Park & Preserve

The Great Sand Dunes are the largest dunes in North America, and although this park gets overshadowed by the Rockies a few hours away, visitors often rank it as one of their favorite national park experiences. It's also particularly kid friendly, offering opportunities to sled down enormous sand dunes and cool off by tubing in the waters of Medano Creek. This national park also offers up the rare beautiful *and* well-maintained national park campground, but it's not large so you'll have to plan in advance if you want to snag a spot.

May through June is often considered the best time to visit since the Medano Creek is usually running at its peak annual height and the heat and frequent thunderstorms of July and August have not yet arrived. Of course, this is when the park is most crowded as well. Early fall is also a favorite for temperate weather and fewer crowds. The park is open through the winter, but it is cold and snowy, so come prepared.

# CAMPGROUNDS INSIDE THE PARK

## Piñon Flats Campground

▷   Mosca, Colorado

▷   nps.gov

▷   RV and Tent Sites

Piñon Flats Campground is an absolute gem of a campground just steps away from the Great Sand Dunes. This is one of the best pairings of a national park campground and a national park in the entire country. Almost every site at Piñon Flats is delightful, with great views of the snow-capped Sangre de Cristo Mountains and the nearby dune fields. Piñon trees and sagebrush provide some shade and landscaping, and the overall look of the campground is enchanting and otherworldly. There are only eighty-eight sites here, and they are always booked solid when the Medano Creek is flowing through the Great Sand Dunes in late May and early June—so if you want to visit during that time, you will need to book when sites become available six months earlier, or find a campsite outside of the park. High winds can be problematic here, so stake up your tent tightly, and keep the RV awnings in if you can. Other than that be prepared for a magical camping experience under night skies filled with stars.

---------- **The Night Sky at Great Sand Dune** ----------

This is a certified International Dark Sky Park, and much of what makes this destination so special can only be seen after the sun goes down. There are two completely opposite recommendations for walking the dunes at night—planning a moon-free visit and planning a full moon visit. Both are equally special and different ways of enjoying the magic of a dark sky location. A moonless night will allow the Milky Way to put on its best show. A full moon reflecting off the sand creates an otherworldly experience. Use a tool like sunrisesunset.com—which allows you to filter by national park—to find the perfect time to visit for your preferred adventure. Also make sure to check out an evening ranger program to learn more about the dark skies.

# CAMPGROUNDS OUTSIDE THE PARK

## Zapata Falls Campground

▷ Bureau of Land Management Special Recreation Management Area

▷ Mosca, Colorado

▷ fs.usda.gov

▷ RV and Tent Sites

The road into Zapata Falls Campground is a bit rough, but once you arrive the views of the dunes and the surrounding mountains are magnificent. The campground, which is 7 miles from Great Sand Dunes National Park, is operated by the Bureau of Land Management and is something of a hidden gem. The landscape here on the Sangre De Cristo Mountain Range is a bit harsh, but some sites do have shade and a bit of tree cover—and they are all spaced far apart, so you won't have neighbors nearby. There are only twenty-three sites here altogether, which is quite remarkable considering the size of this campground. The first loop is for tent campers only, and the second loop can accommodate RV configurations about 50 feet long. There is no dump station here, so plan on dumping your tanks at one of the local gas stations with services. The hike to Zapata Falls is short and challenging— but worth every step!

## ------------ Bring Fido (but Watch His Paws) ------------

Great Sand Dunes is incredibly pet friendly, and dogs are permitted in all of the preserve and most of the main areas of the park. However, during the summer months sand temperatures can reach up to 150°F during the day, so it is extremely important to protect your furry friend's paws. Bring plenty of water for your pups when out exploring, and watch for the prickly pear cactus spines in the desert grasslands surrounding the dunes.

# Great Sand Dunes Oasis

▷ Mosca, Colorado

▷ greatdunes.com

▷ RV and Tent Sites, Cabins

If you can't find a site at Piñon Flats or Zapata Falls, or you just prefer to camp with full hookups, then Great Sand Dunes Oasis is a solid option. The views are good, the sites are level, and the camp store serves breakfast, lunch, and dinner. Great Sand Dunes National Park is just a short drive away. Pets are allowed at individual campsites, but not in the cabin rentals.

## - Top Tips for Visiting Great Sand Dunes National Park -

1. Hike the dunes in the morning before the sand gets too hot during the summer months.

2. Rent the right equipment for sandboarding and sand sledding. Don't bother trying your snow gear. The ones made for sand have an extra slick base and special wax. Splurge on the fee.

3. Cool off in Medano Creek during the warmest parts of the day. If you are lucky, you'll experience the mysterious "surge flow."

4. This is a designated International Dark Sky Park, so make sure to catch one of the many night sky programs.

5. Pick up a Junior Ranger program booklet when you first arrive. This is an amazing national park for kids!

## Pedal It!

Road and mountain bikes won't do you much good in this national park, but fat bikes—with extra wide tires to navigate the sand—are permitted on Medano Pass Primitive Road, which traverses dunes and crosses the Medano Creek nine times. Feeling extra adventurous? Bring your tent gear and camp overnight at one of the free, first-come, first-served designated campsites in the national preserve.

## What Is Surge Flow?

The elements have to align just right for surge flow to occur, and Medano Creek is one of the few places in the world where it happens, with the stream creating rhythmic waves as it flows. There's a video on the Great Dunes park website explaining the science behind the rare phenomena. The creek changes drastically in depth and width throughout the year, with May and June seeing the highest water levels—and the highest number of visitors.

## Hiking Star Dune

Currently tied with Hidden Dune as one of the two tallest dunes in North America at 741 feet tall, a roundtrip hike to the summit and back is 6 miles. The sand and elevation make this a much different experience than hiking a typical trail—the park service recommends planning for six to nine hours to complete the hike and bringing plenty of water. It's an arduous climb, so think carefully about whether you are up for taking on the challenge. You may be better off just appreciating the view of the dune from the cool Medano Creek waters at the base.

## Side Trip: Zapata Falls Recreation Area

Just 5 miles south of Great Sand Dunes National Park & Preserve, Zapata Falls is located on Bureau of Land Management land. The main attraction is a 30-foot waterfall just a half-mile hike from the parking area with some fun rock scrambling. There is also a Bureau of Land Management campground here (see Zapata Falls Campground profile on page 251).

# Rocky Mountain National Park

Rocky Mountain National Park, like other parks near metropolitan areas, brings millions of visitors every year to experience stunning mountain views, alpine lakes, and wildlife spotting. Straddling the Continental Divide, it's one of the highest national parks, with altitudes over 12,000 feet. First-time visitors can avoid crippling altitude sickness by drinking ridiculous amounts of water, avoiding alcohol, and taking a day or two to acclimate before heading up the Trail Ridge Road to the highest parts of the park.

Although the park is open year-round, many of the most popular areas and attractions in the park are only accessible from late spring to mid-fall. If you want to avoid the stifling summer crowds, visit in September. An extra bonus of visiting in the fall is the golden aspen foliage that spreads across the mountains. If you are only able to visit during peak summer months, aim for the weekdays to avoid the Denver weekend crowds.

The most beautiful camping options here are inside the park, but they are also the popular options, so planning ahead is critical. Most, but not all, of the park campgrounds allow reservations up to six months in advance. They fill up immediately during July and August. If you need hookups, or can't nab a campsite in the park, know that the best of the private campground options tend to be a bit pricey for the amenities offered. Understand this is valuable real estate and the camping season is short, so that's just the economics campers are dealing with here. Make sure your expectations are in line.

# CAMPGROUNDS INSIDE THE PARK

### Moraine Park Campground

▷ **Estes Park, Colorado**

▷ **nps.gov**

▷ **RV and Tent Sites**

Many of the sites at Moraine Park Campground (which sits at an elevation of 8,160 ft) have stunning views of snow-capped mountains that defy description. With almost 250 sites, this is the largest campground inside of Rocky Mountain National Park, but sadly it is still incredibly difficult to book in the summer months. Those who can score a coveted site have a very good chance of spotting elk, mule deer, and wild turkeys wandering through the campground—so have your camera ready but keep a safe distance and follow all park safety guidelines for wildlife encounters. There are some absolutely magical tent sites nestled into the woods here, and there are also some sites that can accommodate RVs up to 40 feet, so Moraine makes many of its visitors happy campers—no matter how they choose to camp. Access to the park's shuttle system is close to the campground—and you should plan on using it if you want to do a popular hike like Bear Lake, where the trailhead parking lot fills up very early. Trailheads for Cub Lake and Fern Lake are also close to the campground, and both hikes are beautiful. Ambitious hikers can visit both lakes on the same day. Just remember to bring lots of water and bear spray.

## Glacier Basin Campground

- ▷ Estes Park, Colorado
- ▷ nps.gov
- ▷ RV and Tent Sites

Glacier Basin Campground is a terrific second choice if you can't get a site at Moraine. The campsites here are lovely, and most are shaded and semiprivate thanks to rows and rows of lovely Lodgepole and Ponderosa Pines. The maximum length for RVs here is 35 feet, and most of the RV sites are easy to navigate. And much like Moraine, tent camping is delightful. Sadly, some sections of the campground have had their tall trees removed because of the Pine Beetle epidemic. Because of this, mountain views have opened up in certain sections of the campground. Glacier Basin is peaceful and relaxing and restorative to the soul. When first-time campers score a site here (or anywhere else inside the park for that matter) they often fall deeply in love and spend the rest of their lives trying to come back.

## Timber Creek Campground

- ▷ Grand Lake, Colorado
- ▷ nps.gov
- ▷ RV and Tent Sites

Timber Creek Campground is the only NPS campground on the west side of the park, and it is worth recommending for that reason alone. The location is quiet and beautiful, but there is little to no shade due to the removal of all of the trees here caused by the Pine Beetle infestation in this section of the park. This has opened up mountain views in every direction—but who wouldn't prefer a campground filled with healthy full-sized trees? Timber Creek and the entire west side of the park are well worth visiting. Excellent trailheads are less crowded, and Grand Lake (which is 20 minutes away from Timber Creek) is absolutely stunning. Grab a house-made beer and a Jumbo Bavarian Pretzel at the World's End Brewpub after a long hike in the park.

Relaxing at this delightful brewery is the perfect way to end a day on the west side of the park.

## Other Campgrounds Inside the Park

-⤙⤙ **Aspenglen Campground**
-⤙⤙ **Longs Peak Campground**

# CAMPGROUNDS OUTSIDE THE PARK

### Jellystone of Estes

▷   **Estes Park, Colorado**

▷   **jellystoneofestes.com**

▷   **RV and Tent Sites, Cabins and RV Rentals**

If you want to experience a Rocky Mountains National Park adventure and have full hook-ups and plenty of fun amenities and activities for the kids back at the campground, then Jellystone of Estes is an obvious choice. This Jellystone Park is nestled among the Colorado Rockies and the Roosevelt National Forest and has panoramic views of the surrounding mountains. Proximity to the gateway town of Estes Park is also really good—you can be there in about ten minutes. The cabins here are excellent, and many of the sites are too—but big rigs should call ahead and make sure that they get one that is suitable. The campground is built along the side of a mountain, and some sites are steep and difficult to back into. After spending the morning hiking and exploring in the national park ,the kids will love coming back here and going for a swim or playing a round of mini-golf. Organized activities like craft time, karaoke, and dance parties are also abundant here, particularly during the high summer months and weekends.

## Estes Park KOA Holiday

▷ Estes Park, Colorado

▷ koa.com

▷ RV and Tent Sites, Cabins

This KOA has some major benefits, and a couple of significant drawbacks. The location's proximity to Rocky Mountain National Park is excellent—the Estes Park entrance is just five minutes away. But it is located right next to Route 34, which makes the campground noisy—tent campers and those in RVs with canvas siding may want to look elsewhere. Many of the sites are also small and cramped—so those in larger rigs, or those who dislike camping close to their neighbors, might want to think twice before booking. But for those who can get past the noise and smallish sites, the views of the Rocky Mountains are stunning, and the customer service is friendly and knowledgeable. It is tough to find a magical site anywhere outside of Rocky Mountain National Park, and it is extremely difficult to book one of the many magical sites inside the park. So despite its flaws, we find this KOA to be a very good option for many campers.

## Sun Outdoors Rocky Mountains

▷ Granby, Colorado

▷ sunoutdoors.com

▷ RV and Tent Sites, Airstream Rentals, Conestoga Wagons, Cabins, Lofts, Lodges

Sun Outdoors Rocky Mountains (formerly River Run RV Resort) offers a true RV resort experience on the west side of the National Park, about 20 minutes away from the gateway town of Grand Lake. This delightfully luxurious campground has a terrific pool and hot tubs, live music in the evenings, and even a mini bowling alley for the kids, but it is certainly not the closest campground to the park. If you want proximity, look elsewhere. If you want an unforgettable glamping experience and don't mind a short commute into the quiet side of Rocky Mountain National Park, then welcome home. This will be your happy place.

# Quick Guide to Rocky Mountain National Park

## When to Go

Summer and fall are the best—and most crowded—times to visit. Trail Ridge Road, the crown jewel of the park, is usually open from mid-May to late October, depending on snow accumulation. Visit during the week, if possible, to avoid the weekend crowds from nearby Denver.

## Before You Go

Read *Moon Rocky National Park Travel Guide* and stay up to date on ever-changing timed entry requirements.

## East or West Side?

The east side of the park is known to have better mountain views and more popular hikes and attractions. It's also closer to Estes Park, where many visitors choose to spend the majority of their time when not in the national park. The west side is quieter and known for better wildlife viewing. If you are determined to see moose, the west side is where it's at.

## Where to Stock Up

Estes Park: one of the more popular national park gateway towns, Estes Park has everything you need for any of your Rocky Mountain Adventures. The small city is full of great shopping, restaurants, wineries, breweries, and outfitters.

Grand Lake: the gateway town for the west side of the Rockies, Grand Lake is quiet and charming, but still has a larger grocery store, plus a handful of small, local food markets.

## Permits and Reservations

As with many of our most visited national parks, Rocky Mountain National Park has been experimenting with timed-entry tickets as a way to manage crowds. These are changing every season, so stay up to date on current policies in advance of your arrival.

## How to Get Around

The shuttle buses run from late May to early October, and it is wise to use them whenever possible to avoid extremely crowded and small parking lots at popular park attractions. There are no shuttle buses on the west side of the park or on Trail Ridge Road, so you'll have to drive that one yourself.

## Where to Eat

Many of the most famous national parks have a network of lodges that offer a variety of dining options. Not so at Rocky Mountain National Park. There are actually no lodges in the park and very few food service locations. Pack a cooler with food and beverages if staying in the park for the day. Otherwise, both Estes Park and Grand Lake have great restaurant options.

## Top Attractions

▷   Trail Ridge Road

This drive is 48 miles of beautiful vistas and awe-inspiring wildlife sightings. The road cuts from the east to the west of the park, rising above the tree line to over 12,000 feet at its highest elevation. Stop at Rainbow Curve, Forest Canyon Overlook, Alpine Visitor Center, Milner Pass, and Fairview Curve.

▷   Alpine Visitor Center

Located at the junction of Old Fall River Road and Trail Ridge Road, the visitor center is roughly halfway between the east and west ends of the drive, and there are rangers available for park information along with a gift shop and snack bar. Hike Alpine Ridge Trail while there.

▷   Old Fall River Road

This is the older, unpaved scenic drive in Rocky Mountain National Park, constructed in 1920. It's a one-lane gravel road with hairpin turns and switchbacks, and grades nearing 16 percent, so be prepared for a little white-knuckle driving. The road is one way uphill, so you'll return on Trail Ridge Road once you reach the junction at Alpine Visitor Center.

▷   Bear Lake Area

Take the shuttle to this area of the park because it fills up early in the morning and parking is near impossible during the summer months. Pack your hiking gear and plenty of water and snacks, and don't forget your binoculars for wildlife viewing. There's an interpretative 0.8-mile loop trail around the lake, and a ranger station on-site for more information about the variety of hikes in this area.

▷  Nymph/Dream/Emerald Lake Trail

This hike appears on many people's best of Rocky Mountain National Park lists, and many campers claim it's the showstopper of their park visit. The 3.2-mile hike is considered moderately challenging and starts at Bear Lake then leads hikers up to Nymph Lake, then Dream Lake, then Emerald Lake.

▷  Alberta Falls

See the falls by hiking the easy 1.8-mile out-and-back Glacier Gorge Trail located off Bear Lake Road.

Great Basin National Park is one of the least visited units in the National Park System with well under 200,000 visitors a year. Zion National Park and the Grand Canyon are in the general vicinity of Great Basin, and they are probably the reason why this park is so underrated. But we think that Great Basin National Park is pretty grand in its own right. This park has mountains (Wheeler Peak at 13,000 feet) and underground caves (Lehman Caves, by guided tour only) for above and below ground exploration. It also has groves of bristlecone pines and some of the darkest night skies in the country. Thankfully there are six campgrounds to choose from, and all of them are awesome. Four of the six campgrounds (Upper and Lower Lehman Creek, Wheeler Peak, and Grey Cliffs) require reservations from Memorial Day to Labor Day. Baker Creek Campground and Snake Creek Campground are first-come, first-served. These six campgrounds are each pretty small—if you come without a reservation on a weekend or during peak season, make sure you have a backup plan. Camping on BLM land outside the park may be your best bet if you cannot snag a site inside the park.

# CAMPGROUNDS INSIDE THE PARK

## Wheeler Peak Campground

▷ Baker, Nevada

▷ nps.gov

▷ RV and Tent Sites

Wheeler Peak Campground is yet another gem in the NPS system of campgrounds, and while it may get busy on summer weekends, it is surprising how few campers have heard of it. RVs under 25 feet are allowed in Wheeler, but the campground sits at an elevation of almost 10,000 feet, so make sure your truck or SUV can handle the drive up before going. The views of Wheeler Peak from the campground are awesome, and you can see it from some of the sites. There are several small streams that cut through the campground, so taking a stroll around and dipping your feet in them is an absolute delight—but the water is cold! The temperatures can also get downright chilly at night, even in the middle of the summer. So come prepared with extra layers and blankets. Wild deer often wander through the campground in the morning and evening hours, and other wildlife are also abundant here. The hiking around the campground is also excellent with some rigorous options for those who are more adventurous.

## Upper Lehman Creek Campground

▷ Baker, Nevada

▷ nps.gov

▷ RV and Tent Sites

Upper Lehman Creek Campground offers a classic camping experience that is much more down to earth than camping at Wheeler Peak. The smell of ponderosa pine and the sound of crystal clear mountain streams gurgling in the background make this another unforgettable camping experience in Great Basin National Park. There are only twenty-three sites here, and they must be reserved from late May until late September—so plan ahead if you want to grab one in season.

## Lower Lehman Creek Campground

▷  Baker, Nevada

▷  nps.gov

▷  RV and Tent Sites

Lower Lehman Creek Campground only offers eleven sites, but they are each lovely. Mountain views surround the campground, and the sound of the creek can be heard from every site. The sites are pull-off sites, so they are easy to navigate, but some are close to the road. The trees here provide lots of shade and smell lovely, and the campground is open all year. It is the only one in the park that is open year-round. Sites here are hard to book on summer weekends but more readily available during the fall and spring.

## Other Campgrounds Inside the Park

↦  **Baker Creek Campground**

↦  **Grey Cliffs Campground**

↦  **Snake Creek Campgrounds**

-------- **What Is an International Dark Sky Park?** --------

Great Basin National Park is one of 195 International Dark Sky Parks in the world. According to darksky.org, a Dark Sky Park is "a land possessing an exceptional or distinguished quality of starry nights." These parks are often on public land but can also be on private land if the owner agrees to grant the public permanent access.

## Astronomy Tours in the Park

During the peak summer season, the park offers two-hour astronomy talks three times per week. Check Great Basin's website for exact dates. The talks take place in the Astronomy Amphitheater, and you must park at the Lehman Caves Visitor Center. Space is limited, and when the parking lot fills the rangers stop admitting new attendees—so get there early! The talk is only about thirty minutes—during the next hour and a half visitors can take turns viewing the night sky with telescopes set up by the National Park Service.

## Lehman Caves Tours

Lehman Caves can only be entered by taking ranger-led tours, which are offered every day except for Thanksgiving, Christmas, and New Year's Day. The caves are crazy, creepy, and cool. Two tours are offered: the Gothic Palace Tour and Grand Palace Tour. Both sell out regularly, so get your tickets early.

Death Valley is full of superlatives—it is the driest, hottest, and lowest national park with elevations falling as low as 282 feet below sea level. It's also the largest national park in the continental United States, encompassing over 300 million acres of designated public land. The landscape of mountains, canyons, meadows, and valleys is as unbelievable as the climate. With a record high temperature of 134°F and a record low of 15°F, many species that thrive here do not exist anywhere else in the world.

Planning your visit and taking safety precautions is always important for a national park trip, but even more so when you are visiting such a remote, extreme environment. Many folks are not prepared for the lack of cell service—or other services for that matter—when venturing into the designated wilderness areas that make up 93 percent of the park. If you stay within the popular and more developed Furnace Creek area—with the visitor center, gas station, campground, and hotel—there isn't much to worry about. If you plan on exploring more remote areas, be smart and be safe.

One of the smartest things you can do is not visit during the long summer season, extending from May through October. The spring months of March and April offer wildflowers and warm, sunny days. The Death Valley Dark Sky Festival takes place in early spring, and the campgrounds and hotels are booked far in advance for this time of year. Fall and winter are also great opportunities for camping, and ranger programs run from November through April each year.

In this chapter, we only highlight camping options inside the park, because there are abundant and diverse camping options within the boundaries of Death Valley, and there is no reason to look outside at less compelling choices. Death Valley offers an incredibly unique range of campgrounds in the park, some run by NPS concessionaires and some run by private companies. You'll also find many options for mixed accommodations with campgrounds next to hotels. This is great for folks traveling in groups with non-campers.

# CAMPGROUNDS INSIDE THE PARK

### Furnace Creek Campground

▷ Furnace Creek, California

▷ nps.gov

▷ RV and Tent Sites

Furnace Creek Campground is base camp option number one for most tent campers and RV owners. The campground itself is not exactly beautiful, but it is surrounded by the stark beauty of Death Valley, and it is centrally located near the visitor center and many of the park's most popular spots. There are almost 140 sites here, and eighteen of them even have electrical hookups for RVs. These sites have no shade, but even so, they are very difficult to reserve. Many of the other sites are quite nice. They are large, level, easy to navigate, and have partial shade but little to no privacy. Dishwashing stations with drinking water are available and conveniently located for tent campers and

RV owners who are trying to conserve water. The stargazing is spectacular here, so plan on returning to your campsite at night and taking it all in. Early mornings are also gorgeous, so don't stay up too late! If you can't get a site here you can probably find one at Sunset Campground, which is basically an overflow parking lot right next door.

## Texas Springs Campground

▷ Furnace Creek, California

▷ nps.gov

▷ RV and Tent Sites

Texas Springs Campground is located near Furnace Creek at a slightly higher elevation, and it offers stunning views in a very quiet and tent-camper-friendly environment. Generators are not allowed here, so most RV owners prefer Furnace Creek. Restrooms and dishwashing stations are clean and charming and close to the campsites. There are great hiking options right near the campground. Just make sure you bring lots of water when temps are warm, even if you are not venturing far from your site.

## Stovepipe Wells RV Park and Stovepipe Wells Campground

▷ Death Valley, California

▷ deathvalleyhotels.com

▷ nps.gov

▷ RV Sites and Hotel Rooms at the RV Park, RV and Tent Sites at NPS Campground

At first glance, the fourteen full hook-up sites for RVs at Stovepipe Wells RV Park look like an afterthought thrown together next to a reasonably nice hotel, bar, and restaurant. But if you can get past the small, dusty, and generally unimpressive sites and appreciate the spectacular location near Mosaic Canyon and Mesquite Sand Dunes, then there is a lot to love about staying here.

The NPS-run Stovepipe Wells Campground is located right next door to the hotel and RV park. Campers staying at the campground can use the pool at the hotel with the purchase of a shower pass at the front desk. The campground is sparse and basic but benefits from the same excellent location in the park.

## Panamint Springs Resort

▷ Panamint Springs, California

▷ panamintsprings.com

▷ RV and Tent Sites, Cabin, Cabin Room, and Tent Cabin Rentals

Panamint Springs Resort offers a variety of accommodations about 10 miles inside of the west side of Death Valley National Park. It is almost an hour away from Furnace Creek, so don't plan on using it for a base camp for exploring the best of Death Valley—but it may make for a nice, relaxing stop on your way in or out of the park. This is a rustic resort that is a bit shaggy around the edges, but it is clean and well-kept and has an authentic western vibe. The cabin, cabin room, tent cabin, and hotel room options make this a great place for meeting up with friends who don't camp.

## Other Campgrounds Inside the Park

↦ **Sunset Campground at Furnace Creek**

↦ **Mesquite Spring Campground**

↦ **Emigrant Campground**

↦ **Wild Rose Campground**

↦ **Thorndike Campground**

↦ **Mahogany Flat Campground**

↦ **Fiddler's Campground at the Oasis at Death Valley**

### Big Bang for Your Buck: Five Easy Hikes in Death Valley

1. Badwater Basin Salt Flats Trail, 1.9 miles

2. Death Valley Natural Bridge Trail, 1.4 miles

3. Dante's View Trail, 1.0 mile

4. Devil's Golf Course, 2.6 miles

5. Mesquite Flat Sand Dunes, 2.8 miles

# Things to Do in Furnace Creek

Furnace Creek is the most developed hub in Death Valley National Park. Here are the best things to do.

▷ Stop in at the Furnace Creek Visitor Center and see the interpretative displays. Watch the twenty-minute park film, and pick up a Junior Ranger packet if you are looking to earn another badge.

▷ Tour Harmony Borax Works site by taking the 0.25-mile, paved trail through the ruins of the old plant and town. Learn the history of this place that has been a central feature of Death Valley National Park since it was established.

▷ Drive through Twenty Mule Team Canyon where scenes from *Star Wars: Episode VI—Return of the Jedi* were filmed.

▷ Head south to Artist Drive Scenic Loop, which brings you to the beautiful Artists Palette, a colorful display on the hills created by volcanic deposits.

## Yosemite National Park

Yosemite is one of the oldest and most beloved national parks in this country. Its towering granite cliffs, cascading waterfalls, and ancient sequoias are what many people picture when imagining the ideal national park experience, and these astonishing natural wonders also make it one of the more congested parks. Seventy-five percent of visitors arrive between May and October, so if you can schedule a visit outside that peak window, you'll be rewarded with a much more peaceful park experience.

Many of the country's most popular national parks have a wide range of camping, RVing, and lodging options in proportion to the millions of visitors that arrive each year. Yosemite is an exemption to this. This park is on the smaller side geographically for a destination that often welcomes more than four million visitors per year—it's smaller than Yellowstone, Glacier, and the Grand Canyon—and campground infrastructure has not been updated consistently over the years. Plus, the demand for a limited number of campsites is extremely high. Almost 13,000 campsites have been booked in minutes when the reservation system opened up in recent years.

Unfortunately, there isn't a strong presence of highly reviewed private campgrounds nearby that fill in the gaps for the demand. All of this to say: temper your camping expectations when planning a visit to Yosemite National Park and consider any campsite you can nab as a great option.

# CAMPGROUNDS INSIDE THE PARK

## Upper Pines Campground

▹ Yosemite Valley, California

▹ nps.gov

▹ RV and Tent Sites

Wake up surrounded by the delicious smell of ponderosa pines, the gentle sounds of the Merced River, and views of Yosemite's granite cliffs at this iconic national park's largest campground. Upper Pines has 238 sites that can handle trailers up to 25 feet and motor homes up to 35 feet, and it is a tent camper's paradise. There are three other campgrounds inside of Yosemite National Park, but this is our top pick because of the wide variety of sites for small- and medium-sized RVs. The back-in sites on the exterior side of each loop are preferable because there will be no one behind you. Interior sites are still great if that's all you can get—but you will have less privacy and more neighbors. You can walk directly from your site to several of the park's most famous hiking trails—some of which are easy, like the hike to Mirror Lake, and some of which are incredibly difficult, like the hike to Half Dome. Getting reservations can be tricky—so try to make your reservations right when the booking window opens. Cancellations do happen—so if at first you don't succeed, try, try again.

## Lower Pines Campground

▹ Yosemite Valley, California

▹ nps.gov

▹ RV and Tent Sites

Many Yosemite aficionados, who have camped throughout the park, consider Lower Pines to be the prettiest campground in the park. It is nestled along the Merced River and is located near many of the park's most iconic destinations. For the most part, the campground is shady and deeply wooded, but some sites have incredible views of Half Dome in the not-so-far distance. The sites here accommodate everything from tents and pop-up campers to larger RVs. You will have to be a reservation ninja to get a site here in the summer—so start your training now, and plan on trying to book at the exact moment when reservations open up. They get snapped up in seconds.

## Wawona Campground

▷ Wawona, California

▷ nps.gov

▷ RV and Tent Sites

If you can't get reservations in the valley, then Wawona is worth considering as a backup. It's a forty-five-minute drive from Yosemite's most iconic locations, but so are most of the private campgrounds outside of the park. Wawona is rustic and peaceful, and it has great site options for tent campers and those in small- to medium-sized RVs. We prefer the B and C loops to the A loop. The sites along the South Fork Merced River are the best in the campground, so get one if you can. Plan on bringing tubes and spending some time floating in the river. It's a magical spot for a quiet afternoon away from the madness of the crowds in the valley.

## White Wolf Campground

▷ Tuolumne County, California

▷ nps.gov

▷ RV and Tent Sites

Located north of the Yosemite Valley, the White Wolf is a family favorite. Kids love climbing around on the large rock formations and playing in the stream that runs through the campground. More so than any other campground inside of Yosemite, White Wolf has the look and feel of a natural playground that is perfect for the Junior Rangers in your family. Regional campers love to return here again and again to try different sites, partly because each one is sized and shaped differently. Just like Wawona, White Wolf offers a peaceful respite from the more crowded campgrounds in the valley. Sites are also a bit easier to score.

## Other Campgrounds Inside the Park

- ⇥ **North Pines**
- ⇥ **Camp 4**
- ⇥ **Bridalveil Creek**
- ⇥ **Hogden Meadow**
- ⇥ **Crane Flat**
- ⇥ **Tamarack Flat**
- ⇥ **Yosemite Creek**
- ⇥ **Porcupine Flat**
- ⇥ **Tuolumne Meadows**

# CAMPGROUNDS OUTSIDE THE PARK

## AutoCamp Yosemite

▹ Midpines, California

▹ autocamp.com

▹ Airstream Suites, Luxury Tents, Classic Cabins, Studio Suites

Ever dreamed of owning an Airstream and touring our iconic national parks? You aren't the only one, that's for sure. AutoCamp's Yosemite property can give you a taste of that dream at a fraction of the price. Its custom Airstream rentals will make you swoon, and so will its midcentury modern clubhouse and lounge areas where food, wine, and beer are served for hungry and thirsty hikers returning from the park. If Frank Loyd Wright and Wally Byam had a love child, this property would be it. Everything here feels delicately carved into the landscape, including the private patios and outdoor fireplaces at each site. Luxurious glamping tents and comfortable and stylish tents and suites are also available if you don't want to live riveted. There are no sites for transient RVs and tent campers—we suspect that would risk the stylish and curated feel of just about every inch of this unique property. Yosemite National Park is about forty minutes away, and a shuttle is available if you don't want to drive in and search for parking. The hip little town of Mariposa is nearby and offers quirky shopping and a handful of excellent places for food and drink. AutoCamp Yosemite offers a unique combination of comfort and connection to the great outdoors. Modern glamping doesn't get much better than this.

## Yosemite Lakes RV Resort

▷  Groveland, California

▷  thousandtrails.com

▷  RV and Tent Sites, Cabins, Yurts, Hostel Beds

This campground presents something of a devil's bargain for those who want to camp just 5 miles away from the west entrance to Yosemite—and score an RV site with hookups. The south fork of the Tuolumne River runs through this beautiful campground and is delightful for swimming and fishing. However, the facilities could use updating and basic things like showers and toilets are often broken. If you are self-contained in your own RV, then this might not be a problem. If you aren't too picky about the condition of the amenities, then this might serve as a great base camp for Yosemite.

## Yosemite RV Resort

▷  Coarsegold, California

▷  rvcoutdoors.com

▷  RV and Tent Sites, Cabin, Yurts

Yosemite RV Resort is located about forty minutes away from the park and, like Yosemite Lakes RV Resort, is a bit of a mixed bag. The customer service is friendly and helpful, but the sites can be tight and unlevel. Getting a big rig into a site here can be a tight squeeze, but the campground is pretty and worth considering if you are a seasoned RVer (with modest expectations) who can navigate challenging sites. The cabins and yurts also make a solid option for those without RVs.

## Take the Shuttle!

Traffic jams in Yosemite often take first-time visitors by surprise. It can take hours to drive a short distance from one photo op to the next. The Yosemite Valley Shuttle System travels to visitor centers, campgrounds, and trail heads. Use it wherever possible to avoid traffic headaches. Find a spot for your vehicle before 9:00 a.m. in the lots near Yosemite Village, Curry Village, or Yosemite Falls and park it for the day while you get around on public transportation.

## The Merced River

Starting as early as April with the seasonal snowmelt, rafting adventures are available on the Merced River. The rapids calm down into the summer months and offer relaxing floats by July and August. Rent rafts right in Curry Village and cool off in the river on a hot summer day. If you don't want to splurge on a rafting trip, take a swim in the river at one of the sandy beaches like Sentinel or Cathedral Beach.

## Three Iconic Yosemite Photo Ops

- ▷ El Capitan Meadow provides a picture-perfect view of El Capitan and Cathedral Rocks.
- ▷ Tunnel View offers a stunning shot of Half Dome, El Capitan, and Bridalveil Fall.
- ▷ Sentinel Meadow gives a fantastic framing of Yosemite Falls.

# Before You Go

## Read

▷ *Gloryland* by Shelton Johnson

▷ *The Wolf Keepers* by Elise Broach

▷ *The Camping Trip That Changed America: Theodore Roosevelt, John Muir, and Our National Parks* by Barb Rosenstock

## Watch

▷ *Free Solo*, an intense National Geographic documentary about Alex Honnold free climbing the face of El Capitan.

# Redwood National & State Parks

The stretch of coastline that is home to Redwood National and State Parks is one of the most majestically beautiful places in the Golden State and in our entire country. Visitors find themselves at a loss for words after hiking through primordial redwood forests with trees that are over 1,000 years old. Some find themselves referring to movies in order to explain the majesty—*Star Wars* or *Jurassic Park*—and in fact, filmmakers have pursued their muse in a variety of locations in and around the park.

Redwood National and State Parks is a unique collaboration between the National Park Service and three California State Parks (Prairie Creek, Jedediah Smith, and Del Norte). They manage this national treasure collectively, and so we will approach it that way here. Camping options are excellent inside the park, and there are a handful of good options outside the park. But good sites can be hard to find in most of the featured campgrounds unless you plan ahead—and even that is no guarantee.

This is a long, narrow park situated along the popular and highly trafficked Highway 101. Pay careful attention to geography when choosing your camping base camp. Eureka is the southernmost gateway town. Klamath is in the heart of the park, and Crescent City is up in the north close to the Oregon border. It can take close to two hours to drive from the north end of the park at Crescent City to the southern end at Eureka. You'll also want to check for road closure alerts before and during your stay. Mudslides and scheduled construction can turn an already long drive into an unbearable one.

A quick budgeting note—Redwoods National Park is free to visit. However, the three state parks do collect day-use fees at certain popular locations. Note that your America the Beautiful pass is honored at the state parks, so bring it with you when you visit.

# CAMPGROUNDS INSIDE THE PARKS

### Jedediah Smith Campground

▷ Jedediah Smith Redwoods State Park

▷ Crescent City, California

▷ nps.gov

▷ RV and Tent Sites, Cabins

The location of the Jedediah Smith Campground is storybook stunning. Camping among the old-growth redwood trees along the Smith River is peaceful and restorative to the soul. Campers can spend the entire day swimming and splashing in the river while you relax on the shoreline and dive in for a dip if you get hot. More adventurous souls should swim across the river and enjoy some very mellow rock jumping on the other side. This is also a great spot for kayaks, so bring 'em if you got 'em. Plan on attending the evening ranger programs that provide an excellent introduction to the star of the show—the redwood trees. Sites are perfect for tent campers, and cabin rentals are simple and charming, but RV sites only accommodate trailers up to 21 feet and motor homes up to 25 feet. The 1-mile Hiouchi Trail is accessible via footbridge from the campground during the summer months when the river is low. The easy hike runs along the Smith River and takes you to Stout Grove, one of the most picturesque old-growth forests in the park.

## Gold Bluffs Beach Campground

▷ **Prairie Creek Redwoods State Park**

▷ **Orick, California**

▷ **nps.gov**

▷ **No Trailers Allowed; Vans, Motor homes, Truck Campers up to 24 Feet; Tent Sites**

Gold Bluffs Beach Campground is one of the most stunning campgrounds along the California coast. It is located on a wild and windswept stretch of coastline, and good sites are coveted by those in the know. The road leading to the campground is long and bumpy, and no trailers of any kind are allowed, making this spot perfect for van lifers, truck campers, and tent campers. Flush toilets and showers are available, but bathhouses are in need of updating. High winds can make pitching your tent a high-stakes affair in the fall and winter, but if you can visit during good weather, or brave the coastal elements, then this place may be the highlight of your California road trip. The campground is also just 2 miles from Fern Canyon, where you can hike a 1-mile loop along Home Creek that runs through a deep 80-foot canyon.

## Mill Creek Campground

▷ **Del Norte Coast Redwoods State Park**

▷ **Klamath, California**

▷ **nps.gov**

▷ **RV and Tent Sites**

▷ **No hookups at sites**

Visitors to Mill Creek Campground feel like they are camping in the midst of a coastal California fairy tale. The sites here are surrounded by smaller redwood trees and the stumps of larger trees long gone. The campground is busy and bustling in the summertime, but every site has some privacy—even the smaller ones. Sites max out at 24 feet for trailers and 28 feet for motor homes.

### Elk Prairie Campground

▷ Prairie Creek Redwoods State Park

▷ Orick, California

▷ nps.gov

▷ RV and Tent Sites, Cabins

The drive into this campground past gigantic redwood trees is breathtaking and the campsites are idyllic, with many of them backing right up to Prairie Creek. The bathrooms, however, are old and in desperate need of repair. Tent campers may be dismayed, and those with self-contained motor homes (27 feet or less) or trailers (24 feet or less) may be happiest here. Keep your eyes peeled for Roosevelt Elk in Elk Prairie.

## CAMPGROUNDS OUTSIDE THE PARK

### Crescent City/Redwoods KOA

▷ Crescent City, California

▷ koa.com

▷ RV and Tent Sites, Rustic Cabins and Deluxe Cabins

This KOA feels like two separate campgrounds on one property. The "first" campground offers pretty standard fare—it has a recreation room for rainy days, hearty pancake breakfasts, and playgrounds and bike rentals for the kids. The RV sites are suitable for big rigs but offer little privacy or scenery. The cabins are comfortable and well equipped. The "second" campground is actually inside a 10-acre redwood forest and it is absolutely magical. Tent sites, rustic cabins, and sites for small RVs are surrounded by towering redwoods and the deep shade that they provide. This is the rare KOA that may be better for tent campers than RV owners. Proximity to Crescent City and the national and state parks is also excellent.

## Ramblin' Redwoods Campground & RV Park

▷ Crescent City, California

▷ ramblinredwoodsrv.com

▷ RV and Tent Sites, Cabins

Ramblin' Redwoods is a great place for some good old-fashioned Northern California redwoods camping. There's nothing fancy here, but there doesn't need to be. Under "Amenities" on its website it lists "close to Redwoods National Park," which tells you just about everything you need to know. The location here is terrific—it's a short drive to Crescent City and a short drive into some of the most famous sections of the park. The sites are roomy and shaded and feel like state park campsites, but they have full hookups and sites for big rigs and small. Prices are also more than reasonable.

--------------------- **Read Before You Go** ---------------------

*The Wild Trees: A Story of Passion and Daring* by Richard Preston. This is a breathtaking nonfiction book about Steve Sillett and an adventurous group of botanists and naturalists who seek to discover and climb the largest trees in the world. Reading this while visiting Redwood National and State Parks will allow you to look up and picture the complex universe that exists in the upper reaches of these ancient giants—and give you an epic read for evenings around the campfire. *The Wild Trees* is a legitimate page-turner and one of our favorite outdoor adventure books of all time.

# Our Favorite Hikes

### Hiouchi Trail to Stout Grove (5 miles, out and back)

This hike starts directly across from Jedediah Smith Campground and runs along the Smith River. At the time of this writing, there are fallen trees blocking the path that eventually takes you into the cool and mysterious shade of Stout Grove, where some of the trees are over 2,000 years old. More adventurous souls are not letting the fallen trees stop them from getting into Stout Grove from this trail.

### Ladybird Johnson Grove Trail (1.5-mile loop)

This lovely and easy loop hike, which Richard Nixon dedicated to Lady Bird Johnson in 1969, is one of the most popular in the park. We recommend taking a ranger-led walk here. You will leave with an in-depth knowledge of the conflicts that led to the founding of the park and experience an even greater sense of awe for its magnificent trees.

### Yurok Trail to Hidden Beach (2.25 miles)

You may come to Redwood National and State Parks to gaze in wonder at ancient trees, but make sure you also explore the 37 miles of wild and untamed Northern California coastline that fall under its dominion. This easy hike is the way to do it. Plan on bringing a picnic lunch and hanging out at hidden beach for a few hours.

### Fern Canyon (1.1-mile loop)

This is one of the most popular spots in the park, so get here early and skip a weekend visit if possible. Also plan on bringing waterproof shoes or getting your hiking shoes soaking wet, as you crisscross over playful streams and walk through a sparkling creek bed. Fern Canyon was used as the setting for several scenes in *Jurassic Park 2*, so watching it before you go might be a fun way to spend an evening.

# Scenic Drives

### Northern Redwoods (Crescent City): Newton B. Drury Scenic Parkway

This 10-mile drive off U.S. 101 will take you through the old-growth forest in Prairie Creek Redwoods State Park. You'll also pass the Elk Prairie Visitors Center, Cal Barrel Road, and the Ah Pah Trail.

### Central Redwoods (Klamath): Coastal Drive

This 9-mile drive is accessed via Klamath Beach Road and has sharp turns, steep curves, and stretches that are unpaved. Explorers will be rewarded with panoramic views of the Pacific Ocean. Bring binoculars and scan the water and rocky coastline for whales, sea lions, and pelicans.

### Southern Redwoods (Humboldt Redwoods State Park): Avenue of the Giants

This 31-mile drive runs parallel to U.S. 101 and hosts some of the most iconic redwoods featured in decades worth of calendars, coffee-table books, and brochures. Download the auto map in advance. There are eight main stops—clearly marked along the highway—where drivers can pull off and park for short walks or photo opportunities.

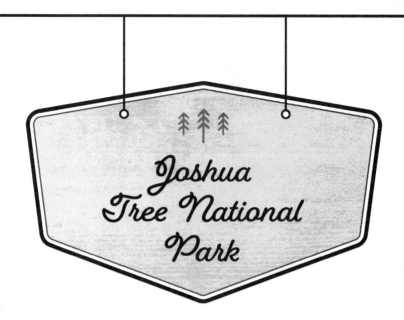

# Joshua Tree National Park

The iconic, twisty, spiky, Dr. Seuss–like trees that are the centerpiece of this national park were named by Mormons and made even more well known by U2, the band that named a Grammy-winning album of the year after them. Joshua trees are not actually trees; they are succulents and a member of the agave family, masters at storing water and surviving in punishing desert conditions. They are only found in areas of the Mojave Desert between 2,000 and 6,000 feet above sea level, and almost three million people come to this national park each year to see these natural wonders in their habitat.

Like Death Valley, Joshua Tree National Park is just a few hours from Las Vegas and Los Angeles, and it's a very popular outdoor destination during the spring when temperatures are mild and the wildflowers are in bloom. The fall is another lovely time to visit, and the crowds are often lighter than in the spring months. Summers are scorching hot, some campgrounds are closed, and most ranger programs are on pause. Winters bring wildly fluctuating temperatures and a chance of snow, so campers will most likely want to avoid these two seasons.

Most of the 500 campsites within the park boundaries are available to reserve up to six months in advance. The campgrounds at Joshua Tree National Park are excellent when compared to other national park offerings, but it can be very difficult to nab a site, especially if visiting during peak seasons, holidays, and weekends. If your dates aren't flexible, try to reserve something on the day it becomes available on recreation.gov. There are also three first-come, first-served campgrounds in the park as well as two BLM areas open for camping outside the national park boundaries.

# CAMPGROUNDS INSIDE THE PARK

## Jumbo Rocks Campground

▹   Twentynine Palms, California

▹   nps.gov

▹   RV and Tent Sites

Camping at Jumbo Rocks can feel like camping on another planet. The rock formations look like they belong on the moon, not in California. These dusty looking formations change dramatically from one end of the campground to another, so the sites here are all quite different. Some of them are level, spacious, and shaded, while many others feel jammed up right against the road. You need to be a superhero to grab the most desirable sites here, so most mortals are happy to take what they can get. To say this campground is popular would be a massive understatement. It is incredibly popular, and only three hours away from Los Angeles. Smaller RVs under 20 feet can get into many of the sites here, but generally speaking, longer RVs are out of luck. Jumbo Rocks is much better for tent campers who can take any site and get a bit more creative setting up their kit. Bathroom facilities are limited considering the size of the campground. There is no water here, so come prepared with everything you need for the length of your stay.

## Indian Cove Campground

▷ Twentynine Palms, California

▷ nps.gov

▷ RV and Tent Sites

Indian Cove is in a much more secluded section of the park than Jumbo Rocks. You may find yourself driving quite a bit more if you camp here, but the campground is beautiful and the sites are typically large and private. It may not be the best place to explore the most famous parts of the park, but it is one of the best camping experiences in the park. This is a great spot for your second trip to Joshua Tree, or if you are just looking to get away from it all, climb around on some rocks, and cook some great food at your campsite.

## Ryan Campground

▷ Twentynine Palms, California

▷ nps.gov

▷ RV and Tent Sites

Joshua Tree rookies rarely look to pitch their tents or park their RVs at Ryan Campground first, but it is an absolute favorite among those who have experience camping in the park. The campground is small (there are only thirty-one sites), and it has a mystical, spiritual quality to it. Joshua Trees are abundant here—and so are peace and quiet. Make sure you get back to the campground for sunsets and stargazing—there is no better place in the park for both.

## Other Campgrounds Inside the Park

↦ **Black Rock**

↦ **Cottonwood**

↦ **Hidden Valley**

↦ **White Tank**

↦ **Belle**

# CAMPGROUNDS OUTSIDE THE PARK

## Palm Springs/Joshua Tree KOA

 ▷ Desert Hot Springs, California

 ▷ koa.com

 ▷ RV and Tent Sites, Glamping Tents, Cabins

KOA campgrounds are at their best when they combine KOA's iconic design sensibility while also capturing regional vibes and textures. Thankfully many of them (especially those that are locally owned) do just that. The Palm Springs/Joshua Tree KOA is a perfect example of this aesthetic. Whether you are walking your dog in its fenced-in Kamp K-9 area, or swimming in its hot springs–fed pool, you will know that you are camping at a KOA, but you will also feel completely immersed in California's Coachella Valley. Everything at this KOA just clicks. The amenities, like hot tubs and pickleball courts, are excellent, and so is the location. Palm Springs is nearby, and Joshua Tree National Park is about forty-five minutes away. So if you want to take a vacation that is not exclusively about exploring Joshua Tree, then this might be your place. If you come back from the park and don't feel like cooking, then grab a bite at the Desert Oasis Cafe and let your kids explore the campground. The bike pump track and rock-climbing wall are both a blast for kids of all ages.

## AutoCamp Joshua Tree

 ▷ Joshua Tree, California

 ▷ autocamp.com

 ▷ Airstream Rentals, Rental Suites

Auto Camp Joshua Tree hits people in different ways. Some love the swanky (and expensive) Airstream rentals that come well stocked with glampy linens, bath towels, and soaps. But others feel the location near a busy highway is less than desirable. If you want complete solitude in a desert location, then this is not your place. Look for an NPS site in the park instead. But if you want to hang with the hipsters in an Airstream rental in an environment where everything, including the food and drink, is delightfully curated, then go ahead and make the splurge.

## Joshua Tree Lake RV and Campground

▷   Joshua Tree, California

▷   joshuatreelake.com

▷   RV and Tent Sites

Located just 9 miles from the Joshua Tree Visitor Center, this charming, rustic, and affordable campground is a terrific option if you can't get a site in the park and don't need fancy amenities. This is also the best option for a campground near the park with hookups for RVs. The sites here are pretty basic and made with dirt and gravel. But there are nice privacy hedges between some of them. The restrooms are also clean, and the staff is knowledgeable about the park and the area in general.

---------------- **Free Camping on BLM Land** ----------------

There are two BLM areas outside of Joshua Tree National Park boundaries that are open for camping. This is a great option for folks who aren't able to reserve a campsite months in advance and also great for those on a budget, since camping is free here. The northern BLM area is near the town of Joshua Tree, and the southern BLM area is close to Cottonwood Springs. Get GPS coordinates from the BLM.gov website to accurately locate the designated areas. The southern dispersed area is very easy to access off I-10, which means it can also get a bit crowded on the weekends. Note that both of these areas are favorites of the off-roading crowd, so if noise from UTVs bothers you, this may not be a good option.

# Quick Guide to Joshua Tree National Park

## Before You Go

▷ Read: *Joshua Tree: The Complete Guide, Joshua Tree National Park* by James Kaiser

▷ Listen: U2, *The Joshua Tree*

## Where to Stock Up

▷ Twentynine Palms: This small city is home to the main entrance of Joshua Tree National Park and has plenty of must-see attractions like the Harmony Motel, where U2 stayed while touring the Mojave Desert and writing the *Joshua Tree* album.

▷ Joshua Tree Village and Cottonwood Spring are also smaller gateway towns with entrances to the park.

## How to Get Around

Although the NPS has periodically experimented with pilot shuttle programs, there is no extensive or reliable public transportation available in Joshua Tree. A personal vehicle is required to see most of the sites in the park. Cell service can be extremely spotty, and it is unwise to rely on GPS for directions. Detailed, up-to-date paper maps are the most reliable option.

## First Stop: Visitor Center

The recently opened Joshua Tree Cultural Center in the newly developed Freedom Plaza in Twentynine Palms is a must-visit park attraction in and of itself, with a bookstore, information center, and rotating educational exhibits. The other visitor centers include Joshua Tree Visitor Center, Cottonwood Visitor Center, and Black Rock Nature Center.

## Permits and Reservations

The park has no timed reservation requirements for entry. Tickets are required for the ninety-minute, ranger-led Keys Ranch Tour, and they can be purchased ahead of time at recreation.gov. Permits are required for back-country camping.

## Rock Climbing

Rock climbing is one of the most popular activities for visitors to Joshua Tree National Park. It's a world-class climbing destination, and all but the most experienced will want to find a guide from the wide selection of outfitters permitted to lead classes and excursions in the park. If you are going it alone, make sure to read the detailed guidelines on the park website that are in place to protect the fragile ecosystem.

## Hiking

▷ **Hidden Valley Nature Trail:** easy, 1-mile loop near Twentynine Palms.
▷ **Cholla Cactus Garden:** very easy, 0.2-mile loop trail near Twentynine Palms.
▷ **Skull Rock and the Discovery Trail:** easy 1.7-mile loop trail offering views of one of the most famous rock formations in the park.
▷ **Arch Rock:** easy 1.4-mile out-and-back trail with lots of boulders near the White Tank Campground.
▷ **Ryan Mountain Trail:** moderate 2.9-mile out-and-back trail with an intense elevation gain and beautiful views at the top.

## Stargazing

Joshua Tree is a designated International Dark Sky Park. Check the schedule upon arrival for stargazing ranger programs that run weekly.

# Sequoia & Kings Canyon National Parks

Sequoia and Kings Canyon National Parks offer up an embarrassment of riches when it comes to camping. These jointly managed parks have fourteen campgrounds, and it is not an exaggeration to say that every single one of them is beautiful. Some are located near crystal-clear swimming holes, and some are located right next door to some of the best hiking trails in the state of California. So how can you possibly choose where to camp next? Depending on the time of year that you visit, you may just need to take what you can get. But if you are visiting during the week or in the off-season, and you have choices, then you might be able to pick a camping experience that best suits your personal camping style. Some of these campgrounds are huge and bustling, and others are relatively quiet and peaceful. So follow your bliss and get camping, camper. Some of the world's largest and most magnificent trees are waiting for you—and some of them have been waiting for centuries.

# CAMPGROUNDS INSIDE THE PARKS

### Lodgepole Campground

▷    Three Rivers, California

▷    nps.gov

▷    RV and Tent Sites

Lodgepole Campground offers up a classic California camping experience in the heart of Sequoia National Park. Almost all the sites here are surrounded by shady and fragrant pine trees. The Marble Fork of the Kaweah River cuts through the campground, and you can hear it running by from many of the better campsites. Many of the sites are clustered close to the road, but they are lovely, nevertheless. With over 200 sites, Lodgepole can get quite crowded in the summertime, but it holds the crowd well with loops that are not right on top of each other. Lodgepole Campground is attractive for the masses because it is close to Lodgepole Village, which has a cute market and a visitor center where you can view exhibits and watch a film about these two epic national parks. Hiking near this campground and then coming back and cooling off in the river is heavenly. In terms of large, popular NPS campgrounds in the West, it doesn't get much better.

## Azalea Campground

▷    Grant Grove, California

▷    nps.gov

▷    RV and Tent Sites

For many, Azalea Campground serves as a great base camp for exploring Kings Canyon. Some of the sites here are open year-round, and more open as the weather gets warmer. It is located less than 4 miles away from the Kings Canyon Entrance and offers a deep, woodsy camping experience under thick evergreen trees. You are in bear country here, so please take precautions and store your food appropriately. The sites here are larger and more private than the sites at Lodgepole—so if you want to take a step away from the madding crowd, this might be your place.

## Sheep Creek Campground

▷ Cedar Grove, California

▷ nps.gov

▷ RV and Tent Sites

The mountains peek up through the conifer trees at Sheep Creek Campground, which, despite being in need of some repairs, is still a magnificent place to park your rig or pitch your tent in Kings Canyon. The river runs right next to the campground, and you can hear it from many of the sites as you fall asleep at night. There are several good spots for swimming nearby, and the rugged beauty of the area around the campground makes this a spot that California campers return to again and again.

### Other Campgrounds Inside the Parks

⇴ **Dorst Creek Campground**

⇴ **Sunset Campground**

⇴ **Crystal Springs Campground**

⇴ **Canyon View Campground (group only)**

⇴ **Sentinel Campground**

⇴ **Moraine Campground**

⇴ **Atwell Mill Campground**

⇴ **Cold Springs Campground**

⇴ **Buckeye Flat Campground**

⇴ **Potwisha Campground**

⇴ **South Fork Campground**

# CAMPGROUNDS OUTSIDE THE PARKS

## Sequoia RV Ranch

▷ Three Rivers, California

▷ sequoiarvranch.com

▷ RV and Tent Sites

Sequoia and Kings Canyon National Parks are blessed with an abundance of great campgrounds for tenting and dry camping in vans and RVs. But if you want a private campground outside of the park with full hookups and amenities, then we think Sequoia RV Ranch is the only show in town. Located only 8 miles away from the entrance to Sequoia National Park, this campground is open year-round and offers a beautiful setting and excellent customer service. The sites on the Kaweah River are, by far, the best sites in the campground. Your kids will love cooling off and playing in the swimming hole area—so plan on coming back to the campground each afternoon to kick back, relax, and get wet. Many of the other sites are close together and lack privacy, though the pull-throughs can accommodate big rigs of all shapes and sizes. Campers traveling with pups will also love the large dog park. This campground, like so many other private campgrounds, is very pet friendly.

## Two Miles or Less

Sequoia and Kings Canyon National Parks have some truly terrific hikes that click in at under 2 miles long. Here are our five favorites:

1. Roaring River Falls Trail (0.3 mile)
2. The General Sherman Tree Trail (0.8 mile)
3. Crystal Cave (0.8 mile)
4. Tokopah Falls (1.7 miles)
5. Buena Vista Peak (2 miles)

## The General Sherman Tree

The world's tallest tree and the world's largest tree both reside in California, and can you blame them? Hyperion (located somewhere in Redwood National and State Park) measures in at 380 feet and takes the prize for tallest tree. The 275-foot General Sherman tree (in Sequoia) is, however, the world's largest tree when measured by volume. Its base is almost 29 feet wide.

## ------- **Susan Thew: A Great Woman of the Parks** -------

Susan Priscilla Thew is an unsung hero in the history of Sequoia and Kings Canyon National Parks. Her advocacy and her photography of this magnificent section of the California Sierras resulted in the tripling in size of what was then Sequoia National Park. A report that she created and sent to Congress sealed the deal and led to the preservation of some of the park's most beloved locations.

# Grand Canyon National Park

The Grand Canyon was one of the top five national park sites visited in 2021, and it's probably one of America's most iconic vacation destinations. Around five million visitors arrive each year to gaze at the largest canyon on earth, formed over millions of years by the flowing waters of the Colorado River. Although the park is popular and well known, it can also present a planning challenge for first-time visitors. Aside from enjoying the view—which can easily gobble up hours of the day—many of the most compelling experiences require advanced planning, permits, or reservations. See our sidebar How Do I Plan for a Grand Canyon National Park Visit? on page 305.

The South Rim is the most visited area of the park, closest to the two largest NPS campgrounds and also most easily accessed from campgrounds in Williams, the starting point for the Grand Canyon Railway. The South Rim offers the most amenities, along with activities for young children and plenty of accessible paths. The North Rim—only open between mid-May and mid-October—is a whopping 200 miles away and much less developed. It's also a favorite for folks who want to soak up the beauty of the canyon without fighting the crowds. If you plan on visiting both areas of the park, you will most likely want to pick a campground at both rims and spend a few days at each location. The West Rim (situated on Hualapai Indian Reservation land and home of the Skywalk) and the East Rim (close to Antelope Canyon) are both long drives from the South Rim area as well.

Although the South Rim is open year-round, the spring, summer, and fall seasons are the most popular. In the summer, temperatures can easily top out over 100°F. Visitors should plan on taking advantage of cooler temperatures during the morning and evening hours, and carefully note any heat advisories before embarking on long hikes. Visitors in the spring and fall will enjoy comfortable high temperatures between 60 and 70°F during the day but will need to be prepared for significant drops at night. Many consider late May or early September as ideal times to visit.

# CAMPGROUNDS INSIDE THE PARK

### Mather Campground

▷    South Rim, Grand Canyon National Park

▷    Grand Canyon Village, Arizona

▷    nps.gov

▷    RV and Tent Sites

With over 320 sites, Mather Campground is significantly larger than the other two NPS-operated campgrounds inside Grand Canyon National Park. Fifty-five of the sites at Mather are tent only. Some, but not all, of the rest of the sites can accommodate motor homes up to 30 feet and trailers up to 27 feet. Smaller RVs will have more options—but that is always the case in our national park campgrounds. The loop roads within the campground are also tight—so again, the advantage goes to tent campers and those with smaller RVs. Mather's campsites do not have any hookups, but there is a free dump station on-site. The location of the campground is excellent and puts you incredibly close to everything that the South Rim has to offer. Campers of all kinds love the shaded and semiprivate sites, which are significantly prettier than those in the Grand Canyon Trailer Village RV Park—though deer and elk roam through both places. Just about everything about Mather campground is delightful, especially the smell of the Ponderosa Pines, which smell like vanilla and butterscotch—especially if you get up nice and close!

## Grand Canyon Trailer Village RV Park

- ▷  **South Rim, Grand Canyon National Park**
- ▷  **Grand Canyon Village, Arizona**
- ▷  **visitgrandcanyon.com**
- ▷  **RV sites**

Full hookup RV sites inside Grand Canyon National Park? And less than a mile from the South Rim? Yes, thank you very much! It may not be the most scenic national park campground, but the proximity is literally unbeatable if you are looking to take your RV—or RV rental—to the Grand Canyon. The sites are basically all the same, and there is nothing fancy about this concessionaire-managed campground, but it is well-loved by even the pickiest RVers. Some sites have more shade than others, and most are a bit tightly packed. But few complain about the simplicity of the sites because they get to run their AC during the heat of the summer. If the heat isn't unbearable, you can walk to the visitor center, but a wide-ranging shuttle is available as well. This shuttle is clutch for those renting RVs who don't have cars with them. Nothing about this simple campground is magnificent—but everything about the Grand Canyon is. The Grand Canyon Trailer Village RV Park is a place to sleep and eat and take breaks from the heat during your visit to one of the most breathtaking places on earth. Wi-Fi is not available, but cell phone service is, depending on your carrier. But we do recommend unplugging completely if your work schedule allows it!

## North Rim Campground

▷ **North Rim, Grand Canyon National Park**

▷ **North Rim, Arizona**

▷ **nps.gov**

▷ **RV and Tent Sites**

The North Rim Campground is significantly smaller than Mather because not as many campers make it to the North Rim. This campground is a great base camp for exploration of the North Rim, and it is enchanting in every way. It sits at an elevation of 8,200 feet, so it is cool even in the summer months. Mather is also easy to navigate, and the sites are large. But the design of the campground is a bit quirky for RV owners. A one-way circular loop road surrounds the campground with five one-way roads cutting through the middle. The campsites on the bottom (when looking at a campground map) are preferable because your RV's door will face into your private site, instead of facing the road. If you have a site on the top of these roads, your RV's door will face the road. The rangers insist that all cars, trucks, and RVs face the right way on the one-way roads in case the campground must be evacuated during a wildfire, so don't even think about pulling your RV in the wrong direction. None of this matters for tent campers of course. The North Rim Campground is open from May 15 to October 31 and can accommodate a total length of 40 feet for a motor home without car or a truck and trailer combo. The general store here is also surprisingly well stocked with coffee, snacks, and other essentials.

## Desert View Campground

▷ **South Rim, Grand Canyon National Park**

▷ **Grand Canyon Village, California**

▷ **nps.gov**

▷ **RV and Tent Sites**

Desert View Campground offers forty-nine sites (30 feet total length) and is located 25 miles east of Grand Canyon Village, so while it may not be the first

Where Should We Camp Next? » National Parks

choice for many campers seeking proximity to services, amenities, and the most popular section of the park, this is still an absolute gem worth considering. It can also serve as a great backup plan if you can't get a site at Mather or the Grand Canyon Trailer Village. The famous rail to the Desert View Watchtower is short and lovely, and the views of the sunrise here are epic.

# CAMPGROUNDS OUTSIDE THE PARK

## Under Canvas Grand Canyon

▷ Valle, Arizona

▷ undercanvas.com

▷ Glamping Tents

This glamper's delight is only twenty-five minutes away from the South Rim entrance to the Grand Canyon. This is an excellent location, and options for getting closer to the majesty of this treasured NPS site are few and far between. Under Canvas offers three types of glamping tents on 160 peaceful acres of juniper forest. The Suite Tent is suitable for adventurous families and has its own shower, sink, and toilet so you don't have to wander out of the tent at night for potty breaks. But we like the Stargazer Tent the best—it has a viewing window above the king bed so you can fall asleep while gazing at the stars. Under Canvas Grand Canyon has its own "adventures" concierge who will help you choose each day's outing. When you get back to base camp you can take a few minutes to relax in the Zen garden before enjoying delicious pan-roasted trout or mushroom ravioli for dinner. When you return to your tent you will find that housekeeping has cleaned your room and refreshed your selections of organic soaps. If you feel like socializing, head out to the communal campfire for s'mores.

## Grand Canyon Railway RV Park (and Hotel)

▷  **Williams, Arizona**

▷  **thetrain.com/lodging/rv-park/**

▷  **RV Sites and Hotel Rooms**

The Grand Canyon Railway RV Park is part of the refurbished and luxurious Grand Canyon Railway and Hotel, and guests at the RV park have access to all the hotel amenities. They also have access to the Grand Canyon train, which has been transporting visitors into the National Park since 1901. This neat and tidy RV park is located only two blocks from downtown Williams and historic Route 66, and there is pretty much nothing not to love about it. Williams has long been called "The Gateway to the Grand Canyon," but it is a fantastic stop in its own right with great food and drink and lots of funky "out west" shopping.

## DeMotte Campground

▷  **Kaibab National Forest**

▷  **Fredonia, Arizona**

▷  **nps.com**

▷  **RV and Tent Sites**

Located just 7 miles from the north entrance to Grand Canyon National Park, the Demotte Campground is a terrific backup plan if you can't get a site at the more conveniently located North Rim Campground that is located inside the park. This National Forest Service gem is clean and tidy and offers some shade and privacy between its thirty-eight sites. There are no hookups at the sites here, but the pit toilets are clean and the price is right. If you are a tent camper, or have an RV that is self-contained, then this rustic and pretty campground is sure to please and makes a great base camp for your North Rim adventures.

# Williams/Exit 167/Circle Pines KOA Holiday

▷ Williams, Arizona

▷ koa.com

▷ RV and Tent Sites, Covered Wagon, Teepee, Cabin Rentals

If you are willing to camp about an hour away from the Grand Canyon and use Williams as your base camp, or if you are just looking for a place to stop for a night on your way into the park, this KOA is a very solid option. The heated indoor pool is a great place to take a dip after a long day of exploring, and the dedicated bike path is a fun place for kids to unwind after a long drive. The Bear Trax cafe is a solid option for breakfast or dinner and the customer service is friendly. If you are tent camping, please take note that the interstate is right next to the campground and it is noisy. This KOA is a better option for RVers in self-contained units without canvas bed ends.

---

### Pedal It!

Rent a bike from Bright Angel Bicycles, located at the visitor center near Mather Point, and "ride the rim" instead of fighting with auto traffic and navigating small parking lots. Bright Angel Bicycles also offers three-hour guided bicycle tours, where you can learn about geology and anthropology while you cycle.

---

### Should I Ride the Rails?

The Grand Canyon Railway has been shuttling guests from Williams into the park since the early 1900s. The train departs at 9:30 a.m., depositing riders in the Historic Village at the South Rim, and returns at 5:45 p.m. The ride is about two hours each way, and ticketed passengers have three hours to explore the park. The tickets are not inexpensive—the cheapest are $67 for adults and $32 for children. Bottom line? While this may be an enjoyable and memorable way to see a small bit of the Grand Canyon, it's definitely not for everyone.

# How Do I Plan for a Grand Canyon National Park Visit?

1. Purchase an entrance pass in advance at recreation.gov (if you don't already have an America the Beautiful annual pass) to avoid long lines at the entrance stations.

2. Plan to use the free shuttle buses. Traffic in this park can be a buzz-kill, especially in peak summer months. Check out bus schedules and routes in advance and use them whenever possible to access points of interest.

3. Enter the online lottery for an overnight stay at Phantom Ranch fifteen months in advance if interested.

4. Purchase Grand Canyon IMAX tickets in advance. The tickets are discounted when purchased online and are good for any showing at the visitor center.

5. Carefully research any hike you are planning on taking. Even experienced hikers are challenged by the elevation changes, rocky terrain, and temperature fluctuations. The Grand Canyon NPS website gives an average length of time for each hike as these can be longer than expected, especially if the hike includes climbing out of the canyon.

6. Make reservations up to thirty days in advance for lunch or dinner at the historic El Tovar dining room, with views of the canyon and murals on the walls reflecting the customs of the Hopi, Apache, Mojave, and Navajo tribes.

7. Book one of the famous mule rides down into the canyon. These sell out months in advance, so don't drag your feet on this one. For a true bucket-list experience check out a Bright Angel Trail mule ride, where guests stay overnight at Phantom Ranch and eat lunch at Indian Garden.

8. Book river rafting trips in advance. The park annually licenses certain outfitters to run half-day, full-day, and multi-day rafting trips within park boundaries. Links to these outfitters are available on the park website.

9. Book a helicopter tour. Another popular—and pricey—way to experience the grandeur of the canyon is by helicopter tour. A link to licensed air tour operators can be found on the Grand Canyon NPS website.

# Discover Route 66 in Williams, Arizona

A vacation that covers a bucket-list national park and a landmark Route 66 destination in one fell swoop? That's about as American as it gets. Williams is often referred to as the "Gateway to the Grand Canyon," but it's also one of the best preserved stops along the Mother Road. Here are some highlights you won't want to miss.

1. Stop in at the Railway Avenue Visitor Center to get your bearings and some personalized advice from the knowledgeable staff.

2. Visit the Train Depot—a designated landmark constructed between 1909 and 1910—even if you aren't taking a train ride to the Grand Canyon.

3. Take time to enjoy the shops along Main Street.

4. Drive through the Bearizona Wildlife Park in your own car or via tour bus.

5. Feed the deer at the Grand Canyon Deer Farm.

6. Visit the Wild West Junction for a beverage at the Longhorn Saloon or some BBQ at the Branding Iron Restaurant.

7. Shop for handcrafted cowboy boots or a hat at Western Outfitters.

8. Order a slice of famous pie at the Pine Country Restaurant.

# More NPS Sites in Arizona

The Grand Canyon gets all the press, but there are many other NPS sites in Arizona that are worth a visit. In particular, Arizona is home to remarkably well-preserved cliff dwellings and other artifacts of indigenous populations in North America. Travel back in history at these other national park locations:

### Petrified Forest National Park

**Petrified Forest, Arizona**

Explore petroglyphs, sandstone ruins from the 1200s, and the Painted Desert Inn National Historic Landmark.

### Montezuma Castle National Monument

**Camp Verde, Arizona**

Here you'll find one of the best preserved cliff dwellings on the continent, which were home to the Sinagua people for over 400 years.

### Saguaro National Park

**Tucson, Arizona**

The Tucson region is home to this country's largest cacti, and these giant plants are protected at this NPS site.

### Walnut Canyon National Monument

**Flagstaff, Arizona**

The 1-mile Island Trail and 0.75-mile Rim Trail provide visitors with access to more than twenty-five cliff dwellings from the 1100s.

### Sunset Crater Volcano National Monument

**Flagstaff, Arizona**

Formed by a series of eruptions around 1085, this volcano is the youngest cinder cone in the San Francisco Volcanic Field.

---------------------- **Meteor Crater** ----------------------

This site is less than a half hour's drive from Williams, Arizona. It's mainly a really big hole in the ground, but those with an interest in astronomy will enjoy the visit. There are elevated lookout points, an educational film, and a museum. Pets are not allowed inside the crater, but the location provides a "Pet Ramada" where guests can kennel their dogs during their visit.

# Haleakalā National Park & Hawai'i Volcanoes National Park

For most visitors from out of state, Hawaii will not be a camping—or national park–centric trip. But those willing to fly in and rent a campervan or get their hands on tenting equipment will have an NPS experience that they will never forget. You can even rent a tent at Hawai'i Volcanoes National Park if you can't bring your own. The campgrounds at Hawai'i Volcanoes offers up some of the most incredible camping in the entire NPS system, but sites are limited. So plan on booking before they fill up.

Sites are also quite limited within Haleakalā National Park. Kīpahulu Campground only offers twenty sites—fifteen are drive-up and five are walk-in only. Hosmer Grove Campground sits at an elevation of nearly 7,000 feet and only offers six tent-only sites. So to say that very few people get to experience this magical place would be the camping understatement of the year. Reservations for this rarely visited NPS gem can be booked at recreation.gov.

# CAMPGROUNDS INSIDE THE PARKS

## Volcano House, Nāmakanipaio, and Kulanaokuaiki Campgrounds

▷ Pāhoa, Hawaii, and Volcano, Hawaii

▷ nps.gov

▷ Lodge Rooms, Cabins, Tent Sites

Hawai'i Volcanoes National Park is home to two of the world's most active volcanoes. It is also home to an excellent lodge and two small, but charming, campgrounds—one of which has adorable cabins. The Volcano House offers thirty-three comfortable rooms that are, in our humble opinion, almost glamping. Like many national park lodges, they are lovely, but not luxurious. The lodge sits at the edge of the Kilauea Caldera, providing guests with views of the volcano from the dining room and many of the guest rooms. If the price for a volcano view is a bit too rich for your blood, then try one of the cute A-frame cabins in Nāmakanipaio Campground just 3 miles up the road. These cute-as-a-button cabins sleep four and are bright and cheery inside— but a bit sparsely decorated, so plan on bringing your own cozy blankets and pillows to glamp it up a little. The two campgrounds at Volcanoes are very small and do not accommodate RVs—which are rarely seen in Hawaii—but you can rent a tent from the concessionaire (who will set it up and break it down for you) or bring your own and do it the old-fashioned way.

## Kīpahulu Campground, Hosmer Grove Campground

▷ Hana, Hawaii, and Kula, Hawaii

▷ nps.gov

▷ Tent Sites and Campervan Sites

Haleakalā National Park is a stunning national park for those with an adventurous spirit. The park has two districts that both have distinct features— and thankfully, each of them has a campground. The Kīpahulu District is accessed by driving 12 miles on the beautiful—but occasionally dangerous—Hana Highway. But once you arrive (hopefully in one piece), you will be treated to once-in-a-lifetime ocean views, waterfalls, and incredible options for swimming and hiking. You can hear the sound of waves crashing onto ocean cliffs just a short walk away from your site at the Kīpahulu Campground. There is no water available here, so bring your own, or plan on getting it nearby at the visitor center. The Summit District of Haleakalā is like no other place on earth. At an elevation of over 10,000 feet, this place gets cold, and you may want to think twice about going if you have health issues. The Hosmer Grove Campground is tiny and intimate, and it puts you pretty close to the summit—and there is drinking water. But even campers at Hosmer Grove need reservations to see the sunrise at the top. You can get them at recreation.gov.

# Looking to Rent a Campervan?

Outdoorsy and RVShare are both peer-to-peer RV rental companies, and many small rental companies in Hawaii also list their rigs on these sites. The search features, reviews, and clear cancellation policies make these websites our favorite for RV rentals. We've used them both in the past and had only good experiences. Campervan Hawaii is a well-reviewed rental company that showcases its RVs on the Outdoorsy platform and on its own website. Its selection of rentals includes a Jeep Rubicon pop-top, a VW Westfalia, and other modern and well-equipped class B van options.

## A Few Tips for Renting an RV

1. Make sure basics like linens and cooking equipment are included. You do not want to fly to Hawaii and shop for sheets.
2. Read the reviews carefully and pick an owner with a lot of positive feedback.
3. If you are new to RVing, pick an owner who is happy to provide a lot of education and support.
4. If it's your first time visiting Hawaii, pick an owner that offers local camping and travel expertise. Renting from a great RV owner can also mean getting the best insider destination tips.
5. Check cancellation policies carefully. They vary from platform to platform and owner to owner. Consider purchasing your own travel insurance, if necessary.

PACIFIC NORTHWEST & ALASKA REGION

# Olympic National Park

Olympic National Park is vast and can seem like a variety of national parks squeezed into one otherworldly dreamscape. Where else can you hike among snow-capped mountains, ramble along a wild and windswept coastline, and explore a cool rain forest filled with hanging moss and ferns? Thankfully, you can also camp in or around each of these equally magnificent sections of the park. A trip to Olympic is best when you take your time and stay at several different campgrounds for a few nights each.

Why not stay in Port Angeles for a few days, then head to the Hoh Rain Forest for a few nights, and then round out your trip with a site overlooking the ocean at Kalaloch or South Beach? We understand that you might not have enough time, but stretch out your trip to this top-tier national park for as long as you can! We think it is every bit as good as Glacier, Yellowstone, or Yosemite—and so many visitors that we have talked to left wanting more.

A shorter trip is still well worth taking. If you only have a few days, we recommend staying in or around Port Angeles or near Lake Crescent. Spending hours driving around Olympic is not such a bad thing. With the right attitude, and a willingness to pull over and chase some waterfalls, it might just be the best part of your trip.

# CAMPGROUNDS INSIDE THE PARK

## Kalaloch Campground

▷  Forks, Washington

▷  nps.gov

▷  Tent and RV Sites

For those adventurous souls who want to experience coastal Olympic National Park in all of its rugged glory and are willing to camp without hookups or shower facilities, there is no better place than Kalaloch Campground. There are a wide variety of site sizes and only a handful have ocean views, but all of them have easy access to the beach just below the bluff upon which the campground sits. The mile-long Kalaloch Creek Nature trail also makes for a lovely walk as you follow the water to its drainage point in the wild Pacific. Plan on spending hours at Kalaloch just exploring tide pools and looking for crabs and sea urchins. But make sure you keep your eyes peeled just past the waves because dolphins and whales make more than occasional appearances. Swimming is allowed but please take caution. Riptides and gigantic floating logs pose real dangers. Smaller RVs will have more success finding suitable sites at Kalaloch. Those in tents should pay close attention to the possibility of rain and strong winds.

## Log Cabin RV and Campground

▷  Port Angeles, Washington

▷  olympicnationalparks.com

▷  RV and Tent Sites, adjacent to Camper Cabins at Log Cabin Resort

The Log Cabin RV and Campground is located directly on Lake Crescent with epic views from just about every site. It can accommodate RVs up to 35 feet, and sites have full hookups. The location is also just a hop, skip, and jump away from amazing outdoor adventures. The only drawback is that the concessionaire that runs the campground does not keep it neat and tidy. When we were there, we would have mowed the lawn ourselves if we had access to a lawnmower.

## Sol Duc Hot Springs RV & Campground

- ▷ Port Angeles, Washington
- ▷ olympicnationalparks.com
- ▷ RV and Tent Sites

This concessionaire-run location offers two options for campers and RVers that are both located within walking distance of Sol Duc Hot Springs Resort. The RV park offers seventeen full hook-up sites that can accommodate rigs from 26 feet to 36 feet. It is basically a parking lot in a great location for those who want to hike to Sol Duc Falls and then get a massage or soak in the hot springs afterward. The separate "campground" location accommodates smaller RVs and tent campers and is much prettier than the RV section.

## Hoh Rain Forest Campground

- ▷ Forks, Washington
- ▷ nps.gov
- ▷ RV and Tent Sites

An ideal camping trip to Olympic National Park would include a variety of stops in its richly varied landscapes. One of those stops should be at the Hoh Rain Forest. Many campers make the long day trip to Hoh, but we think it is worth an overnight stop at the Hoh Rain Forest Campground. There is so much to see and explore in this cool, ancient forest. Might as well set up camp and stay for a little while.

## Fairholme Campground

▷ **Port Angeles, Washington**

▷ **nps.gov**

▷ **RV and Tent Sites**

Fairholme Campground is located near Lake Crescent and offers up a classic NPS camping experience for tent campers and those with RVs 21 feet and under.

## South Beach Campground

▷ **Forks, Washington**

▷ **nps.gov**

▷ **RV and Tent sites**

Located a pinch over 3 miles south from Kalaloch, South Beach campground offers another oceanfront spot for camping within earshot of crashing waves. Be forewarned, it can be quite windy here.

# CAMPGROUNDS OUTSIDE THE PARK

## Salt Creek Recreation Area

▷ **Port Angeles, Washington**

▷ **clallam.net/parks/saltcreek**

▷ **RV and Tent Sites**

When we post pictures of Salt Creek Recreation Area on social media, our followers flip out and demand to know where it is located. It is just that beautiful. The campground is situated on a bluff above the Strait of Juan de Fuca, and the vast majority of the sites have views of the sparkling water. When we pulled into the campground our cell phones welcomed us to Canada—which is located directly across the Strait. The location of this campground is stunning and dramatic in every way. The tide pools located just steps below the campsites kept our young kids occupied for hours, as did the basketball and volleyball courts. Outdoor activities abound for thrill seekers and nature lovers. Whether you love hiking, biking, kayaking, bird-watching, or surfing, there is something for you on-property or nearby. Downtown Port Angeles is also close and filled with hip food, coffee, and shopping. If summertime on the Olympic Peninsula isn't near wild heaven, then it sure does come tantalizingly close.

## Olympic Peninsula/Port Angeles KOA

▷ Port Angeles, Washington

▷ koa.com

▷ Camping Cabins, Deluxe Cabins, Tent and RV Sites

Olympic is filled with rustic NPS campgrounds without hookups or amenities. But if you are willing to camp outside the park (near downtown Port Angeles), you can get full hookups, a pool, a hot tub, and other fun amenities at this charming KOA. There are still gorgeous mountain views, but the highway is nearby and you will have some serious driving to do to get deep into the park.

## Elwha Dam RV Park

▷ Port Angeles, Washington

▷ elwhadamrvpark.com

▷ Cabin, Studio, House Rental, RV and Tent Sites

Elwha Dam RV Park is a great option for campers who want to be close to gorgeous spots in the park like Crescent Lake but still have full hookups and amenities. The owners and staff are kind and knowledgeable, so make sure to ask for intel about best hikes, best food, and best day trips inside the park. Guests can help themselves to vegetables from the community garden, and pet-sitting services are available. Dogs are not allowed in most sections of the park—so this service is clutch for those who camp with their pups. E-bike rentals are also available through Elwha eBike Adventures. Let's go!

## Coho Campground

▷ Olympic National Forest

▷ Montesano, Washington

▷ fs.usda.gov

▷ RV and Tent Sites, Yurts

Willing to venture outside of Olympic National Park? The Coho Campground is a peaceful lakefront gem in a quiet and somewhat remote region of Olympic National Forest. Come prepared with full tanks and coolers—nearby services are slim to none.

---------------------- **Free Camping** ----------------------
Boondocking is allowed in Olympic National Forest. Check the forest service website or a local field office for guidance and regulations.

---------------------- **Gearing Up!** ----------------------
Swain's General Store in downtown Port Angeles claims to have "everything!" and we can confirm that this is close to true. But we must confess that we spent most of our time perusing its well-stocked and neatly organized camping section. Walking through the doors of this general store was like stepping into a time machine and going back to 1957, when this local landmark first opened its doors.

# Quick Guide to Olympic National Park

Olympic can be a tricky national park to navigate because it is spread out over nearly 1 million acres and encompasses multiple ecosystems, from the coast to a rain forest to snow-capped mountains. You'll need a plan and the willingness to spend some time in the car, driving to all the amazing park highlights.

## Visitors Centers

The main **Olympic National Park Visitor Center**, located in Port Angeles, is the perfect place to get acclimated and speak with the park rangers about your plans. The interpretative exhibits are engaging, but you shouldn't bother watching the video, in our humble opinion. There are two short but sweet hikes at the visitor center as well: **Living Forest Trail** (0.4 mile) and **Peabody Creek Trail** (0.5 mile).

You should also visit the **Hurricane Ridge Visitor Center** and the **Hoh Rain Forest Visitor Center** when arriving in those areas of the park. Both places were helpful for us as we mapped out our adventures for the day.

## Areas of the Park

### Hurricane Ridge

The **Hurricane Ridge Trail** is our favorite hike in the whole national park (and one of our favorite hikes ever). It's about 3 miles round trip and offers magnificent views along the entire trail.

### Sol Duc Falls

The **Sol Duc Falls Nature Trail** is an easy 1.6-mile, out-and-back hike that runs through an old-growth forest and across one beautiful spring-fed creek after another, offering views of three waterfalls. You can also visit **Marymere Falls** and **Madison Falls** nearby. Our kids particularly loved the **Sol Duc Hot Springs**, which basically look like pools with varying temperatures that smell like sulfur. This wasn't a highlight for the adults, but the kids begged to go back throughout our trip.

## Lake Crescent

This lake is a great place for a day trip since it offers hikes, a picnic area, and recreation opportunities. The **Spruce Railroad Trail** runs for about 6 miles along the edge of the lake, but you can just hike for as long as you choose and then turn back. We enjoyed renting a canoe from the concessionaire, and there are also kayaks and paddleboats.

## Ruby Beach

If you are staying near Port Angeles, this will be a bit of a drive (1.5 hours), but do not miss visiting this part of the national park. Check the tides (rangers at the visitors center have the tidal charts) and make sure to visit during low tide, when visitors can hike out to the sea stacks and find colorful sea stars and sea anemones. Bring a change of clothes.

## Hoh Rainforest

Yes, there really is a rain forest in Olympic National Park, and it is one of the most beautiful places we have ever seen. There are two loop trails with trail heads right at the Visitor Center: **Hall of Moses** (0.8 mile) and **Spruce Nature Trail** (1.2 miles). These short trails are an awesome way to experience the wonders of the temperate rain forest. Note that this is a very remote part of the park, so plan ahead for meals and be prepared for no cell reception. The town of Forks is about an hour away and has limited food options.

# North Cascades National Park

North Cascades National Park is consistently ranked as one of the ten least visited national parks in the country—which absolutely befuddles us for a variety of reasons. This Pacific Northwest gem is located less than three hours from Seattle, and its snow-capped peaks, evergreen forests, pristine lakes, and rushing rivers are absolutely magnificent. The campground options inside the park are also excellent, but those looking for reliable private campgrounds outside of the park will be disappointed. So plan on pitching your tent or parking your RV inside the park if you want to camp here next. And get ready for outdoor adventure if you come. The hiking here is wonderful and encompasses everything from short family strolls to wild peaks only fit for the heartiest alpinist. When we think of North Cascades we think of rushing streams, fragrant trees, and wide-open spaces that are not overcrowded—even in the middle of the summer.

# CAMPGROUNDS INSIDE THE PARK

## Colonial Creek South Campground

▷ Rockport, Washington

▷ nps.gov

▷ RV and Tent Sites

Colonial Creek South Campground in North Cascades National Park is the best campground you've never heard about. Its ninety-six sites are rustic and rough around the edges—and that is an absolute plus in our book. Some of the sites are nestled right up against the cold, blue waters of Diablo Lake and make for perfect launch points for campers with kayaks and canoes. There is a public boat launch as well—so anyone who wants to paddle will love it here. When you come, make sure you bring your comfortable hiking shoes, because the Thunder Creek trailhead starts right in the campground. It's a terrific hike for families, but be forewarned—dogs are not allowed on the trail. This campground is remote with few services nearby, but it is still popular with regional campers on summer weekends—so don't show up on the Fourth of July without reservations. Colonial Creek North Campground is just a short walk away from South and offers an additional forty-one sites for tent campers and RV owners.

## Newhalem Creek Campground

▷ Marblemount, Washington

▷ nps.gov

▷ RV and Tent Sites

Newhalem Creek Campground is a bit closer to civilization than Colonial Creek, and it is also a lovely option for camping in North Cascades. The sites here have paved pads and back into dense and shady woods, offering great privacy for campers. Newhalem is situated right next to the Skagit River, but only a handful of sites are really close to the water, and those are "hike to" sites without parking.

## Goodell Creek Campground

▷  Marblemount, Washington

▷  nps.gov

▷  RV and Tent Sites

Located across the river from Newhalem Creek Campground, Goodell Creek only offers nineteen sites for tents and small RVs—but some of them are downright magical. Grab one of these sites on the water and avoid those closer to the highway for a classic North Cascades camping experience.

## Other Campgrounds in the Park

⇥  **Gorge Lake Campground**

⇥  **Lower Goodell Creek Group Campground**

⇥  **Colonial Creek North Campground**

-----  **Three Ambitious Day Hikes in North Cascades**  -----

North Cascades National Park is filled with epic day hikes that will lead you to lake overlooks, past rushing streams, and to stunning views of mountain peaks. Here are three classic day hikes for those who like to push themselves a little bit.

1.  Diablo Lake Trail (7.6 miles round trip)

2.  Easy Pass Trail (7.4 miles round trip)

3.  Thornton Lake Trail (10.4 miles round trip)

---------- **Crazy Names in the Pickett Range** ----------

One hundred years ago, Lage Wernstedt of the National Forest Service mapped and named the Pickett Range, which is an incredibly rugged set of peaks in a remote section of North Cascades National Park. He must have had a dark sense of humor, because the names he selected for many of these peaks are downright scary. Here are a few of the highlights:

▷ Poltergeist Pinnacle

▷ Mount Terror

▷ Mount Fury

▷ The Chopping Block

▷ Crooked Thumb Peak

▷ Mount Challenger

# Mount Rainier National Park

Mount Rainier is less than two hours from Seattle and is one of the country's oldest and most visited national parks. It's also the tallest mountain in the Cascade Range and an active volcano. Although most campers will look to visit during the sunniest and driest time of the year—summer or early fall—Mount Rainier is a year-round park, where visitors swap out hiking boots for snowshoes once the winter snowfall arrives.

Understanding the geography of this national park is important when planning a trip to this destination, because the crown jewel, Mount Rainier, sits in the middle and there are no direct routes through the center. There are four entrances to the park, and popular hikes, drives, and overlooks are mostly clustered around those areas, so you may want to pick a campground—or campgrounds—based on your park itinerary wish list. No matter where you stay, you'll probably do a lot of driving during your visit, but that is a great way to soak in the variety of landscape and natural beauty on the most glaciated peak in the contiguous United States.

Even if you do plan to visit during the dry season, always pack your rain gear and plenty of layers when visiting this part of the country. The weather changes can be rapid and extreme, especially when exploring the 14,410-foot mountain.

# CAMPGROUNDS INSIDE THE PARK

### Cougar Rock Campground

▷ Ashford, Washington

▷ nps.gov

▷ RV and Tent Sites

Cougar Rock Campground is very popular among tent campers and RV owners because of its spacious and deeply wooded sites. Many of them make you feel like you are camping in your own private slice of magical forest. There are almost 200 sites at Cougar Rock, and it is fun to walk around and pick your favorites for future trips. Each site is different, and almost every single one of them is excellent. The campground is easy to get to, and RV owners will face little to no stress navigating the loops and getting situated in their sites. The maximum length for motor homes is 35 feet, and travel trailers can't be longer than 27 feet. Cougar Rock is located near several excellent waterfall hikes, and the epic 93-mile Wonderland Trail picks up right across the street from the campground. You will often see exhausted but elated hikers crashing for the night here after finishing the trail. Make sure you catch a ranger talk at the amphitheater, which looks like an ancient Pacific northwestern gathering place...or a set created by Walt Disney World's Imagineers.

## Ohanapecosh Campground

▷ Randle, Washington

▷ nps.gov

▷ RV and Tent Sites

Ohanapecosh is even more beautiful than Cougar Rock, largely because the Ohanapecosh River cuts right through the middle of the campground, making this a destination worth exploring in its own right. Spending an early morning wandering the grounds of this delightful place with a cup of coffee in hand is a great way to start a day on your Mount Rainier vacation. The trade off at Ohanapecosh (when compared to Cougar Rock) is that the roads are tighter and harder to navigate for RVs, and the sites are smaller and less private for tent campers looking for peace and quiet. Ohanapecosh is located in the southeast section of the park.

## White River Campground

▷ Ashford, Washington

▷ nps.gov

▷ RV and Tent Sites

The White River Campground sits at a higher elevation than Cougar Rock and Ohanapecosh, so it typically opens about a month later than its sister campgrounds to the south. It is also about half the size of those more bustling campgrounds. Some sites in loop D have majestic mountain views, so grab one if you can. The White River provides a blanket of sound that drowns out campfires and conversations from nearby sites. It is a wonderful spot to fall asleep on a cool summer night.

---------------- **A Day in the City: Seattle** ----------------

If you want a break from hiking, drive about two hours to Seattle for the day, eating your way through Pike Place Market, visiting the observation deck of the Space Needle, and cheering for the Seattle Sounders at a soccer game.

# CAMPGROUNDS OUTSIDE THE PARK

## La Wis Campground

▷ Randle, Washington

▷ fs.usda.gov

▷ RV and Tent Sites

The Ohanapecosh River flows past La Wis Campground, which is in Gifford Pinchot National Forest, with a gentle rushing sound. Campers returning from a day of exploring Mount Rainier can often be found kicking off their hiking boots and cooling off their feet in its emerald green waters. The campsites here are woodsy, rustic, spacious, and semiprivate, though some are poorly marked and a little bit unlevel. The sites along the river are the most level, and the most inviting with private launch points for tubing and lounging at the water's edge. There are no showers here, and the toilets are pit toilets—so this campground is usually filled with pretty hard-core campers—or those with self-contained RVs. The Purcell Falls Trail and the Blue Hole Trail start at the campground and both lead to fun places to get wet and cool off, so put a towel in your backpack and bring snacks and water!

## Silver Springs Campground

▷ Enumclaw, Washington

▷ fs.usda.gov

▷ RV and Tent Sites

Silver Springs Campground is every bit as good as the campgrounds inside Mount Rainier National Park—so getting a site here is no compromise at all. The campground is situated along the sparkling waters of the White River within Mt. Baker-Snoqualmie National Forest. Many of the campsites are nestled among old-growth forest and offer great privacy and shade, while other sites (the most desirable ones) are located directly on a natural spring that cuts through the campground. Most sites are back-in and surprisingly level, but some of the turns in the campground are tight and there are low hanging trees, so be careful if you are in an RV. There are abundant options for hiking and fishing nearby, but it can be hard to find your way around. Check in at the Silver Creek Guard Station for more information about exploring the area.

## Mounthaven Resort

▷ **Ashford, Washington**

▷ **mounthaven.com**

▷ **RV and Tent Sites, Cabin Rentals**

If you are looking for full hook-up sites near Mount Rainier National Park, then this is your option. Thankfully, it is a very good one. The campsites at Mounthaven are nice and the Nisqually entrance to the park is just a half mile away. There are also cute cabins here that have bathrooms, kitchens, and fireplaces or wood-burning stoves. Larger vacation rentals that sleep up to ten are also available. Some of these charming rentals even come with hot tubs, grills, private decks, and more. Mounthaven also offers tent camping if you can't find a site inside the park.

# A Quick Guide to Mount Rainier National Park

## When to Go

Mount Rainier is open year-round, but the summer and early fall are the driest and warmest months. The wildflowers bloom from late July to late August, making this a beautiful but crowded time to visit the park. Plan popular hikes during the week to avoid weekend day trippers from nearby Seattle.

## Before You Go

Pack high-quality rain gear—including footwear—so you don't have to stay inside whenever the skies open up, which happens a lot no matter the time of year in this region of the country.

## Park Entrances

There are four main entrances to Mount Rainier National Park, and each one provides access to a different popular area of the park.

- ▷ Carbon River Entrance is in the northwest corner near Carbon River.
- ▷ White River Entrance is in the northeast corner near Sunrise.
- ▷ Nisqually Entrance is in the southwest corner near Longmire and Paradise.
- ▷ Stevens Canyon Entrance is in the southeast corner near Ohanapecosh.

## Park Highlights

### Paradise

Hike the easier Alta Vista Trail (1.8 miles) or the Nisqually Vista Trail (1.1 miles). If you are up for a challenge, tackle the more strenuous Skyline Trail Loop, a 6.2-mile hike that takes you past Myrtle Falls and then up the slopes of Mount Rainier. Have a meal at the Paradise Inn, where you can enjoy a cocktail, warm up near the fire on a chilly day, and listen to live piano music. Visit the Longmire Museum and learn the history of one of our oldest national parks.

## Ohanapecosh

Explore the old-growth forest area of the park by hiking the short but sweet Grove of the Patriarchs Trail (1.1 miles), Hot Springs Nature Trail (0.4 mile), and the Box Canyon Loop Trail (0.5 mile). Drive to Reflection Lakes and see the reflection of Mount Rainier in the crystal clear water. Snap a selfie or family portrait at Inspiration Point with perfect views of Mount Rainier in the background.

## Sunrise

This is the highest area of the park that you can access with your vehicle, and here you'll arguably find the best views of the mountain along with a wide variety of hikes. Drive up Sunrise Park Road and pull off at the many overlooks for one stunning view after another. Walk the short path around Tipsoo Lake (0.5 mile) or hike the longer Naches Peak Loop Trail (3.4 miles), especially during wildflower season. The Sunrise Nature Trail starts from the Sunrise Picnic Area and offers great views of the mountain on clear days.

## Carbon River

The Rain Forest Nature Trail (0.3 mile) leads visitors through an inland temperate rain forest. The Carbon Glacier Trail (17 miles) heads to the lowest elevation glacier in the lower forty-eight. Although it's a long hike, it's not exceedingly strenuous and most folks complete the trail in under eight hours. Pedal the 5-mile Carbon River Road closed to vehicles but perfect for ambitious mountain bikers. Eat a packed lunch at the Mowich Lake Picnic Area.

# Crater Lake National Park

Crater Lake National Park is Oregon's only national park and home to the country's deepest lake. Crater Lake was formed almost 8,000 years ago when the volcano Mount Mazama collapsed, creating a basin of pure and visually spectacular water. Plan on mentioning the almost unreal color of the water at least a thousand times during your visit.

Picking the best time to visit Crater Lake can be a challenge. The large majority of people visit between Memorial Day and Labor Day, so the crowds can be intense, especially in the afternoon hours through July and August. Planning a trip during the shoulder season may help you avoid the crowds, but it will present a different set of challenges. Crater Lake is about 7,000 feet above sea level and sees an average of 43 feet of snow per year. The park's northern entrance and West Rim Drive close between mid-October and mid-May. The entirety of the Rim Drive is not usually open until mid-June to early July. If you are looking to avoid the crowds but still see all the park highlights, an early September trip may be your best bet.

This is a relatively small national park, and many visitors are content with spending one or two days exploring. We recommend planning for at least three camping nights, which will give you two full days in the park. There are only two campgrounds in the park, but there are many national forest–serving camping options in the nearby area, and we highly recommend checking them out before deciding on a base camp.

# CAMPGROUNDS INSIDE THE PARK

### Mazama Campground

- ▷   Crater Lake, Oregon
- ▷   nps.gov
- ▷   RV and Tent Sites

Mazama Campground (named after the ancient volcano Mount Mazama—where Crater Lake resides) typically opens in early June and closes in late September. The camping season is short because Mazama sits at an elevation of 6,000 feet, and snow is not uncommon in June and September. Everything about this campground, which has 214 sites nestled in an old-growth forest, is lovely and enchanting. Many of the campsites are spacious and shaded and provide a relaxing place to spend an evening around the campfire after a day of exploring Crater Lake. Some sites are challenging to navigate for larger RVs, even if you are supposed to fit in that site. So take your time when backing in. The Annie Creek Canyon Trail is an easy-to-moderate 1.7-mile loop hook that begins behind the amphitheater in the campground. Annie Creek is crystal clear and provides the water source for the campground. The trail is filled with wildflowers and hemlock. Nearby Crater Lake may be bustling and busy all summer long, but Mazama Campground tends to feel like a quiet retreat that is perfect for a good night's sleep surrounded by the sounds of nature.

# Lost Creek Campground

▷  Crater Lake, Oregon

▷  nps.gov

▷  Tent Sites Only

Lost Creek is every bit as beautiful as Mazama. The sites are huge and shaded, and the campground provides a peaceful retreat after a day of exploration. While there is much to love here, it is a difficult place to include in your plans. The campground is tiny and only has sixteen tent sites. All sites are first-come, first-served. The camping season here is also very short. Lost Creek typically opens in early July (when the snow is cleared and pit toilets can be delivered) and closes in October. If you are winging it, this may be an epic place to try. But if uncertainty stresses you out, you may want to skip it.

------  **Just One Day in Crater Lake National Park?**  ------

1.  Begin your day by watching the educational film at the Steel Visitor Center. NPS visitor center movies are rarely impressive, but this one is crucial to understanding the geological history of Crater Lake and interpreting the sites you will see during your visit.

2.  Enjoy the breathtaking Rim Drive, a 33-mile loop with thirty overlooks. This is a narrow road with tight curves and potential rockslides. The driver will need to remain laser focused, pulling over to enjoy the views. You can take a ranger-guided trolley tour from the Rim Village if you prefer not to drive yourself.

3.  Hike the Garfield Peak Trail, which brings you to stunning lake views. The 3.4 miles is made challenging by more than 1,000 feet of elevation gain. Take your time and enjoy the spectacular sites.

4.  End the day with cocktails on the Crater Lake Lodge terrace. Try your best *not* to talk about the color of the water the entire time.

# CAMPGROUNDS OUTSIDE THE PARK

### Collier Memorial State Park

▷ Chiloquin, Oregon

▷ stateparks.oregon.gov

▷ RV and Tent Sites

Oregon's state park system is a national treasure and a great source of state pride—especially for those who love to camp. Collier Memorial State Park is an awesome choice for those who want full hook-up sites and don't mind making a manageable drive into Crater Lake National Park. It is also a great second choice for those who can't get a site inside of the park. This campground has almost fifty full hook-up sites that are spacious and shady, and several are ADA compliant. The Williamson River and Spring Creek Trail are just steps away from the sites. Spring Creek is an amazing spot for tubing or kayaking—the water is crystal clear, relatively shallow, and mellow to navigate with little ones. The Collier Logging Museum is also located within the park, and the self-guided tour is well worth taking.

### Diamond Lake Campground

▷ Umpqua National Forest

▷ Crescent, Oregon

▷ fs.usda.gov

▷ RV and Tent Sites

Diamond Lake Campground is an absolute gem in the National Forest Service's network of campgrounds. Located about 25 miles north of Crater Lake's park headquarters, this large campground in Umpqua National Forest has 238 campsites, with over 50 of them located directly on the magnificent lake. All of the sites are large and private—and these lakeside sites have stunning views of the water. This is God's country for fishing, boating, and hiking—and the natural beauty of the location rivals that of a national park. But be forewarned: Mosquitoes can be bad. So come prepared.

## Broken Arrow Campground

▷ Umpqua National Forest

▷ Crescent, Oregon

▷ fs.usda.gov

▷ RV and Tent Sites

Like nearby Diamond Lake campground, the mosquitoes are often quite bad here, but if you are just looking for a place to sleep at night during a trip to Crater Lake National Park, then this might be a solid option for you. Some tent campers do not like having their sites right next to sites with large RVs because of the noise from generators. RV owners tend to do well here because the sites are large and level and easy to back into.

# MORE NATIONAL FOREST SERVICE CAMPGROUNDS NEAR CRATER LAKE

## Natural Bridge Campground

▷ First-come, first-served campground good for tenters and RVers up to 30 feet.

▷ (541) 560-3400, *fs.usda.gov/rogue-siskiyou*

## Thielsen View Campground

▷ Reservations are required from mid-June to early September, and this campground can host tents and RVs up to 35 feet.

▷ (541) 498-2531, *fs.usda.gov/umpqua*

## River Bridge Campground

▷ First-come, first-served campground with sites for tents and RVs up to 25 feet.

▷ (541) 560-3400, *fs.usda.gov/rogue-siskiyou*

## A Trip to Wizard Island

Wizard Island is a 763-foot cinder cone that rises from the middle of Crater Lake. Two boat shuttles depart every day during the summer months—one in the morning and one around noon—bringing visitors from the mainland to the island and allowing them to explore for three hours before heading back. This adventure will take the larger portion of the day, but if you have the time, it promises to be a memorable part of your visit to the park.

Reserve your tickets in advance, but only if you and the rest of your party are up for the strenuous 1.1-mile hike down to the boat dock via Cleetwood Cove Trail, which boasts an impressive 700-foot elevation change. Don't forget you'll have to hike back up upon return.

The boat ride takes approximately thirty minutes, and you'll pass the time learning about the area's history and geology from a park ranger. You are free to enjoy the three-hour visit to the island however you wish. We recommend hiking the 2.3-mile roundtrip Wizard Island Summit Trail, which brings you to a 90-foot crater at the top of the cinder cone, and then taking a dip in the frigid lake waters.

## Popular Stops and Overlooks on the Rim Drive

There are thirty designated overlooks on this scenic drive. Some offer a bit more bang for the buck, so here are the stops you really don't want to miss. The Rim Drive is a two-way road all the way around, but these stops are listed in clockwise order, starting at Steel Visitor Center and heading out on the West Rim Drive.

- ✧ Sinnott Memorial Overlook
- ✧ Watchman Overlook
- ✧ North Junction
- ✧ Pumice Point
- ✧ Cleetwood Cove
- ✧ Palisade Point
- ✧ Cloud Cap Overlook
- ✧ Pumice Castle
- ✧ Phantom Ship Overlook
- ✧ Pinnacles Road
- ✧ Sun Notch

# Denali National Park & Preserve

The basic statistics on Denali National Park and Preserve almost defy comprehension. Denali encompasses 6 million acres of pristine land. Its centerpiece is the highest mountain in North America, which stretches upward toward the heavens and reaches 20,310 feet. The park and preserve has only one major road bisecting its interior—and compared to other parks of its stature has few marked hiking trails. This is true wilderness, and it attracts those who seek solitude and majestic beauty on an epic scale. Some adventurous RV owners buy their motor homes or travel trailers just to go to Alaska, and for them, Denali is often the main event. Tent campers also love Denali, but coming prepared for chilly nights, even in the middle of the summer, is an absolute must.

Considering how remote Denali is, there are a variety of options for dry camping inside the park. Options for camping outside the park are extremely limited—so make sure you plan far ahead if you want to camp with hookups outside of the park. No matter where you are camping during your stay in Denali, make sure you pick up the annual Milepost Alaska Travel

Planner. It is an essential reference for those traveling anywhere in Alaska. Thankfully, the National Park Service's website for Denali is also jam-packed with information about visiting the park. The message from the NPS seems to be that all are welcome here, but please come prepared and informed to be awed by true wilderness.

# CAMPGROUNDS INSIDE THE PARK

### Riley Creek Campground

▷  **Denali Park, Alaska**

▷  **nps.gov**

▷  **RV and Tent Sites**

With 6 million acres of wild land, Denali is almost hard to comprehend. Ninety-two-mile Denali Park Road is the only road in the park—and during the summer months (late May to early September) private vehicles are only allowed to traverse the first 15 miles of road to a spot called Savage River. For further exploration in the park, you have to take a tour bus for a fee or a park transit bus for free. Denali can be seen as early as mile 9 (on clear days), and wildlife can certainly be seen on this stretch of road—but delving further into the park on a bus will guarantee more wildlife and more magnificent mountain views. There are two campgrounds on the paved stretch of road. Riley Creek is the biggest campground in the park, and it offers the most services and the most convenient location. The campground is right inside of the park's entrance, and it offers almost 150 sites for tents and RVs up to 40 feet. Sites are semiprivate and situated near fragrant spruce trees near Riley Creek. This campground is a good choice for most people because it is close to the visitor center, which is a hub for hiking trails, and the Riley Creek Mercantile, which offers basic camping supplies, groceries, and fresh coffee.

## Savage River Campground

▷ **Denali Park, Alaska**

▷ **nps.gov**

▷ **RV and Tent Sites**

Savage River Campground is located at mile marker 14 and offers spacious, private, and beautiful RV and tent sites with fewer amenities (and fewer people around!) than Riley Creek Campground. But on clear days you can take a short walk from your site and see Denali in all its magnificent splendor. There is also an easy hiking trail that takes you down to the Savage River where you might see caribou feeding along its banks and playing in the water. Bring your camera and always keep a safe distance from the abundant wildlife in the park.

## Teklanika River Campground

▷ **Denali Park, Alaska**

▷ **nps.gov**

▷ **RV and Tent Sites**

Most vehicles in Denali National Park must turn around at mile marker 15, but a special exception is made for those camping at Teklanika River Campground, which is located at mile marker 29. So camping here feels like a special adventure just beyond the reach of civilization. But once you are settled into Tekanlika (which has a three-night minimum for those who drive into the campground), your vehicle must not leave the site and you are required to travel by foot or use the park's bus system to get around. The sites here are large and semiprivate and easy to back into. Campers love taking the short walk to the river bed and exploring, though the path is occasionally closed due to bear activity near the water.

## Wonder Lake Campground

▷ Denali Park, Alaska

▷ nps.gov

▷ RV and Tent Sites

For the most magnificent views of Denali, tent campers head to Wonder Lake Campground. Located at mile marker 85, this is the campground that gets you deepest into the park and closest to Denali, which is only 26 miles away. On a clear day the view of Denali, and its reflection in the lake, is absolutely stunning. Bring layers and a cold weather sleeping bag. Summer temperatures can drop rapidly at night.

## Other Campgrounds Inside the Park

⇥ **Igloo Creek Campground**

⇥ **Sanctuary River Campground**

# CAMPGROUNDS OUTSIDE THE PARK

## K'esugi Ken Campground

▷ Trapper Creek, Alaska

▷ dnr.alaska.gov

▷ RV and Tent Sites, Cabin Rentals

The grand opening ceremony for this modern state park campground was in 2017, so in campground years it is a brand-new baby. Many veteran campers consider this to be the best state park campground in Alaska. It also makes for an excellent stop on your way to Denali National Park, or on your way back home. It is over an hour away from the national park and situated in Denali State Park, so using it as a base camp would probably require a bit too much driving. The RV sites at K'esugi Ken have electric hookups and accommodate the biggest of big rigs. The tent sites are also large and private, and some of them border a peaceful stream. The cabins are adorable but sparse and have wood stoves for heat. A few of the campsites have stunning views of Denali, but everywhere you look here is beautiful. This is a near perfect campground in one of the most beautiful places on earth. The Curry Ridge Trail is accessible from the campground, and there are multiple viewpoints where you can catch breathtaking views of Denali and the Alaska Range. If you are headed to Alaska in an RV or with a tent, or if you are a cabin camper, this is where you should camp next.

## Denali RV Park and Motel

▷   Healy, Alaska

▷   denalirvpark.com

▷   RV and Tent Sites, Motel Rooms

If you want to bring your RV to Denali but want full hook-up sites, then this is your best option. Denali RV Park and Motel is located just 7 miles from the entrance to the national park. This is no-frills camping to say the least, but the customer service is friendly, the RV sites are spacious and can accommodate big rigs, and the views around the campground are lovely. Dog walking services are also available for an additional fee if you plan on spending a long day in the park and don't want to leave your pup alone for the entire day.

--------------- **Public Use Cabins in Alaska** ---------------

If you aren't interested in RVing, and tent camping is off the table, Alaska's public use cabins may be the perfect way for you and your family to enjoy a trip to and from Denali. Alaska's state park system has more than eighty of these cabins reservable through Reserve America. The cabins are located in remote locations, and some are not even accessible by vehicle. There is a cabin access page online that will give details about each individual location. Bird Creek Campground is a great place to try out a public use cabin. The cabins are situated near the Seward Highway, an easy drive from Anchorage.

## -- Fly and Camp in Katmai National Park and Preserve --

Looking to add another Alaska national park to your bucket list and venture beyond Denali? Then book a flight on a small plane to Katmai National Park and Preserve for a tent camping adventure you will never forget!

## ---- Alaskan Adventures from a Local's Perspective ----

Plenty of folks visit Alaska and write about their experiences. But if you want some great recommendations from a local's perspective, check out Erin Kirkland's blog *AKontheGo*. Erin is a travel expert who has lots of camping content on her blog. She's even got some RV rental recommendations.

# Hiking and Biking Inside Denali National Park

Hiking inside Denali National Park and Preserve is a once-in-a-lifetime experience. But be forewarned, there are very few marked trails in Denali. This is an intentional decision by the National Park Service, as it hopes to preserve a trail-less wilderness experience in this majestic national park. This may sound daunting to the average camper—but it does not need to be. Speak to a park ranger for directions and safety tips before you lace up your boots. Those wishing to hike on trails will find a variety of options near the Denali Visitor Center. The Horseshoe Lake Trail is the prettiest and the most popular in this area.

Those brave enough to bike in Grizzly Country may decide to bring bikes and take a memorable ride on Denali Park Road. Those biking must have a "safety chat" with a ranger and earn a Denali Cycling Token before heading out on the road. The NPS is quite clear that cycling in Denali is "inherently dangerous" and that you cannot outrun a bear on a bicycle. But nevertheless, common sense and basic bear education should keep you safe. The NPS has excellent resources for bikers on Denali's website. There is a lot to learn about biking in Denali—but those passionate about doing it will enjoy boning up. E-bikes are allowed in the park, but they still can't outrun a grizzly. So don't get cocky, okay?

# The RV Pilgrimage: Alaska Files

It seems to be a rule: if you are a popular RV YouTube personality, you must film the journey to Alaska. This means there is much quality, helpful content out there to help you plan your own Alaskan pilgrimage. Here are our favorite series of videos for your binging pleasure.

- *The Long, Long Honeymoon*: This Alaskan YouTube playlist has eight videos on planning, budgeting, and various destinations.

- *Gone with the Wynns*: This Alaskan playlist has eighteen videos and some of the best cinematography of any videos on YouTube. The Wynns specialize in dispersed camping if that is your jam.

- *Less Junk, More Journey*: This channel has thirty-eight videos on the Alaska playlist. You'll get lots of good campground insight, but the videos focus fairly heavily on family situations.

- *Keep Your Daydream*: This fifteen-video Alaska playlist also tends to focus more on personal stories than straight-up travel intel, but there are videos on the Alaskan Highway and other specific destinations like Seward and Homer.

- *Mortons on the Move*: This couple teamed up with Lance Campers to make a twenty-episode series called *Go North*. They took a truck camper on an epic 15,000-mile journey to Alaska and the Arctic Ocean. Their goal was to camp in some of the most remote locations possible.

# Appendix:

## CAMPGROUNDS BY STATE

# ABOUT THE AUTHORS

 Jeremy Puglisi is the co-host of The RV Atlas podcast and managing editor of The RV Atlas. He is the coauthor of *See You at the Campground*, *Where Should We Camp Next?*, and *Where Should We Camp Next?: National Parks*. His work has been published in *RV Magazine*, *AARP The Magazine*, *ROVA*, and dozens of online publications. You can also check out his RVing shows on GoRVing's YouTube channel. He loves nothing more than camping with his wife and three sons, and he is always ready to hitch up and head out for the next RV adventure.

Stephanie Puglisi is the co-host of The RV Atlas podcast and the Vice President of Content for Roadpass Digital. She is also the coauthor of *See You at the Campground*, *Where Should We Camp Next?*, and *Where Should We Camp Next?: National Parks*. She most appreciates that RV camping has allowed her to embrace her semi-outdoorsy personality—sleeping in the great outdoors while simultaneously enjoying a hot shower and soft bed. Even though she loves traveling with her family, she recently acquired a very small RV with only enough room for herself and sweet Maggie the Camping Dog. Some solo trips are in her near future.